Richard's Story;

The Choice

by

IVIE JONATHAN SHELTON, ESQ,

Visit us at; www.thechoicelovestory.com

DEDICATION

Although our encounter was brief, I dedicate this book to Richard Washington for sharing his life story; his love story ... with me.

PREFACE

Do you know what love looks like and how safe you feel when **l**ove is real? **H**ave you spiritually felt the confidence of knowing that he or she will always **l**ove you... will never leave you?

What are you willing to gamble to find love?

How far are you willing to step outside your comfort zone to get what you want?

What are the Limits? How extreme are the risks?

Richard told me his story and I felt, saw and envisioned the most substantive and intense love story...ever

Would you like to see... **l**ove?

I saw it. I felt it.

I was eighteen years old with less than three dollars in my pocket. He was homeless. It was a late Wednesday winter night. A heated argument between my parents and I commenced, flared, and erupted to the point that I stormed away from their home, my dwelling place of residence.

That dark winter night, while driving without direction, my automobile overheated, stalled, and then stopped

4

within the once bowery sector of downtown Detroit, Michigan.

Being too proud to call my parents for assistance (after heatedly departing from them just hours prior to my misfortune) and little money to afford having my automobile towed to some distant service station for repair, I was forced to either reside the night in a downtown bowery-type flophouse or sleep within a cold, immobile automobile. I chose the warmth and stench of the downtown flophouse.

It was here that I met Richard. He was a kind, homeless man who tried to comfort me in these desperate surroundings. He was a different derelict, although they all have their own story. Richard spoke with eloquent English, was seemingly well educated, and although he appeared to be an elderly street beggar, upon close examination I could detect he was a rather young man who was once relatively good looking.
Something had drastically aged him.

A conversation between he and I ensued whereupon I probed for the answer to how a young, educated man as himself could end up in the bowery. Richard told me that he was married. *He had fallen on bad times and was looking for his wife.*

I continued to probe and Richard commenced to reminisce and tell me the most sensuous and terrifying love story I had ever heard; a story which continues to both arouse and distress me to this very day.

It was a story of love, a story of passion, a story of commitment, a story of sexual obsession incorporating a series of nonnegotiable real life choices and the resulting aftermath of those decisions. Richard's story has lived and gnawed in my spirit ever since that chance encounter many, many years ago.

The story is true. It is a true love story based upon a true love relationship and how unforeseeable dilemmas and the choices associated with same can enhance or destroy the nucleus of one's love and standard of one's life.

I was in awe of the passion, commitment, zeal, obsession, risk and sensual terror of Richard's story and perspective on love.

Would you like to see... love?

Then come...travel with me. Travel with me as I recreate Richard's life and story of . . . "*The Choice.*"

*A*UTHOR'S NOTE

I refer to my style of writing as faction. Richard conveyed this story to me when I was eighteen years of age and from the mood of that brief encounter, I have written this book. However, for legal and literary purposes, the names of most places and players, sequence of actual events, and the dialogue conveyed throughout this story was developed in accord to my interpretation of character, environment, and dramatic effect.

CHAPTER 1
September, 1945

A bright blue sky absent of clouds, allowed a gleaming red Saturday sun to dominate the heavens. Below, a troop of military men clad in green army fatigues and short-sleeved white T-shirts, toiled at landscaping the barrack grounds.

World War II was over.

These men were to be released from active military duty within seven days. They were the fortunate few, alive with all of their physical faculties intact.

Sergeant Major Crawford, a medium built, neatly attired officer in his mid-thirties, came out of his quarters with a large brown leather bag slung over his left shoulder. He walked into the barrack grounds with an air of peace and tranquility, slowing down to look at a bed of flowers clamoring tastefully against the officers' club near the center of the camp.

The enlisted men dropped their shovels and other garden utensils and proceeded to walk briskly toward him, it was time for mail-call. Sergeant Crawford began to give the letters to his men as he called their names,

"Larry Welsh, Douglas Moran, John Dybek,. . . Richard Washington."

As Richard made his way toward Crawford to pick up his mail, Crawford satirically questioned him,

"By the way, Lieutenant Washington, would you please tell your mother to hold up on sending these damn baked pastries so much? *Mommy's widdle buoy's deliveries are taking up over twenty-five percent of my mail bag*!" he growled.

The enlisted men cajoled in laughter.

"Yes Sir," Richard meekly answered as he took the large cake and pastry boxes from Crawford's hands. When mail-call was over, a non-stop group of service men gathered around Richard to share his pastry treasure chest.

Richard was the most liked and respected officer on camp. He had received numerous medals during the war, including the Presidential Citation for bravery. He stood a slim six feet tall, quiet, soft-spoken and unusually good-looking for his twenty two years. The senior officers in the company had tried to persuade him to consider making military life a career. They baited their persuasive arguments with promises of higher commissions and levels of responsibility. However, after four years of military life, Richard's mind was made up; he wanted out.

Larry Welsh, a company private, saw a birthday card from Richard's mother beneath the cake. Larry informed his peers and superiors of his discovery and they unanimously agreed to throw a birthday celebration in Richard's honor at *Club Creole*, located five miles from the base. The word was spread. Military men on base and beyond were aware that tonight was to be Richard's night.

****

Richard arrived at Club Creole at nine o'clock p.m., totally unaware of the party being given in his honor. As he walked through the barroom doors, a barrage of military men of various rank bellowed birthday greetings coupled with warm wishes of future civilian success and happiness.

The evening was soft, sophisticated, with table candles supplying the lighting effect. At around eleven o'clock p.m., the feeling of freedom and world peace had turned the affair from soft to insane. One hundred watt light bulbs replaced the candles, alcohol was flowing freely, spirits were unrestrained, and some soldiers openly wept about leaving military life and their friends behind.

Richard sat alone at a corner table away from the bar. He smiled at the total lack of discipline being projected by the officers and subordinate soldiers of his unit. It was good to see the formal masks removed and genuine smiles of happiness dancing across their mouths.

"But what's next?" He pondered.
In a few days he'd be released from military service. Outside of his mechanical talents to repair diesel and commercial vehicles, he had no marketable skills.

"What's next?" he whispered to himself. "What's next?"

Frank Henderson, a young, arrogant, polished, well-manicured first lieutenant who had never witnessed military action, approached Richard's table with two whiskey sours in his hands.

"Mind if I join you, war hero?" Henderson sarcastically asked with a painted smile.

"I'd prefer it if you wouldn't," Richard answered while looking up from his glass of red wine.

"Why not?"

"Because if you do, I might throw up."

"You really envy me, don't you, Richard? C'mon, admit it," he smiled while seating himself.

"No, Frank. I don't envy you. I just don't like you."

"Why not, Richard? Because I wasn't on the front lines offering my life as target practice to the enemy?" he shot back bitterly.

"No Sir, that has nothing to do with it. I don't like you because you talk down to and disrespect everyone you meet. I've often wondered, though, how did you escape military action, anyway?"

Frank moved his chair in closer to Richard's table as if to tell a secret.

"Well, it's like this, Rich. My folks have got money, *lots of money*," he answered with a smirk while downing the first whisky sour.

"So what?"

"Don't be naive, Richard. My folks bought my safety."

"I didn't think that kind of thing went on during periods of war," Richard replied, unimpressed by Frank's response.

"*It goes on especially during periods of war, Richar*d."

"It's not fair!"

Frank grew uncomfortable. He always admired the cool-headedness Richard generally conveyed. He found it difficult to deal with this air of bitterness.

"Here, have a drink," Frank responded while pushing the second whiskey sour toward him."You don't seem like yourself tonight, Richard. It's obvious you want to be alone so I'll check back with you in about an hour . . . *if I'm still sober,"* he smiled.

Frank got up from his seat and joined a group of boisterous servicemen at the bar.

Richard made a mental review of the possible career options he might consider. He did not want to make a career in auto mechanics. His father and grandfather were automotive mechanics and they convinced him that he should aspire to be something more. His ambitious mother, Tina, wanted him to be a doctor, but Richard had seen enough blood and guts during the war to know that he didn't have the stomach for it.

The night continued to thunder with barroom laughter until Frank got drunk. While sitting at a table occupied with oversized Marines, he got into a debate with Bulldog Allen. The topic of the debate was centered on which branch of servicemen were more responsible for the American victory. In the height of the argument, Frank declared that the Marines were an overweight bunch of sissies who had done nothing during the war except look ugly. To further complicate things, Frank pointed his finger in Bulldog's face, laughed out loud and said that he was the "*leader of the uglies.*"

Allen was six feet five inches tall, weighing in excess of two hundred eighty pounds. He obtained the nickname "Bulldog" because of his muscular hunchback build and sagging facial features which accompanied a hostile disposition. Bulldog was proud to be a Marine and was prejudiced against other armed forces. His prejudice against the Army was secondary to his dislike for Henderson. Their argument continued until it reached a climax.

Richard, lost in his own thoughts, happened to look up from his table. It appeared as if Frank had acquired wings and was flying through the air. When Frank finally landed in the corner, Richard jumped up out of his seat to help him up.

"What happened?" Richard asked, as Frank lay sprawled on the floor.

"A brick building fell on me," Frank answered while shaking his head and trying to regain consciousness. As Richard tried to help Frank to his feet, Allen marched briskly toward him, apparently to finish Frank off. Richard left Frank on the floor and appealed for Allen's sympathy.

"Look Allen, the guy's drunk and damn near unconscious, give the guy a- now wait a minute, Allen!" Allen had angrily pushed Richard out of his path. He lifted Frank's wobbly-kneed body from the floor and knocked him across two barroom tables.

The short, skinny, bald, middle-aged proprietor began jumping up and down from behind his bar, roaring for the fight and destructive violence to stop.

No one heard him.

Frank was unconscious, yet Allen went after him with increasing fury. He began throwing chairs out of his way, in pursuit of Frank's body. It was obvious, Bulldog planned to seriously injure Frank. When Allen reached Frank's unconscious body, he lifted him up from the floor with one hand and proceeded to hit him again and again with the other until Richard stepped in front of him and grabbed his arm.

"Dammit, don't hit him again!!" Richard yelled.

Richard didn't like Frank's character any more than the others, but he had no intention of being a witness to manslaughter.

A mild hush fell over the barroom.

Bulldog was stunned. No soldier in the Army, Navy or Air Force had the gall to talk to him in such a fashion. While holding Henderson by the shirt collar with one hand, Allen looked around the room to observe over one hundred and thirty military spectators eagerly awaiting the next move. Allen was confident that Richard's slim physique was no match against his Goliath frame. However, Allen respected Richard's military accomplishments and easy character. Furthermore, Richard was a higher ranking officer, irrespective of the Army/Marine distinction. On that basis, he wanted to avoid a confrontation with him.

"My fights not with you!!" he roared in a warning tone of voice.

"If you attempt to hit him again, Allen, your fight will be with me!" Richard emphatically warned.

Allen slowly lowered Frank's unconscious body to the floor, turned, and swung at Richard's face. Richard, expecting street tactics, ducked from Allen's attack and bombarded him with a series of connecting assaults to multiple parts of his upper body. The fight continued across the tiny dance floor until Allen finally timbered over two chairs and fell to the floor.

The barroom exploded with cheers.

Richard turned from Allen's fallen position and went back to the corner of the bar to assist the others in reviving Frank. As Frank sat incoherently in a chair at the corner table, Richard tried to arouse his consciousness with the smelling salts he received from the bartender. With his mind on Frank's condition, *Richard was unaware of the soldiers in his unit yelling for him to turn around.*

Allen, angry, had gotten up from the floor, and was walking speedily toward Richard's back. Once alerted, Richard turned and escaped Allen's attack. During their slugfest, Richard struck Allen multiple times, but Allen appeared able to absorb more of Richard's blows. However, Allen did not possess the quick hands and offensive speed as displayed by Richard. Richard got tired and careless as the fight continued, and dropped his guard. Allen delivered a body punch to his stomach. Richard's legs buckled from the pain as he saw his entire life pass before his eyes in a matter of seconds. He quickly regained his boxing form and sent Allen falling to the floor for the second time.

Richard had delivered his best attack on Allen. He stood for a moment over Allen's fallen body to determine if he wanted to continue the fight. Richard was convinced that the fight was out of him. Arm weary and physically exhausted, Richard slowly walked to the corner table. Frank appeared to be conscious and well. A feeling of relief lighted Richard's face.

He was less than two feet from Frank's table when the soldiers in his unit *again* warned Richard to turn around. As he turned, he saw Bulldog slowly getting up from the floor and walking toward him with vengeance in his eyes. Allen was determined not to let an Army lieutenant of smaller physical stature claim victory over his awesome Marine body. It was a matter of pride. Richard was flabbergasted. He stood mute by the table and watched that giant of a man come at him like a slow, powerful locomotive.

"*Holy Shit!*" he whispered, while engaging himself for yet another round of physical battle.

CHAPTER II

Valery Hall was nineteen years of age when the world was brought to peace. She bore a sexual yet saintly beauty which left most acquaintances drawn and spellbound by her appearance. One always witnessed a warm smile passing over her lips and a soft touch exhibited during the course of a conversation.

Coupled with her beauty was a legendary name synonymous with wealth, power, and prestige within the small town college community of Camden State University.

Behind the blocks of her father's white marble home, the rehearsed smile would usually disappear. It was a mild September evening. After preparing a late night dinner for her tired father, she searched for peace and solitude. She found such solitude when she walked outside the front doors and witnessed the array of bright stars dancing across the night sky.

Valery sat on the white stone banister of her father's large porch clad in an elegant, white, silk robe. She appeared to be hypnotized by the night stars as she pondered upon her future.

Clifford walked out of the house and approached her. He wore an expensive, maroon-colored smoking jacket and puffed on a captain's pipe which emanated a rich aroma in the immediate vicinity.

"Valery."

She did not answer.

He touched her and she startled.

"Oh! . . . Father"

"What's on your mind, child?" he asked while seating himself next to her.

"Life," she solemnly answered.

"What's wrong, daughter?" he asked while stroking her black hair with his fingers and trying to create eye contact.

She would not look at him.

"Nothing seems to be going my way," she sighed.

"I don't believe you said that, Valery. *Everything is going your way!* You're young, beautiful, in excellent health, attending a good university, and the daughter of a very prominent, wealthy and handsome banker," he smiled.

"But I'm not happy," she responded, not amused by his humor.

Clifford was at a loss. He was growing concerned by the sporadic high and low moods of her depression. Her loved mother had died of cancer during the early years of her life. That death had thrust father and daughter into a stronger allegiance and dependence upon one another. Clifford, however, did not possess her mother's talent of alleviating Valery's depressed moods.

"How are things between you and Damien?"

"Okay," she answered nonchalantly.

"He's a fine boy, Valery. He comes from a strong family. I see a solid future for the two of you. Be patient, Valery. Happiness will come."

Clifford stood up and kissed his daughter on the forehead.

"It's getting cool out here, Valery. Don't stay out too much longer or you'll catch cold."

"I won't, Father. Good night," she replied while returning to her private thoughts and the dark night skies.

"Good night," he answered while opening the screen door and walking into their home.

****

Richard continued to be in awe as this giant of a man continued to march toward him.

"You're going to be sorry you ever knew me!'" Allen roared as a table of peer Marines cheered him on.

Two Army privates, who were sitting on the bar for a better ringside view of the battle, realized that Bulldog was too much animal for one man. As Allen walked past the bar toward Richard, the two privates jumped off the bar and onto Allen's shoulders, crashing together to the floor. About two dozen Marines, sitting at adjacent and surrounding tables, retaliated by emptying their seats and joining in the fight. The Army soldiers at the remaining tables charged into the fracas. It was a military barroom brawl, Army against the Marines. Various soldiers from the Air Force and Navy joined in the brawl on general principle.

The bartender resumed jumping up and down from behind the bar like a boy with both feet on fire yelling obscenities to deaf ears for the battle and destructive violence to stop. He finally got on the phone and called the Military Police to come and stop their destructive violence.

Frank was fully recovered and decided to join the activities. Bulldog Allen was busy annihilating the two Army privates when Frank snuck up behind Allen's back and hit him over the head with a broomstick. The stick broke over Allen's head like a wooden match breaks between two fingers. Allen turned, while scratching his head, and saw Frank, *in terror*, slowly retreating away from him. A sinister smile crept on Bulldog's lips.

He grabbed Frank with his left hand, lifted him into the air by his shirt collar, and proceeded to hit him with his free fist.

Richard, observing Frank's dilemma, ran to give him assistance. Allen was enraged to see Richard again coming to Frank's rescue. Richard speedily approached Allen. Allen, with a roar, grabbed Richard by the front of his shirt collar with his right hand, and with his awesome strength, he lifted both Richard and Frank up into the air and over his head.

As they were slowly being lifted up into the air, Frank looked at Richard. Richard, helpless, shocked and fascinated at the present state of events, looked at Frank. They were both astounded by this man's unnatural strength.

Richard looked into Bulldog's eyes and said,

> "Well, uh . . . look Bulldog, uh, listen, uh, why don't we talk this thing over? It seems to me that, uh,-"

Allen answered by hurling both of them out of the club, crashing through the barroom doors, and onto the dark concrete streets. Every bone in their bodies felt broken.

Frank slowly got up from the pavement and extended his hand to Richard still lying on the ground.

"C'mon, War hero. Get up. Let's get out of here."

"No, Frank. You go on. I'm going back in."

"Hey, man, this isn't the war, let's-"

A military police siren was blowing. In the distance, Frank could see four jeeps of Military Police wagons finally responding to the bartender's call.

"Get up, Richard! The M.P.'s!!"

Richard, still lying on the ground, turned his head and saw the headlights of the jeeps speedily approaching them. He took hold of Frank's extended hand and they both ran down an alley next to the club and escaped a military arrest. Their run slowed down to a walk. They circled back to the bar and witnessed the arrest of all of the soldiers within the club. When the trucks were gone, Frank turned to Richard and laughed.

"How about that for luck, Richard?"

Richard swung at Frank. Frank ducked.

"What's wrong with you?!"

"You! . . . You arrogant, fat ass, smart-talkin', two bit, good-for-nothing'---"

"Hey! What'd I do?"

"What did you do!??" Richard angrily swung again, but again his slow tired aching body missed its moving target.

"You should be at the head of those arrested soldiers, Henderson!! You're the cause of all this shit!"

Richard angrily crossed the street. He didn't want to walk on the same side of the street as Frank.

"Wait, Richard, I've got my car. I'll drive you."

"No thanks! I'm walking!"

"*But camp's over five miles away!*'

Richard kept walking.

"Well, hell with you, Washington. I didn't ask for your damn help anyway!" he yelled, while kicking an empty can in his path.

Frank looked at his red two-seat sports car shining brightly under a street light. He looked at Richard walking in the distance and crossed the street. He walked about a half block in back of Richard. After three miles, Frank silently walked next to him.

Richard appeared more calm.

"What's on your mind, Rich?"

"I don't know."

"Yes you do, man. I know you're upset with me and-"

"Forget it."

"How can I forget a man who-"

"Forget it!"

20

As the walk continued, a calm air of tranquility soothed Richard's spirit. After a brief silence, Richard turned his head toward Frank and initiated conversation.

"What are you doing after you leave the Army, Frank?"

"I'll probably work as a financial consultant in my father's agency."

"Is that interesting?"

"I don't know, Richard. But it's lucrative. Besides, I majored in finance in college."

"How do you know you'll like it?"

"I like any clean job that delivers big money, Richard."

Richard grew solemn and continued to walk in silence along the dark rural streets toward camp. Frank saw a deep look of depression on Richard's face.

"What are you doing after your release, Richard?"

"I don't know."

"What are you prepared for?"

"Nothing!"

"Are you going to college?"

"I wouldn't mind, but who am I kidding? What would I use for money?"

"How would you like to go to Camden State University?"

"Camden State University??" That's one of the most elite schools in the country. I couldn't even afford the required books for classes at that University," he laughed.

"Yes, you can, Richard. Listen, my father is a member of the board of directors at State. He can get you in."

"Man, forget it. There's no way I could afford the tuition."

"No problem! He can get you all the scholarships and financial aid you need."

Richard slowed down the pace of their walk.

"How?"

21

"You've got a strong military record and financial need. There are cooperative scholarship programs for veterans subsidized with the G.I. bill of benefits. He could probably swing your financial package in one day."

"You're kidding!"

"No! . . .No! It's all in whom you know, friend," he smiled.

"But what would I major in at college?"

"Why not a business program? Like I said, I majored in Finance."

"I don't know, Frank. That's an awfully prestigious place. I'd stick out like a sore thumb. I read an editorial that the male students wear suits everyday to class. Hey, I own *one* suit, but maybe I could buy more, with what? Scholarship money? What would I major in? . . . But it-"

"Hold on, Richard!" laughed Frank, it felt good to see Richard excited about something. "You haven't got to make all those decisions today. Just keep in mind that I'm for real. You want in? You've got it! You need financial assistance? You've got it. I never believed in friendship until tonight, Richard. You can't stand me and yet you've been a friend. Let me be a friend to you."

****

Three days later, Frank and Richard were released from service. They exchanged telephone numbers, addresses, and promised to maintain contact with each other during their civilian life.

CHAPTER III

"**W**illiam, was that the doorbell?" Tina asked while rolling over in bed to face her husband.

"I think so," he replied getting out of bed and putting on his robe. He looked at the worn white automatic clock on the small wood night-stand.

It read 1:37 a.m.

"Well, who could be ringing our bell at this crazy hour?"

"As soon as I answer the door, Tina, I'll be able to tell you," he sarcastically answered.

"I've got a better idea, husband. Tell me in the morning when I'm awake," she replied while rolling over with a pillow that covered her head.

William, a rugged, muscular, five-foot-nine-inch man with a face as gentle and soft as his character, moved slowly from the room. He sleepily turned on the quaint dining room lights and became temporarily blinded by their radiance.

The doorbell rang again.

"Alright, alright!" he muttered as he walked toward the front door while flipping the porch light switch.

He opened the interior door while trying to wipe the sleep from his eyes. A broad smile covered the face of a tall, good-looking young man wearing an Army officer's uniform.

"A man could freeze to death waiting for you to answer the door, Father."

William opened the door widely and stood in shocked disbelief.

"I'll be damned! . . . I don't believe it!! Are you visiting, gone AWOL, or what?!"

"I'm home, Pop. War's over." he smiled.

"Dammit, I know the war's over, but you didn't say you were going to be released from service this soon. As a matter of fact, you didn't, why you haven't even written in the last four weeks! You know how worried and excited your mother gets when you don't write! Hey! Let me take a look at you. C'mon, turn—"

"Hold on, Father," laughed Richard. "It's getting cold out here. Mind if I come in?"

William, in all his excitement, had blocked the front door entrance with his body. They laughed as William grabbed his son with a bear hug and lifted him into the house.

"C'mon, tough war hero, c'mon home!" he yelled while kissing his son's cheek.

"William, what is that racket out there?! Are you alright?!"

"I'm fine, Tina. Go on back to sleep!"

"Who's at the door, William?" she demanded.

"No one important, Tina . . . Just Richard!"

There was a brief silence.

"Richard?....Our son, Richard?!! William, are you telling me the truth?" she asked while hurriedly getting out of bed and falling over her shoes in excitement. She had not seen her son in over two years. Just as she was about to open and exit from her bedroom door, the door opened.

"Richard! . . . Son! . . . Are you really home?" she cried as Richard picked up his mother in an embrace.
She pulled away from him.

"Boy, do you look good in that uniform! I think he's grown some, too, William, although God in heaven knows he's tall enough. Son, let me touch you," she whispered while moving closer to him.

24

"Are you really home?" she asked while touching the features of his nose and cheeks, trying to retain the emotionalism swelling within her.

Richard hugged his mother as she cried upon his shoulder and kissed his lips.

"Why didn't you tell us you were coming home, son?" she inquired.

"I didn't want a big party and stuff, Mom. I just wanted to share this moment together with you two," he answered with his arms around both of their shoulders.

"Well you can be sure we're going to celebrate this weekend," replied William,

"Ever since you got that medal for bravery, that phone's been ringing off the hook. Everyone's been asking for you. Your cousins, friends, newspapers, even a few enemies I'm sure," he laughed. "Wait till I tell them you're home. Why they'll probably bring this house down"

"Okay," laughed Richard. "But do me a favor, Dad."

"Name it, Son."

"Don't tell anyone that I'm home for at least two weeks, okay?"

"Why not, boy?"

"I just need some time alone, Dad. I . . .   I need some time for me. I need to think. Give me a couple of weeks, okay, Dad?"

William, observing the need and intensity in his son's eyes, replied favorably.

"Thank you, Father."

"Thank you, Son."

"For what?"

"For staying alive and coming back home to your mother and me in one piece."

"Amen," smiled Tina as they continued their conversation with warmth and laughter.

****

Richard had been home for fourteen days. His parents saw very little of him during those days. He said very little, ate very little, and spent most of his time upstairs in the guest room--alone.

It was Monday morning. A rich aroma of coffee soothed his nostrils and gradually awakened him. His watch read 6:33 a.m. As he continued to rest within the neat, though sparsely furnished bedroom, a faint conversation between his parents became more audible to his ears.

"He's changed, hasn't he, William?" asked Tina while pouring a cup of coffee to complete her husband's breakfast.

"Changed? How?" answered William while turning the pages of the newspaper to the sports section.

"He seems about the same to me."

"No! . . . No! I see it in his eyes. He looks hurt . . . confused...alone."

William began to pull the paper down from his eyes. The intensity in Tina's voice was alarming.

> "Tina, the boy's been in the war," he softly replied, "He had to kill people. Enemy soldiers were trying to kill him. That is enough to promote some change in any man. Give him a little time to fit it back together."

"My poor baby," she sobbed.

"He's not a baby anymore, Tina. He's a man," William declared.

> "He should be married! It's not good for a man to be alone."

"Uh, oh . . . There you go! Off onto one of your tangents again," William responded while returning to the newspapers.

"You know it's true!" she snapped. "You know it's time that he settled down, found himself a wife and had children. Why, at the rate my two boys are going, I'll never be a grandmother."

"The boy just turned twenty-two, Tina. Give him time. You've been trying to marry our boys off ever since they were born," he laughed while turning to the next sport's page.

"Well, I give up on Leonard. That nineteen-year old boy of yours is just a gigolo. But Richard is settled. He always has been rather mature for his years."

"He's *only* twenty-two, Tina. Let the boy enjoy life for awhile."

"What are you implying?" she sternly asked, her lips growing tight with anger. "Are you saying that a man can't enjoy life with a wife?"

"No! I'm not saying that," William smiled while looking at the anger in her eyes, *"But he just got out of one war, why be in a hurry to put him into another?"*

William roared with laughter as Tina proceeded to chase him around their kitchen table. Richard fought to restrain the robust hearty laughter boiling for release. His father's sense of humor was always refreshing.

It was good to be home . . . but what's next?

William exited from the house toward his automotive service garage. Richard got out of bed. He shared a cup of coffee with his mother midst small conversation.

He then dressed and went to his father's garage. William had mentioned to Richard the night prior that one of his men had quit the garage and the lack of manpower resulted in a backlog of vehicle repairs. He jokingly inquired if Richard had retained the mechanical talents he had prior to entering the military and of his need for those talents.

William was happy to see Richard walk into his shop. He suited him up in overalls and Richard went directly to work.

Richard possessed strong auto mechanic skills and talents. William's customers were generally flabbergasted by his son's ability to quickly analyze and correct their automotive problems. The female patrons were awed by Richard's good looks.

As a result of Richard's presence, William's clientele grew.

CHAPTER IV

Six months quickly passed. William could sense an air of boredom and despair in Richard's character. At the end of a busy Friday, William walked to his employees and gave them their checks. He then walked over to Richard with his check. Richard refused to accept it.

"What do you mean by you 'don't want it?'"

"You've given me enough, Dad," he answered while wiping beads of perspiration from his forehead.

"I haven't *given you* anything, Son. You've earned every penny of it. You're the best mechanic here."

"Thanks, Dad .... but no thanks. I don't feel right taking money from you," he replied while pushing the check away from him.

"Buy mother a gift with it, Dad."

"I've got a better idea, Son. Why don't I buy you a dinner with it? I think it's past time we talked"

They took a shower at the garage, dressed, grabbed a cab, and went to a well-known supper club. William ordered two large steak dinners for them and rounds of cocktails. Prior to their dinner being served, William initialed conversation.

"It's time for a change. Isn't it, Richard?"

"Is it that obvious, Dad?'

"It is to me, what kind of change did you have in mind?"

Richard told him about his plan to enter college. He felt that a business degree in marketing was the best program for him to pursue. He informed William of the commitment Frank Henderson had made of enrolling him into State University.

"Well, have you talked to him, Richard?"

"No. That arrogant soldier talked a lot of stuff, Dad. I kind of feel that he felt obligated to say something nice to me because I helped him in a fight. I'll bet that if I called him, he would act like he doesn't even know me."

Their dinners were served. Richard made small conversation as they feasted on their meal. William and Richard finished eating at around eight o'clock p.m. The night air felt crisp, clean, and refreshing. They decided to walk home.

As they walked through the quiet, lighted, rural streets, William turned to his son.

"You know what I think?"

"Yeah, Dad. I know what you think. You think I should call Frank."

"Absolutely! What have you got to lose?"

"I don't know. I'm really not State University material. That's a money school, Dad. I don't want that guy to think I'm begging."

William put his arm around his son's shoulder and gave him a small squeeze.

"Son, you can't make it in this life by yourself. Everyone needs a little help at some point in their lives. You help him. He helps you. It all balances out."

"Maybe you're right."

"Maybe nothing. I know I'm right. Call him!"

"Okay, already. I'll call."

"By the way, do you remember my friend, Jim Wyatt?"

"Yes."

"Well, he's got a garage around that University. He's always looking for good help. I'm sure I can arrange a part-time job for you."

"I don't know, Dad, maybe, let's see."

They arrived home at 9:00 p.m. After kissing his mother, Richard hurriedly walked up the stairs to his room and called

Frank's number. He was relieved that the number was still active. A gentleman answered his call.

"Hello"

"Hello, is Frank Henderson in?"

"Yes, speaking."

"Hello, Frank. This is Richard."

"Oh . . . hi, Richard."

"You don't sound very happy to hear from me."

"No . . . it's not that. I just had a long crazy day at the office today. Actually, I expected to hear from you months ago. Well, tell me, how are you doing?"

"Not bad . . . uh . . . look, if you're busy I can call back."

"No, I'm glad you called, war hero. There's something I want to discuss with you. How is the battle for the dollar going?"

"Not too bad. I'm working in my father's garage and, uh, that keeps me pretty busy."

"How do you like it?"

"Well, it's not all bad but…. you know… . . . I kind of feel like I'm accepting charity. . you know - from my father and all."

"Well, I work for my father, Richard. I don't feel like I'm accepting charity. I work my ass off and-"

"Well, that's different!" Richard interrupted.

"You seem a bit up tight, Rich. What's on your mind?"

"Nothin' …….Just some crazy thoughts going through my head. Look, I'll talk to you later."

"Hold on, Richard! Like I said, there was something I wanted to talk to you about."

"What's that?'

"Do you want to do anything with this college scholarship proposal we discussed? If so, it's ready…been ready."

Richard was shocked. He lost his voice. There was silence.

"Richard? Are you there?"

"Yeah, I'm here," he answered, trying to catch his breath.

"Well, what do you think? Are you interested?"

"It depends. What do you mean by the `college scholarship proposal' is ready?"

"Well, it's a cooperative program joint ventured between the military and the university. My father is on the faculty committee that oversees the program.

If you sign the required forms, I can have you in class for the upcoming semester."

"That sounds great!! but . . . uh . . . how much will this cost me? I don't have much money, Frank."

"It won't cost you anything. Your books and tuition are covered plus you get living expense money of about two hundred dollars a month."

"I don't believe it!!"

"Believe it, friend."

"When do I start?"

"The summer semester starts in June, Richard."

"Frank, *that's one month from now!*"

"If that's too early, you can start-"

"No! No! I want it now! What should I do?" he excitedly asked, "I mean . . . to make it official."

"Rich, you're going to have to find an apartment, register for classes, sign the required forms, attend orientation, and find a part-time job. Man, the sooner you get up here the better."

Richard was elated.

"Look, Frank, I'll be there within *one* week!"

"Great! I'll see you then."

They said their goodbyes and Richard got off of the phone. He let out a loud cry of happiness. Tina ran to his room.

"Son, what happened?"

"I'm going to State University, Mom!"

"That's good, Richard," she beamed. "You're going to college. That's great!! But State University is awfully expensive. Can you afford that, Son?"

"I got a scholarship, Mom!"

"A scholarship? A scholarship?! William!!William!!"

William came out of the bedroom.

"Richard got a scholarship to State, William!"

William looked at Richard and smiled.

"I guess the guy came through, right, Richard?"

"Yes, Father, he came through."

Tina looked at William. She seemed disappointed.

"You knew about this?"

"Tina, Richard just told me tonight about this potential opportunity."

Tina turned and looked at her son. There was sadness in her face. She knew that her son moved fast once he made up his mind on something. He had been home for six months; she didn't want him to leave-not yet.

"When are you leaving?"

"In one week, Mother."

"Why so soon, Richard?"

"The semester starts in one month and there's a lot of business I must take care of before classes."

He saw the sadness in both of their eyes.

"C'mon, be happy for me. I would wait until the fall semester, but I'm afraid that if I don't jump on this opportunity quick, that it might vanish. Listen, State's only two hundred and twenty miles from here. I promise that I'll spend so many weekends at home that you'll never have a chance to miss me."

Tina seemed relieved.

"I'll call Jim in the morning, Richard."

"Thanks, Dad."

Leonard came over that evening and Richard informed him of the good news. Leonard was elated and promised to drive Richard to State's campus the following weekend.

Chapter V

Richard arrived at Camden State University at ten o'clock a.m. on a Monday morning. He left his clothes in his brother's trunk. Leonard got out of the car and walked the campus grounds while Richard attended a meeting with Frank and his father in the Dean of Admissions' office.

Frank's father, Henry, had obtained the use of the Dean's office to explain the conditions of the scholarship and advance some money to Richard as provided in the assistance program. Henry also discussed the general instructions for registering into classes, scholarship requirements, expectations, and the date and time for freshmen orientation. Henry then shook Richard's hand and left for his agency. Frank stayed with Richard for two hours and gave him a brief tour of the campus.

Richard was literally spellbound by its beauty and size.

Prior to departing for his office, Frank gave Richard his home address, a key, and insisted that Richard stay with him until he find his own place.

Richard felt Frank had done enough. He found Leonard and they began looking for an off-campus apartment.

Leonard, however, had different plans he wanted to pursue. For years, he had heard about the picturesque hills, beaches, and beautiful coeds at Camden University.

Today, he was intent upon seeing them.

Leonard lowered the top of his 1941 M.G. Midget convertible. He drove down the wide hilly campus streets and out of the tall wrought-iron gates isolating the prestigious University from the not-too-distant beach area.

Richard shook his head in disbelief as they approached the beach zone. He was awed by the unique beauty of the beach's imported variations of trees, the mirror-like reflections of the clear blue waters, the white sands, and the smooth, wide, hilly, perfectly paved streets encompassing the massive beach district. Richard continued to quietly inhale the character of this foreign tropical-type environment as Leonard cruised his restored convertible sports car throughout the mini-hills and slopes surrounding the waters.

The warm west sea wind was lightly fingering through their hair.

"You've changed, Richard," initiated Leonard, while handling the wheel of the car and keeping his eyes on the road.

"Changed? . . . How?" answered Richard while looking at a large school of pigeons gradually ascending higher and higher in unison from the sands of the beach toward the clear blue skies.

"You're more serious, more reserved, more introverted, ...*more square!!*' he answered. "*You know, considering the mannerisms of the stuffed shirts in this city, you should fit in rather well.*"

Richard laughed at his brother's sarcastic remarks.

"No, that's not it at all, Leonard," he replied while looking at the side profile of his brother's handsome face.

"I haven't changed much. I just look at life a little bit differently."

Leonard sporadically took his eyes off of the road and looked at Richard suspiciously,

"Differently?... How??"

"Well, I really didn't think I'd live through the war, Leonard."

"Why not, Rich?"

"Because there was so much death. I routinely would speak to a soldier one minute, turn around and find he had caught a bullet the next minute. They kept us in that front line."

Leonard looked at his brother, shaken by the conversation.

"Who is 'us'?"

Richard looked at his brother and answered in disgust,

> "I don't know. I generally felt that the pattern in the military was to place those infantry soldiers from the poorest families or with the least amount of education on the front lines of action. In other words, the most dispensable lives were lost first. You know, it didn't bother me so much dyin' as did the thought that in the eyes of my superiors, my life really didn't count for much," he answered while looking nonchalantly out of the car.
>
> "Maybe I'm being unfair," Richard continued while sitting up straighter in the passenger seat, "But that's how I felt. I felt vulnerable, empty, alone. Maybe that's why I fought so hard during the war to get recognition; recognition that I was someone of importance . . . Anyway, I made up my mind that if I survived that nightmare then I would come back and be someone of importance."

There was a small space of silence. Leonard was digesting Richard's objectives.

> "Important to who, Richard?" he quietly asked while looking into his brother's eyes.
>
> "Important to me, Leonard," he solemnly answered, returning his eyes back to the beauty of the strong sea waves crashing toward the shores. "Important to me!" he emphatically repeated.

The car screeched and the rubber on Leonard's tires branded the streets as he shifted his car from second to third, then fourth gear.

"Hey, man! What are you doing'?!" Richard yelled, taken ajar by the sudden change of Leonard's driving behavior. The car had jumped from twenty-five to fifty-five miles per hour. *They were driving in a twenty mile per hour beach zone.*

"Hold on, Rich!" replied Leonard as his car zoomed throughout the crowded streets.

The pedestrians, clad in bathing suits, were yelling and screaming obscenities while scampering in multiple directions across the streets as the 1941 M.G. Midget recklessly curved and tipped from side to side as a result of the excessive speed.

"How do you like that horsepower, Richard?" proudly asked Leonard, enjoying the power behind his hands.

"I think it's crazy!" yelled Richard over the screams of the panicked pedestrians, angrily whaling their fists in the air after escaping danger.

"Slow down!!" demanded Richard while holding the dashboard for safety.

"*Speed up? Okay!*" replied Leonard, heartily laughing as he pushed the car to seventy miles per hour.

"You're going to kill somebody, Leonard!" he bellowed, growing increasingly upset by his brother's juvenile actions.

"Ahhh, don't worry about these pompous stuffed shirts, Richard" he responded. "They need some excitement in their dull lives, anyway," he sneered while picking up speed and chasing a distinguished elderly gentleman across the street.

"Well, how about us, Pea brain? You're going to get us killed!" Richard yelled over the noise of the engine.

"Pea brain??! Pea brain??!" Leonard angrily accelerated the car to seventy-five miles per hour.

"Okay, dammit! You're not a Pea brain. Now slow this damn jalopy down or I'm jumping out."

Leonard slowed the vehicle down to a cruising speed. Richard shook his head disapprovingly in disgust. However, the disgust quickly vanished as they became in awe to find themselves alone in a wide open, mountainous stretch of isolated majestic beauty overlooking the water. Leonard drove down the hill toward the open empty beach shore.

Richard and Leonard got out of the car and gazed at the breathtaking beauty encompassing the beach environment.

"Can you believe this place, Leonard?"

"No, Rich. But you know, the whole city is like a tropical paradise. I've never seen such white sands before in my life!"

Leonard pulled up the cuffs of his pants, took off his socks and shoes, and waded in the water. Richard took off his shoes and socks and walked in the sands a short distance from the water.

"I'll say one thing about this wealthy hick town, Richard."

"What's that, Leonard?"

"I have never seen so many gorgeous women in one place as I saw on State's campus this afternoon."

"Yeah, I couldn't help noticing that myself," Richard smiled.

"Speaking of women, how's your love life, Richard?"

"Right now, nonexistent. However, Mom says you've become quite the gigolo."

"Yeah, I've got them coming out of my ears," Leonard nonchalantly replied as a small smirk crossed his lips.

"Well, how do you like that kind of life?"

"I love it. I love it. I love it!!" replied Leonard as he continued to wade through the shoreline waters.

"Why do you ask?"

"I don't know. I guess because I don't think I'd like that kind of life. Too *shallow*."

"Okay, now, big brother. Don't start preaching to me. This is Leonard, I *know you*. How about that *shallow* relationship you had with Kathy?" he smiled.

"Kathy who?"

"Oh, you know, Kathy; the one that caused you to be out all night and late to Dad's garage every morning after you graduated from high school."

"Oh... Kathy,"

"Yeah, Big Brother. How about Linda?"

"Well, she-"

"She my ass! How about Gloria? . . . You wanna talk about equipment? Okay. You've got all the equipment, Big Brother. You're tall, dark, beautiful curly hair, and handsome . . . no! . . .*pretty.*"

Richard began to laugh. He looked off into the distance as they continued their walk.

"*Pretty?*"

"Yeah, pretty. I couldn't stand having you around me in high school. You got all the attention. I was only Richard's little brother. Although, I did get your rejects which were not bad...not bad at all. So don't talk that square shit to me, Big Brother."

Richard put his hands into his pockets and continued to walk the sands as his brother Leonard walked the shallow water. He couldn't understand why Leonard appeared so agitated. After a brief pause, their conversation continued.

"Leonard, I'm not saying that I didn't have any shallow relationships in the past. I think it might even be normal for a young man to relate with a few girls while subconsciously looking for that special someone. Most of my past involvements, however, were brief, meaty experiences without depth. I don't want that anymore. It's not fulfilling. From now on, I want a steak and

40

potato relationship. I want a physical, emotional, spiritual, and intellectual relationship with that special woman; sex alone just isn't enough."

Leonard abruptly stopped wading the waters with Richard. He was baffled by Richard's philosophies. Although they had seldom talked seriously in the past, Leonard had always visualized Richard as a playboy; a suave lady's man. Today, that impression was being destroyed.   Richard turned around and looked at his brother, standing rigid in the waters and eyeing him suspiciously.

"What's wrong, Leonard?"

"I . . .I can't believe you're saying these things to me, Richard. You sound like you're thirty going on forty. *What happen to you!!* You're square, Richard. *You have gotten so damn square!*"

Richard was hurt and annoyed by the way Leonard was reacting to what he felt were adult like perspectives.

"Go play with yourself, Leonard," he bitterly responded while rolling the cuffs down from his pants, and walking towards the car. Prior to opening the passenger side of the car, Richard looked over his left shoulder. Leonard, standing in the water, was taking off his clothes and throwing them towards the shore. Richard was startled.

"Hey, Leonard! What are you doing?" he asked while walking back towards the water.

"I'm going to follow your advice, Big Brother. I'm going to go out there in that wild, wet, blue water and play with myself."

"Leonard, put your damn clothes on!" he demanded as Leonard pulled down his last piece of clothing and began to walk out deeper into the water.

The water covered most of his naked body.

Leonard closed his eyes and appeared to be masturbating himself.

"C'mon, get outta that damn water, Leonard!" Richard demanded, embarrassed and shocked by Leonard's lewd behaviors.

"You oughta c'mon in, Richard. *It feels sooo gooood!"*

Richard continued to stand at the water's edge, gesturing and yelling obscenities at his younger brother. At that moment, two high school girls, carrying their books, appeared at the top of the hill overlooking the isolated beach area. They were shocked and curious by Leonard's strange, erotic behavior.
Fear plagued Richard's mind. What if these girls got the license plate number of Leonard's car and reported him to the authorities? What if the police were to suddenly arrive and observe Leonard's exhibition? Would they get arrested? . . . Yes!!

Would he lose his scholarship as a result of his association with Leonard?...Probably!!

Richard began to nervously talk to himself, kicking the sands and beach pebbles high in the air.

"You're always getting me in trouble, Leonard," he muttered to himself reminiscing about their childhood and adolescence.

"Broke Mr. McCoy's picture window and I got blamed for it. Ate up Mom's chocolate cake, you know she baked that cake for her neighborhood social meeting, and I got blamed for it. I know you did it! I haven't forgotten!!
And Dad always told you never to play with matches and there you were, in the basement, playing cowboys and Indians, tied the babysitter around the pole and set her dress on fire. Poor lady, if she hadn't yelled loud enough, I never would have heard her. You could have killed that woman! She never babysat for us again. And

42

I got hassled for it! Well, you're not getting me in trouble today, Leonard!"

Leonard saw Richard's mouth moving but he couldn't hear anything. Richard picked up Leonard's pants from the sands, searched the pockets, and took out the car keys.

"Hey, Richard! What are you doing?!" Leonard yelled from the distance.

Richard then gathered up all of Leonard's clothes and began to walk to the car.

"Where are you going with my damn clothes, Richard!!?"

Richard got in the driver's side of the car and threw Leonard's clothes in the back seat and yelled,

"Leonard, if you aren't out of that water by the time I count to three, I'm leaving you behind!"

"You wouldn't?"

"One!"

Leonard didn't move.

"Two!" Richard started the engine.

Leonard could sense Richard's anger. He began to quickly run out of the water. He used his hands to cover his exposed private parts.

The young girls on the cliff continued to look on, pointing their fingers, giggling.

"Three!"

Richard began driving away. Leonard jumped over the passenger door of the moving car and landed on the seat as Richard drove up the sand hill, out of the beach zone, and toward the city. Leonard hurriedly put on his clothes in the moving vehicle while looking in shocked disbelief of his brother's actions.

"You must be suffering from combat fatigue or something, Richard. You're no fun anymore. You used to be a pretty wild guy."

"And you're an asshole, Leonard. You're a supreme asshole," replied Richard with his eyes on the road.

"I love you, too, Richard," smiled Leonard while patting him on the right shoulder.

A large, fluffy white cloud covered the radiance of the afternoon sun as Richard drove up and over a steep street hill leading toward the center of town in search of an apartment. The apartment search was disappointing. The lease costs were excessive. Richard finally found an affordable apartment in a slum district less than four miles from campus. The unshaved, unkempt, and overweight manager found an old box spring and mattress to throw in the deal. Richard rented the unfurnished apartment.

Leonard helped Richard move his clothes into the apartment, and they both spent the afternoon cleaning it up. The following morning, Leonard began the long journey back home.

CHAPTER VI

The following Tuesday afternoon, Richard hailed a cab and was driven to Jim's Garage. He walked into the large garage, surprised to find it filled to capacity with disabled vehicles. He counted six mechanics working feverishly under the hoods of expensive, modern automobiles.

After inquiring about the proprietor's whereabouts, Richard found Jim busy working under a 1945 station wagon.

The hood of the station wagon was up. Richard looked down at the engine and initiated greetings to Jim, lying on a flat cart between the vehicles wheels.

"Hello, Jim, How are you doing?"

"Fine, sir. What may I help you with?" Jim inquired while rolling from under the car, standing up, and wiping his hands clean of the axle grease with a cloth that was straddled on the fender of the vehicle.

Jim Wyatt was a stocky built, five-foot six-inch, mid-fiftyish rugged individual with soft facial features and a gentle disposition that resembled the character of Richard's father.

"Well, Jim," Richard smiled. "Dad said that you might need my services so here I am."

Jim looked closely at Richard and responded,

"Your father? Well, who is . . . Richard?? Is that you in there? Well, I'll be damn! Boy, have you grown!" Jim laughed while vigorously shaking Richard's hand.

"Well, Jim, what did you expect?" Richard laughed. "I haven't seen you since I was fifteen years old. Yeah, you came out here, rubbed elbows with the rich and famous, made gobs of money, and forgot all about me," he teased.

"I did nothing of the sort," Jim laughed.

"I haven't rubbed elbows with the rich, I haven't made any real money, and you and your family are always in my thoughts. As a matter of fact, the wife Eleanor and I spent a couple of days with your parents the week before you were released from the military. I'm proud of you, Richard. Your father ranted and raved about that Purple Heart medal for bravery you earned. C'mon, walk with me to my office."

After reacquainting themselves with past histories and discussing their family's health and welfare, they talked business.

Jim offered a good part-time hourly wage. Richard was granted the liberty of a flexible work schedule predicated upon the understanding that he would labor a minimum of twenty five hours a week.

"Well, Richard when would you like to start?"

"Looking at the back- log of vehicles, Jim, I might as well start now."

Jim was elated.

"Great, I have some overalls in the locker room. I am excited about having you here, Richard."

Richard went to work. The day was a success.

****

Richard left the garage at 6:00 p.m. that evening. The night air felt good. He decided to walk the campus town. The restaurants, department stores, and even the novelty shops displayed an air of elegance. The big bright lights of the small city town leaned toward fantasy. Richard passed an obviously expensive restaurant called `Candlelight'.

A good looking young man in his twenties sat with his date at a table next to the window. They were holding hands, looking into each other's eyes, and appeared to be lost in each other's gaze. Richard looked at the girl. He had never seen any woman more beautiful. She, feeling his eyes upon her, looked out of the window at him. They were both intrigued and attracted by each other's appearance. They appeared hypnotized for seconds which seemed like minutes. The woman's date knocked on the restaurant window and forced Richard to come out of his trance. He then motioned Richard to move on. Richard, embarrassed by his own actions, left the immediate area.

****

Richard saw that same beautiful woman walking the campus grounds during the first week of classes. She was practically surrounded by men. She saw him in the distance *and discreetly let him know it.*
 She looked at him; cool, calm, walking nonchalantly in the distance, as the curly locks of his dark hair blew softly in the wind. She questioned her female friends and associates about the mysterious, handsome new student attending the university.
They knew nothing about him.
****

The citizens of the town of Camden were affluent in class and character. The poor were generally ignored and segregated from view within hidden slum pockets of the city. Consequently, there were very few competent automotive repair garages in the city besides `Jim's Garage.' Within a relatively short period of time, many of the elite male students of State University had driven their automobiles into Jim's garage for inspection or repair and discovered that the mystery student, Richard, was a laborer in what they felt was a menial occupation. The word was spread around the campus that he was not one of their stature and was to be avoided.

****

Three academic months had passed. It was Thursday morning and Richard was running late for his marketing lecture. The halls and corridors were practically empty as Richard rapidly moved up the stairwells toward the third floor lecture room.

While recklessly turning the stairway corner and sprinting two steps of the third flight of stairs, he bumped hard into that mysterious beautiful woman, carrying a handful of school books. She screamed as they both stumbled and fell down the stairs onto the stairwell basin. Their books lay wrenched upon numerous steps. Valery was stunned and speechless by the impact. Richard hurriedly picked up her books as she lay, her legs spread, on the basin. She sat up on her elbows, in a daze, trying to figure out what had happened.

> "I'm really sorry! Are you hurt? Here, let me help you," he asked while gently lifting her up by her waist and examining her face for any possible injuries.

She leaned against him, deep in his arms, in a state of semi-consciousness. His arms and body felt warm, strong, safe, and secure. Richard was excited by the feel of her body in his arms and the fragrant smell of her hair. He was distressed with the thought of having possibly injured her. He tenderly held her in his arms and she seemingly allowed herself to be cuddled next to his body. Richard looked into her eyes,

"I'm really sorry. I was running late for class; I wasn't looking. Are you alright?"

he asked while continuing to hold her soft body close and tenderly in his arms, examining her face and arms for any external injuries.

"I think I'm okay," she softly replied.

Damien, and others, having heard her screams following the stairwell accidental impact, travelled to the stairwell scene. Damien was furious to see books scattered in the stairwell and Valery leaning deep in Richard's arms.

He stormed down the stairs in a fit of rage.

"Dammit, what's going' on?! Why don't you watch where you're going!! Did you hurt her?" he roared at Richard while angrily approaching him.

"Are you okay, Baby?" he asked while taking Valery away from Richard's arms into his own.

"I'm fine, Damien," she answered.

Richard picked up the remainder of Valery's books and approached her with them.

"Here, give me those!" Damien bellowed while yanking the books from Richard's hands. Richard continued to approach Valery.

"Please . . . accept my apology," he softly requested while looking deep into her eyes.

His handsome face and mannerisms excited her.

"I accept your apology," she smiled.

"Haven't you done enough, Grease boy?! Why don't you get out of here! Split!" Damien jealously roared.

Richard stood rigid; unafraid.

Damien put Valery's books under his left arm and wrapped his right arm around Valery's waist. Valery looked over her left shoulder and saw Richard leaning against the wall, looking at her as she walked away with Damien. She smiled. Richard smiled back.

****

Again, Valery questioned her female peers about the handsome stranger's background. They informed her of his low economic and social status and urged her to avoid association with him. Additionally, several male students spread vicious rumors questioning his ethnicity in order to dissuade the university coeds from pursuing further interest in Richard. Consequently, during the next six months, Richard and Valery's eyes would warmly acknowledge each other's existence, *but Valery would incessantly avoid any direct or indirect contact with Richard.*

The word was spread. He was not one of their kind.

****

The elite male student body at State University felt insecure within Richard's handsome presence and tended to shun him from their social activities-and their women. He generally moved about the campus-alone.

****

Nine months had passed. Richard had completed the first year of his program and enrolled into the summer program in order to accelerate his academic advancement. Frank Henderson initiated graduate studies at State University during the same summer. Frank eased the tensions held between his wealthy elitist peers and Richard by including him in his circle of campus associates. On Friday, June twenty-third, the Phi Beta Kappa Fraternity held a dance at Frank's home. It was here that Richard formally met that beautiful mysterious woman named Valery.

CHAPTER VII

Their eyes had touched so many, many times -yet they seldom spoke. Nevertheless, at this late evening black-tie fraternity affair, Richard formally met Valery. Richard had been in quiet pursuit of the opportunity to speak to Valery ever since their initial visual encounter upon the campus grounds of State University; nine months ago. He treasured the knowledge of discovering if one who appeared so beautiful and sensuous could possibly be coupled with a mentality to match. Unfortunately, Valery was consistently occupied within the company of various men of various means at various times around the university campus. This lack of access had caused Richard to become invariably exasperated, for he could never catch her, alone. Furthermore, he was convinced that she was purposely and incessantly avoiding him. *Tonight was going to be different.*

Tonight, at this black-tie fraternity affair, Richard was determined to consummate his acquaintance with this beautiful, warm woman with eyes as deeply colored as the rooted darkness of her hair, and talk to her, just talk.

It was a Friday evening semi-formal affair. The season was warm and the day was growing dark when Richard made his entrance into Frank Henderson's home.

It was a massive property with thirty foot high cathedral ceilings and a large foyer entrance that merged into the forty foot wide great room. The great room was joined by a large, elegant, gothic dining room of almost equal size which complemented the majesty of the home.

A small orchestra played in the northwest corner of the great room.

Attendant waiters strolled throughout the crowded venue with gold plated trays offering an assortment of delicacies, pastries and beverages. As Richard continued to walk deeper within the spheres of Frank's home, he observed Valery standing as several men competed for her attention.

There were a large number of attractive young men and women present at this gala affair, handsomely attired in the most expensive and fashionable garments. The bulk of these young people were products of families with strong financial backgrounds, many of whom were graduate students, all of whom projected a consistent air of snobbery. Richard felt somewhat uncomfortable within this elitist environment and maneuvered to blend himself into the woodwork.

He did not desire to be subjected to the typical conversational screening questions of this privileged group. He came here for one reason; to meet and dance with a very particular lady. Conservatively attired in a dark wool suit and tie, Richard leaned against a corner wall and pondered upon a strategy for their ' chance' encounter when,

"Hey, Richard! Richard!! Wake up, man, Where is your head at?"

Startled, Richard awakened from his strategic daydream, turned around and reached for Frank's extended handshake of greeting.

"I don't know, Frank," he smiled. "How long have you been standing here, anyway?"

"Long enough, Richard," grinned Frank while squeezing Richard's right shoulder. "C'mon over to the library and have a drink with me."

In nodded agreement, they commenced their short stride from the dining room quarters and walked around to the elevated library overlooking the great room.

They had exclusive use of the library which featured an intimate built-in bar. Within the solitude of the library, Frank prepared a whisky sour for himself and a requested glass of white wine for Richard.

With beverage in hand, Richard walked to the entrance of the library, sipped the light wine, and unintentionally totally ignored Frank while gazing out surveying the distinguished couples dancing on the open floor of the great room. He again fixed his eyes on that particular young woman. To say Valery was attractive would be a gross understatement. She bore a petite figure of softness within her leggy five-foot- six inch frame. She was blessed with a delicate, mar free olive complexion coupled with a pair of the most hypnotic eyes Richard had ever visually experienced. Her long locks of dark curls trampled below her small shoulders and a sensuous pair of full lips protected her perfect set of teeth.

"Richard!" impatiently probed Frank, "where is your head at?!? I know it's not on this party."

Looking in the direction of Valery, Richard questioned,

"What's her name, Frank?"

"Forget her, Richard."

"What's her name, Frank?" quietly demanded Richard, irritated by Frank's response.

"Valery, Valery Hall."

"She's beautiful, isn't she, Frank?"

"Yes, Richard, she's beautiful."

There was silence.

"Richard...I....I think she once had her eyes on you."

"What?...Are you serious, Frank?"

"Yeah, my sister tells me that Valery once asked probing questions about you when you first registered to State University nine months ago."

"But she won't even speak to me, Frank. It makes no sense!"

"It makes sense to me, Richard."

Richard was puzzled by Frank's response.

"Then explain it to me."

Again there was silence.

Richard turned to Frank and peered into his eyes.

"Explain it to me! And while you're at it, please tell me why you never told me of her interest prior to today, Frank?"

"She happens to be involved with a friend of mine, Richard. I don't like being in the middle."

"Who?... Damien?" questioned Richard.

"Yes. .. Damien."

"What else do you know, Frank?"

"What do you mean, friend?"

"*Why does she avoid me? She literally goes out of her way to avoid even passing me in the school corridors!*" he angrily questioned.

Frank put his hand on Richard's shoulder.

"It's probably the approach/avoidance syndrome, Richard. *She finds you appealing but her world has programmed her to avoid you.* Be forewarned, friend, that she's high class and plays it. Her father is a big-wig banker here, consequently, her heads always in the air. I'm sure she'd look upon you as being economically subservient to her. Besides that, she's engaged to marry Damien, but even If she wasn't, hell, look at your competition."

Richard glanced into Frank's front room and acknowledged Valery being overwhelmed with male attention. Damien had not yet arrived and his competitive peers were voicing unto Valery their verbal appeals for her consideration.

Damien Johnson, a tall, good-looking basketball forward at State University, happened to belong to an extremely wealthy family within the rural campus community.

Besides Damien's athletic prowess, it's been rumored that he has sampled the physical sweetness of the most attractive coeds on campus.

"I don't think she's very happy with him, Richard," continued Frank, breaking up the brief silence.

"Why not?"

"Because she seldom smiles, Richard; she seldom genuinely smiles."

"Do you know her, Frank?"

"Yeah, of course."

"Good, then introduce us, Frank. I've wanted to know her since the day I first saw her on State's campus nine months ago. I can never catch her alone, Frank. Tonight has got to be different....it's got to be!"

"Like I said, Richard, Damien is an associate of mine. I'd prefer not-"

"Just an introduction, Frank!.... Please! Just an introduction!" Richard pleaded in anger.

Frank agreed to make the introduction on condition that it appear to be a chance meeting. Richard agreed to remove himself from the immediate surroundings in order to alleviate any discomfort Valery might have with his initial presence. Frank reluctantly strolled toward Valery and politely slipped her away from the crowd of wooing gentlemen encircling her beauty. He then escorted Valery to his bar for a supposed drink.

She moved slowly, seductively, and with an air of confidence and class. After entering the dimly lit beverage room, she was given her requested beverage of Chablis wine as Richard approached them from the rear. Frank initiated introductions as

Richard approached. Valery was startled and appeared upset as Richard slowly walked toward her.

> "Valery, I'd like you to meet Richard Washington, one of the nicest guys at the University. Richard, meet Valery Hall."
>
> "Pleased to meet you, Richard," she initiated, with a rehearsed smile, "I believe we've seen or bumped into each other several times around campus."
>
> "The pleasure is mine, Valery," smiled Richard while trying to force a confident air of composure.
>
> "How long have you been here, Valery?"
>
> "Well, over an hour. I would have been here earlier but Damien called late and asked me to drive here instead of wait for him. He had a longer than anticipated practice session for Sunday's game," she smiled while looking more at Frank than at Richard.

Frank excused himself from their company in order to give Richard an opportunity to create a dialogue with Valery. Valery appeared visibly nervous about being alone with Richard. Richard continued,

> "I've been told that Damien is State's superstar."
>
> "He is," she bubbled, "I guess that's why I put up with some of his inconsistencies."
>
> "What kind of inconsistencies?"

Valery froze and replied with a half-smile, half whisper,

> "Let's talk about something else, Richard. Have you been here long?"
>
> "No, about forty-five minutes, superstar," he smiled.
>
> "Superstar?"
>
> "Yes . . . Superstar," Richard repeated to her blush. "In my eyes, you've always been State's superstar."

She was impressed by the soft sincerity of his voice and the increasing comfort of his character. Their conversation continued and surprisingly became one of lightness and laughter until the increasingly growing crowd filled the room with verbal, gregarious thunder.

"Valery, it's too loud in here. Allow me a favor."

"What kind of favor, Richard?"

"Allow me the privilege of ten minutes of your undivided attention on the back patio. I really must talk to you."

"I can't."

"Why not?"

"Richard ... I'm . . .why . ... what do you have planned for the weekend?" she asked.

"Are you changing the subject?"

"Yes," she answered, looking away from him.

"For what reason?"

"Richard . . . I think I'd better go," she stated rising from her chair.

"Why? So you can avoid me for another nine months, Valery?" he replied while looking deep into her eyes.

"Richard-"

"Why, Valery? . . .Why?"

She turned her hypnotic eyes away from him.

"Valery .... please . . . look at me," he whispered.

She slowly turned her delicate mar free face in his direction and spoke in a firm, yet gentle manner,

"Look, you've been straight with me, Richard, so I'll be straight with you. I like you. You have an interesting look and a classy, mysterious, dark kind of personality. I'm sure you're a very nice guy. I just want something more."

"More than what, Valery?"

"Look, Damien might get the wrong impression if he saw us sitting here together. I must leave. But it was good having finally met and talked to you."

"Valery,-"

"I'm not interested, Richard," she whispered.

And she left.

Richard, bewildered to find a chair once so full of feminine personality vacant as quickly as it had been inhabited, slowly walked into the great room toward Valery. The orchestra was playing slow and easy listening dance music.

Valery was again besieged by hungry, admiring young men. Nevertheless, amid the cold stares of her male peers, Richard warmly requested the 'privilege' of the present dance. Richard's warm request was warmly refused by Valery, although she happily accepted the same dance request, among others, by the obviously more prominent male members on the floor.

He asked again-and her refusal of his second request exasperated Richard to the point of surrender. Within the emotional abyss of pain and disgust, Richard quietly departed from this affair toward home.

Richard, ego-battered, inattentively drove his car beyond the speed limit toward his residence, a private world of retreat. For Richard, home is still that four-room apartment within the campus slums. However, it's a cozy dwelling with light colored carpeting, quaint living room furnishings and a recently purchased Mediterranean styled bedroom set of dark oak wood. Tonight, however, his apartment is without status.

Why is it, he ponders while disrobing, that he is so attracted to a woman beyond his reach? Why is it, that at the age of twenty-four he cannot patiently endure his present economic situation until he's completed his academic education? He's not doing too badly with his life. His car, a mechanically sound brown Chevrolet, is only three years old. He wears quality clothes, has a job at the garage which he enjoys and, "Dammit, that woman is beautiful!" . . . he's able to play the role of a progressive student on campus.

"So why am I so lonely?" he whispered, when he bears knowledge of several young attractive women who have discreetly offered to come to his apartment by merely a phone call. Why was he wasting his time pursuing her?

Realizing he was making himself miserable reminiscing about this night's negative experience, Richard rationalized reasons why it was probably a good educational lesson.

After all, what does he have to offer a woman of her stature? How could he possibly think of competing against a male member of her peer class?

Thoughts of labor took over Richard's depressed mind, relieving him of present thoughts of loneliness. A couple of long days awaited him at the garage this weekend and sitting, thinking, walking, and sulking over Valery would not shorten their length, only prolong them.

"Get it together, kid," he whispered in comfort to himself.

"Get it together," he repeated, as his mind drifted slowly into the escape of a deep, disturbing, restless sleep.

CHAPTER VIII

The weekend had passed.

The clock alarmed hysterically at six o'clock a.m. the following Monday morning.

The air was crisp, the sun shone radiantly, and the blue skies screamed a greeting to life. After rising and preparing a cup of coffee, Richard found himself buried with the thought of Valery lingering heavily over his mind. He commenced to dress, completed the drinking of his coffee, hurriedly paced out of his apartment, down the stairs to his brown Chevrolet, and away to State's campus.

The dry fallen leaves cracked crisply beneath his black work oxfords as Richard proceeded to make his way through the private landscaped campus of greenery in route to his business marketing class.

Now, close to the business building, Richard ran within eyesight of Frank Henderson.

They closed the distance between them.

"Good morning, Frank?" quietly greeted Richard as the both of them walked in casual unison toward the campus business building.

"Good morning, Richard. Have you recovered yet?"

"Recovered from what?"

"Total rejection," laughed Frank, "*total rejection!*"

"Yeah, I think so," smiled Richard in a retreating half whisper.

"Look, Richard, I think Valery might feel something for you."

"What? Frank, you wouldn't play games with me about something like-"

"No! No, Richard! You know me better than that. Listen, about an hour after you left she walked through my barroom more than once. I got the distinct impression that she was hoping to see you."

"Did Damien show up, Frank?"

"Yeah, late. She appeared rather cool and distant toward him, Richard. Nevertheless, she's engaged to marry the guy so don't get your hopes up. How about lunch in the school cafeteria, Richard?"

"What time, Frank?"

"Ohhh, about noon."

"Okay, good time."

"Great, Richard. I'll see you there."

At 12:15 p.m., Richard walked into the campus cafeteria and ordered his lunch. He then found Frank and associates seated and half glutted at their favorite round table. Richard was the youngest male member of the group and yet these graduate students respected and dealt with him as a peer. He sat next to Frank.

Halfway barreled through his lunch, amid laughter and light conversation, greetings were extended between Frank and an approaching new member to the group. Frank discreetly elbowed Richard to pay attention to the new attendees.

"Hey, Frank, how are you?"

"Fine, Damien, come on over."

As Richard momentarily took his eyes away from his lunch to visually observe Damien, he felt his heart fall to the floor at seeing that particular woman named Valery, clinging to Damien's arm. The hurt upon Richard's face was readily apparent to Frank and Valery, whereupon a trace of sympathy seemingly appeared on her soft face when her eyes gazed upon his.

Frank, in the interim, hoping to detour Damien's attention away from the desire in Richard's eyes for Valery, succeeded by persuading Damien and Valery to momentarily join the group in conversation.

After twenty minutes of athletic double talk between the men, an indifferent Valery grew impatient. She was also growing uncomfortable, for Richard's eyes were continually upon her.

"Damien, class starts in two hours and we still haven't completed our assignment."

"I know, Valery . . . could you believe that shot, Frank? Of course I saw the game, Man, I-"

"Damien, you promised me we'd complete that paper in the library," Valery whispered in a soft, audible tone.

Richard continued to look on at their interactions with each other.

"Right, Valery, . . with just three seconds to go, John, I-"

"Damien!"

Damien's eyes sarcastically rolled up toward the ceiling upon being interrupted by Valery.

"Valery, would you mind going to the library without me right now?"

She gasped with embarrassment and disbelief at his request.

"What about that assignment, Damien? Our marks are predicated upon that paper."

"I know, Val, Listen, I'll be there within thirty minutes."

"Are you sure?"

"Of course, no problem. I'll be there."

Valery, cool yet irritated, complied with his request and pardoned herself from the table of admiring males and left. As

Valery strolled out of the cafeteria doors, Richard discreetly pardoned himself and went in pursuit of her. As he walked out of the cafeteria into the warm radiant sun, Richard saw Valery walking through the large campus garden of roses and greenery en route toward the campus library, alone.

"Valery! Valery!"

She turned; she waited.

"Hello, Richard."

"Hello, Valery. Do you mind if I walk over to the library with you?"

"If you want to."

"I want to," he asserted as they began their campus journey.

"What class are you preparing for, Valery?"

"A sociology elective called `The Family'."

"Sounds interesting."

"It is," she affirmed with a large smile.

"I can easily imagine you with a family, Valery."

"Why is that?"

"You look like the wife/mother type; warm, patient, loving, and so forth, and so forth and so forth," he smiled.

"I hope you're right, Richard," she blushed, "being a good mother means a great deal to me."

"I am," he replied. "I am."

He had captured her attention.

"Tell me something about yourself, Richard," she asked. "How old are you?"

"Twenty-four."

"Are you married?"

"Why do you ask?"

"Because you look married, Richard . . . you know . . settled."

"No, Valery. I'm waiting."

63

"Waiting for what?" she inquisitively asked while looking deep into his eyes.

"For someone like you, Valery," he whispered.   "For you, Valery"

"Oh, no! Not another smooth-talking State Casanova. State's men have got the smoothest lines in the world," she smiled.

"It wasn't a line, Valery. . . and I think you know it."

"You're fast," she responded, caught by the intimacy of their conversation and the chemistry of their personalities.

"After nine months, I think I'm too slow."

"Nine months?"

"It has been that long, hasn't it, Valery?" he whispered.

Valery, uneasy and conveying nervousness, felt herself being drawn toward him by the frankness of the conversation, his deep masculine voice and boyish good looks. She had felt herself attracted to him ever since their initial visual encounter at the 'Candle Light' Restaurant; an attraction she had not allowed to blossom.

Richard desired more than a light-hearted conversation, he needed answers.

"Tell me, Valery, why wouldn't you dance with me last Friday night?" he inquisitively asked with a half smile.

"I didn't want to."

"And why didn't you 'want to'?"

"My own reasons," she evasively responded.

"Which are?"

"This feels like an interrogation, Richard. Let's talk about something else," she abruptly requested. Richard, easily detecting he was getting nowhere fast with Valery, decided he had little to lose by exposing his feelings for her.

After all, he pondered, he may never have another moment with her alone again.

However, for whatever reasons, he said nothing more to her during their walk toward the library.   They walked in silence.

Once the two were seated in the library, Richard asked,

"Do you belong to Damien, Valery?"

"I don't *belong* to anyone," she coldly replied.

"Fine, I'll try again," stated Richard patiently.

"Does your love belong to Damien, Valery?"

Valery, impressed by Richard's wit and persistence in forcing an answer to his questions, quietly responded,

"Yes, I guess it does."

"I find that surprising, Valery, I never considered Damien to be your type."

"What are you talking about, Richard?" she snapped in light anger, "Damien is the most sought after male on campus."

"Is that why you're involved with him?"

"No!"

"Then why, Valery? Why are you involved with Damien? What is there about Damien that turns you on and about me that turns you off?"

Valery was growing uncomfortably irritated.

"I don't care to pursue this crazy conversation any further, Richard! I barely even know you!"

"But that's by design, isn't it, Valery?"

She would not respond. Richard, realizing that Damien would appear in the library within minutes in search of Valery, made a last attempt to reach her.

"Valery, I think there is something you should know about Damien."

"And what is that?"

"I can't tell you right now."

"Why not?"

"Because this isn't the place or time to discuss such a delicate matter; Damien may be here at any moment."

Richard, discreetly enjoying the verbal edge he now possessed in what was a dead-end conversation, continued,

"But there really is something you should know about Damien," he convincingly reiterated.

"When can you tell me?"

"Tonight, tonight around five-thirty p.m., would you prefer if I called or drove over to your house?"

"Neither!" she emphatically answered, wondering if Richard was playing games with her or if he was serious. He looked so intent.

"I'll meet you at the North end campus coffee shop around six o'clock p.m., Richard. It better be good."

"It will be," he declared.

At this point, Richard observed Damien entering the library. He retreated from the table without Damien's attention and casually left the library walls wondering what in the hell he was going to tell Valery about Damien at six p.m. Outside of Damien's physical appearance, arrogance and cold indifference, Richard knew nothing about Damien.

CHAPTER IX

The time was 6:15 p.m., when Richard, gripped with mild fear, walked into the dimly lit sparsely filled North-end campus coffee shop.

He observed Valery sitting alone and apparently daydreaming in a corner back isolated booth. She had planned to give Richard the privacy necessary to inform her of the dark secret she should have knowledge of concerning Damien.

She was beautiful and appeared even softer against the rugged wood-grain paneling of the shop's interior. As Richard approached the table, Valery awakened from her daydream.

"Hello," she coldly greeted.

"Hello", he responded while seating himself "Would you like some coffee?"

Valery nodded in approval and Richard ordered two cups of coffee for the both of them.

"Are you normally around campus this late in the evening, Valery?"

"No, my last lecture ended at four o'clock. I hope this dark secret concerning Damien merits my two hour wait."

While the coffee was being served, a light conversation commenced. Richard learned that Valery had just concluded her sophomore year at State University and of her high academic standings. He wanted to know more. He probed and their conversation became one of depth.

She briefly spoke of her mother's death from cancer during her childhood and her widowed father's prestigious position as a prominent banker in the community.

7:15 p.m-The conversation continued.

Richard learned of Valery's protected childhood and the recognized private schools chosen for her to attend. She modestly discussed her academic scholarships and her plans to be an educator upon graduation from the university.

In this quiet, isolated, coffee shop, Valery looked at Richard. She was impressed by his quiet inner strength, his gentleness, his warmth and his unusual good looks.

She learned that his relationship with Frank was the result of their joint tenure in the Army and of his officer status. She wanted to know more but decided against it. The denial of the attraction was wearing her down. She felt a strong desire to run before her desires for him reveal itself.

8:15 p.m.

> "Okay, Richard," she initiated, "enough of the small talk. What is this big secret that I should know about Damien?"

Richard, peering up from his cup of hot coffee, responded while setting his cup on the saucer.

> "Damien can't possibly love you."

> "What!?!" she echoed in hurt, shock, and disbelief.

> "Damien can't possibly love you . . . as much as I can."

Valery found herself stunned. She didn't quite know how to react. She had been hurt, shocked, relieved, swooned, and flattered within a one minute time interval. Looking at Richard, she then made the most logical, plausible response,

> "*Richard, I think you're crazy! I think you are really nuts*!! You don't know me and I don't know you. I have never given you any encouragement to promote an acquaintance with me. I have refused to dance with you at social affairs and barely acknowledge your existence. You know I belong to Damien whom you really cannot

compare to, and yet here you are professing about all this love you have for me!"

"What do you mean by I can't compare to Damien?"

"You can't!" she emphatically answered.

"What does he have that I lack?" he calmly inquired. She responded,

"Money, status, position, name, heritage-"

"But what does that have to do with love?" he inquisitively interrupted. "There are many men at this university from families with money, status, position, name, and heritage. They pursue you every day. What does Damien have that persuades you to love him in contrast to knowing and loving me? *We're both attracted to each other. We both feel the chemistry! I'm acknowledging it, why won't you?!"*

She couldn't answer his questions and her inability to respond made her uncomfortable. This man was forcing her to face her own questions, something she was finding increasingly harder and harder to do.

"Richard, you've been wasting my time!" she quietly screamed while rising from the table. Patrons sitting at adjoining tables turned in their direction as Valery's voice escalated in anger.

"How, Valery? Because I so desperately want to know you?" he asked while rising and gently grabbing her arm to remain seated.

"Forget it, Richard!!!" she angrily responded, attempting to shake off his embrace.

"*I will, Valery!*" he declared "I give you my word that after tonight *I'll forget it!* I'll never think, feel, or move in your direction again. We'll just be friends, associates, buddies, whatever... if that's the way you want it. But you're here now, Valery, for whatever reasons, you're here; so know me. *Before you reject me, Valery, know me!"*

He moved her.

She had been sought after by many types of persistent men during her young life but none more gently adamant, intense and charming as Richard. His request was small-his request was granted.   With her temper softening and her eyes planted upon his, she slowly seated herself as Richard continued,

"Do you realize I have been trying to talk to you for almost a year?"

"…..Yes," she reluctantly answered, "I think so."

"Then, why haven't I, Valery?"

"What do you mean?"

"Why have you avoided any kind of communication with me?"

"I have no idea what you're talking about."

"I think you do, Valery. You have purposely avoided a verbal or any other kind of interaction with me and I need to know why."

With her eyes turned away from him, she answered,

"Because you scare me, Richard."

"What?!? How?!?" he asked in bewildered amazement.

"I don't really know. Maybe it's your background, or maybe your character; you just do."

"Look at me, Valery," he softly demanded.

She lifted her eyes toward his.

"What do you see?"

"I see a very handsome and persistent young man who is making my life difficult," she answered.

They both laughed.

"What do you want from the man you love and marry, anyway, Valery?" Richard seriously continued.

70

"Do you want Security? Warmth? Attention? Love? Or your name in the social register? If you continue with and marry Damien, your name will appear in the social register, it's inherent. However, forget about warmth, that's a quality he doesn't possess and you know it. If you come my way, eventually, I'll give you both! You will have the love and passion now and I can promise you a significant placement in the social register within a short period of time."

Valery did not like the criticisms being levied against Damien, even though she knew them to be true. Additionally, she was jarred by the level of love Richard professed for her considering their unfamiliarity with each other and indifference she had continually conveyed toward him.

"*This conversation borders on insanity.* You don't know me well enough to make these kinds of unsolicited promises."

"I know that you are what I want and that we work," he replied.

"I have to leave now!" she snapped.

"I'll walk you to your car," Richard sighed in surrender.

"I'm not driving."

"Then I'll drive you home," he offered, hoping for an affirmative response.

Because the night was dark and the air was chilly, Valery nodded in hesitant approval.

They walked out of the restaurant together. Once on the street, Valery lagged a short distance behind him. Richard opened the passenger side of his car and assisted Valery within.

There was silence within Richard's car during the thirty minute drive to Valery's residence. Richard was in awe as he turned off the street and into the long lighted entrance roadway leading to her home. About a block down, wrought iron exterior gates and patrolled guards separated the property from the public. Another winding road followed which led to a fairy tale majestic presentation of Valery's home.

The white marble banisters surrounding the massive front porch entrance of the property quickly emphasized the wealth one could expect from within. He drove into the large circle driveway in front of the home and turned off his engine.

They sat in the car; quietly; without movement.

She was looking out of the passenger window. He looked straight ahead. Richard pondered if this would be the last night that they would ever converse on this matter again. He wanted her badly but it was fruitless if she could not sense nor feel favorable about the possibilities of going forward.

"Valery, how many days have you felt my eyes on you during the past year?"

"Many . . . very many," she quietly conceded.

"Why, Richard?... Why?"

"Why what?"

"Why do you feel you must have me?"

He looked at her intently and told her what was on his heart in a half whisper,

"Because I have loved everything about you since the moment I saw you. I love the way you talk, the way you smile, the way you walk, the way you dress, the warmth in your eyes, the fragrance of your hair, your mannerisms-everything."

She was touched.

She was touched not only by his words but by the intensity, warmth, and sincerity by which he conveyed himself. Momentarily, she could not speak. She was spellbound.

She looked intently into his eyes. He seemingly had everything she ever wanted in a man even though substantively, he had nothing. He had swagger, confidence, honesty, tenderness, and a seemingly raw camouflaged sexuality. The physical attraction was undeniable.

The time was 9:30 p.m.

"I really must go in now," she whispered.

Richard then stepped out of his car, walked around to the passenger side, opened her door and escorted Valery toward the entry of her father's elegant home. There were several tall lighted lamps leading toward the front porch. As they walked in the direction of the massive stone staircase leading to the porch, Richard turned to her,

> "Considering that this is our last meeting and I have professed openly and honestly how I feel about you, please tell me how you feel about me."
>
> "Why?" she answered, shaken by the request.
>
> "Well, I always thought that this attraction I felt for you was mutually shared. I need to know if I was the only one caught up in this fantasy. Give it to me straight. I can take it."

She looked at his side profile as they approached and began walking up the stairs. He turned and looked at her in anticipation of her response. Valery centered her eyes more on the stairs than toward him, seemingly embarrassed by the confession she was about to deliver.

> "Richard, considering that this is our last conversation on this subject, I will give it to you straight. My doctors believe that I suffer with a mild form of depression.
>
> I normally wake up depressed…until I think about the likelihood of being able to see you walking around the campus during the course of the day. *I then begin to feel better.* There have been some days that I have felt unusually depressed and travelled *from building to building, class to class, until I found you. I think I know your class schedule better than you do,"* she laughed.

Richard was stunned by the confession.

"What?!!"

"If you ever tell anyone Richard, I will deny it!" she declared.

"Valery, if you felt that way about me then why have you avoided and ignored me?"

She did not immediately answer and looked away from him. Valery walked toward the front door and opened it. Richard accompanied her into the foyer of the house. The room was dark. A ceiling skylight directed a mist of light into the room. A small shiver of fear ran through her veins. No one was home. The domestic help had left and her father was out of the country. She had never been totally alone with Richard before. However, everything about him excited her and she was no longer willing to deny that reality. Valery sat on the majestic sofa in the foyer and commenced to take off her shoes. Richard continued standing.

"We are from different worlds, Richard, and.."

"I really must see you again," he interrupted.

"How are we going to see each other when I'm engaged to marry Damien?"

"Then break the engagement."

"That's ridiculous! Why would I do that, Richard? You and I don't really know each other. We haven't spent any time together. We don't even know if we are compatible with each other. Furthermore, I would have to give up my life as I know it. My social circle will never accept you. My father will cut me off from my trust. *It just won't work!!"*

Richard walked to her, knelt on one knee and helped her take off the remaining shoe. He looked up into her eyes.

"There is nothing your social circle or father can do to us. However, we do need time together. *So spend some time with me, Valery. You won't be disappointed, I promise."*

Richard was cautiously excited. It appeared that Valery was listening, that she saw the potential of their relationship.

"When?"

"Tomorrow, Tuesday, after classes."

"I can't. I'm scheduled to review the bridal registry with Damien."

The excitement and optimism left Richard's face like air leaving a balloon. He was making a fool out of himself. It was pointless. Richard stood up and began walking toward the door.

"Good night, Valery. I hope you have a good marriage."

Valery saw the pain and disappointment in Richard's face surfacing from his efforts to be with her. He was growing tired. She could sense his despair. Valery stood up and petitioned that he be reasonable.

"*It's a bridal shower registry meeting, Richard; not a wedding*!! It was planned over two weeks ago. You and I will just have to plan for another day!"

Richard stopped, turned and slowly walked back and looked into her eyes.

"Valery, just spend a little time with me. We owe it to ourselves to at least look at us."

"Richard, I don't know. I need time to think," she answered, looking at him tenderly, the masquerade of indifference falling away.

"Don't make me beg! *I need to know that something happens between us beyond tonight!*"

She looked at him. Everything about Richard excited her. A future with him seemed dark. However, tonight, a future without him seemed even darker.

Throughout the school year she had fantasized how their lives might be together. However, she never anticipated actually acting on efforts to materialize the fantasy. It was too risky. Tonight however, she found herself wanting to examine the possibilities.

She stood up and spoke like a college professor.

> "Richard, today I have been straight and honest with you and you equally with me. I need time to think about this. I am agreeable about having one final meeting to resolve this. I will meet you Wednesday after class. However, it will have to be around three o'clock. We can meet at the same off campus coffee shop if that is agreeable."

Richard walked to her and put his hands on her shoulders,

> "Valery, a one hour meeting over coffee is not enough time to determine the possibilities of a relationship. We need legitimate time together."

She continued as if she had not heard his complaint,

> "Is three o'clock Wednesday agreeable, Richard?"

> "Yes, Valery. Three o'clock Wednesday is agreeable," he replied in exasperation.

Valery extended her hand to Richard in the form of a handshake.

> "Good night, Richard," she smiled, "It's been an interesting evening."

Richard looked at her extended hand and smiled in amusement. He approached her. She slowly retreated. He softly grabbed her by her waist and pulled her to him.

> "Richard!...Richard!" she protested.

His right arm encircled her tiny waist and her trembling body was firmly pressed against his. She turned her face away from him in order to avoid the anticipated effort to kiss her. The smell and feel of her body and perfumed hair made him feel drunk with passion. He fought to restrain himself. His left hand reached up to Valery's hair and turned her face to his as he intensely kissed her retreating soft full tender lips. Her lips were delicious; succulent. He hungered for more, much more, one kiss was not enough.

"Wait Richard, wait…" she softly cried trying to gently remove herself from his firm embrace. However, he did not hear her. Her lips had awakened the craving his body demanded for her. The kisses that he had imagined paled in comparison to what he was now tasting. He kissed her again and again; each kiss more sweet, tender and passionate than the last.

Valery's body, previously in retreat, was now at attention. Her arms initially lay motionless by her side, letting him do whatever he wanted to do with her. Those arms were no longer motionless but ascending, desperately wrapped around his neck, passionately returning Richard's kisses as if there were no tomorrow.

His lips were luscious; much more tasty then what she had anticipated. They finally came up for air. Richard continued to hold Valery tightly in his arms. Valery's head lie on his shoulder and her eyes were still closed. She appeared to be in some semi-conscious state of euphoria.

Richard whispered,

"Valery…"

She came back to the present; reluctantly.

"I wish you had not done that," she whispered unconvincingly, trying to catch her breath while still wrapped in his arms.

"Why do you wish that?"

"Because you have confused me even more. What are we going to do, Richard?"

He looked at her tenderly and smiled,

"I don't know. I guess you will tell me at our 'meeting' on Wednesday."

Valery was seemingly jarred back to the present. She fully opened her eyes and softly pulled away from him.

"Yes, Richard. We will discuss it at our meeting on Wednesday."

Richard took Valery's right hand and fingers to his mouth and kissed them.

"Until Wednesday, Valery."

"Until Wednesday, Richard."

And he left.

Valery stood outside her door and watched his vehicle until it disappeared. That night, Valery did not sleep. She did not want to sleep. She wanted to replay the entire evening in her mind and determine what risks, if any, she was willing to take to find happiness outside of her class norms. A public formal wedding announcement, broadcasting the union of she and Damien's family was planned within three weeks. She pondered and questioned the possibilities.

CHAPTER X

Unbeknownst to Valery, two members of the varsity basketball squad had observed Richard and Valery at the North End coffee shop Monday night. They communicated this information to Damien. Damien, attempting to avoid embarrassment, advised them that he was aware of the meeting and that Richard was retained to address the fleet of vehicles of Clifford Hall.

****

The following Tuesday morning, Valery awakened after a sleepless night of self negotiation. *She decided that she was not going to pursue a relationship of any kind with Richard.* She enjoyed the high-shelf lifestyle she lived. She enjoyed the access and the excesses of money, power and wealth. She relished the aristocracy of being the daughter of the most powerful banker in the community.

She was envied by most coeds at State University and pursued by the most reputable men in the country. She took pleasure in the personal attendants who helped her daily with dress and makeup and the boxes of jewelry she could patiently pick from to adorn her body. The clothing she wore were one-of-a-kind pieces that were exclusively designed for her by various tailors who visited her home on a regular basis to display their fine lines of new weaves and wools to Valery and her father. Furthermore, Valery was engaged to marry Damien. A formal state-wide announcement was planned within weeks. Damien loved Valery although not in the way she wanted to feel and be loved. *Valery regarded this as a small inconvenience.* She would teach him how to love her in the manner that she wanted after the wedding. He was teachable, she reasoned.

Valery was aware of the promiscuous reputation of her fiancée; a reputation that same Damien disavowed. Nevertheless, she would change all of that after the wedding.

Yes, she was very much attracted to Richard but felt that these kinds of feelings would have to be controlled or else they would wreck her life. Damien's family built their wealth from oil exploration and refineries. Their prominence was more solid and substantial than that of her own wealthy father. Her father had educated her to understand that her eminence would be elevated by this marriage merger.

The association between Damien's family and Valery's family had existed for decades. They had a history together. Both families had discreetly nurtured and planned this marriage between Valery and Damien for years. *You can't let that history die over some flirtatious attraction, she reasoned.*

****

Valery attended her 9:30 a.m. class. The lecture ended at 10:45. She walked out of the classroom with several of her coed associates. They were conversing and laughing as they exited the room. As she walked out into the corridor, she saw Damien leaning on the opposite corridor wall facing her class. Several of her friends greeted Damien as Valery walked up to him. He appeared distraught.

"Hey, what have I done to deserve this favor?" she smiled.

Damien did not smile back.

"Where were you last night?" he inquired.

"I was at home," she meekly answered.

"Where did you go before you went home?" he suspiciously asked.

"I had a cup of coffee with a friend."

"What friend?"

Valery shuddered. It appeared that Damien was aware of the meeting she had with Richard and she needed to represent that meeting in the most innocent light.

"Well…not a friend, I would say a school associate."

"What associate?"

"It's not important who I had coffee with. Why are you interrogating me like this?"

"Did you have a date with this Richard Washington fellow?" he asked in the tone of a prosecutor.

"No! There was no date! He persuaded me to meet him there under false pretenses. When I determined that he misrepresented certain information, I went home."

The corridor of the hallway was now empty and quiet.

Damien was 6'4" tall weighing in excess of 220 pounds of muscle. Valery was 5'6" tall weighing 115 pounds soaking wet. He was an intimidating figure when angry.

"Your car was being serviced yesterday, how did you get home?"

"Richard gave me a ride home," she meekly answered.

At that point, Damien grabbed Valery by her arm in a vice like grip and pulled her into an empty room.

"Ouch..ouch…ouch!!" she screamed from the pain to her arm.

Damien appeared like a madman.

"You are a liar! You are just a liar!! Are you that fucking stupid to have a date with this nothing while in the same university and environment as mine?!!" he roared.

She tried to remove his grip. The pain was immeasurable.

"Let go of me!" she cried, "let go of me!!"

He angrily pushed her against the blackboard. The back of her body slammed into the blackboard and she slid down the board wall onto the floor.

Suddenly, his character and mood radically changed. He became soft and rational. Damien walked over to assist her up and she slapped his hand away from her.

> "Don't you touch me! Don't you put another hand on me!" she screamed.

She slowly stood up in pain and continued to lean on the blackboard.

> "I can't believe you have the nerve to question my integrity or common sense. How dare you imply my lack of fidelity considering that you have fornicated with practically every coed who has made herself available to you."

> "Well, that's not true. Even if it were true, that's different!"

> "It is true and it isn't any different in my book!"

Damien meekly approached Valery,

> "Valery, I didn't mean to hurt you. You know it makes me crazy seeing these men around you and hearing these stories of you *and this Richard guy!*"

Valery tried to put the engagement and relationship back in focus,

> "We have several bridal shower registry meetings starting at four o'clock. We must be there on time."

Damien stood at the door and declared that he was not going to the bridal registry meetings. His rationale was that the registry was something that brides do and whatever gifts she desired was fine with him. He then left Valery, grimacing in pain, standing at the blackboard.

Valery tried to shake off the horror of this encounter. It was not the first time that Damien's jealous temperament had displayed acts of intimidation toward her. In the past she had excused his jealous outbursts as immature signs of his love for her. Valery now questioned that interpretation.

Valery was flustered, angry and in pain. She was more confused now than ever. She felt that she had to get away from the school, the people, everything. She had promised Richard a meeting at three o clock for the following Wednesday afternoon and decided that it would have to be postponed until she got back later in the week.

The time was 11:05 a.m.

Richard's next class, Economics, commenced at 11:30 a.m. in the Regus Building which was next door. Valery took out her makeup mirror, straightened her hair and proceeded toward the Regus Building. She arrived there at 11:10 a.m. Many of the students and the professor were seated for the Economics lecture. Richard had not yet arrived.

At 11:15 a.m., Richard arrived to class. As he approached the class, he saw Valery standing near the entrance of the lecture room.

"Hello, Valery, this is a pleasant surprise," he smiled. Valery was shaken by how happy she was to see him. A big smile crossed her lips.

He took her hand and escorted her around the short corridor corner to the empty maintenance room.

"Hi, Richard. I promised to meet with you on Wednesday at three o'clock and I wanted to tell you that we have to postpone it for some other day."

"Why is that?" he inquired, disappointed.

"Because I have to get away for a moment. I'll be back this weekend and maybe we can meet next Monday."

Valery bruised easily. Richard noticed the large welts on her right arm.

"Hey, what happen to your arm?" he quietly asked, trying to contain a growing anger.

"Nothing," she answered unconvincingly.

Richard looked at her warily. Valery would not look at him. With his finger, he raised her chin and eyes toward him-and she cried. She turned her head and moved away from him.

"So what kind of trip are you initiating?" he asked while observing her anguish and nervous energy.

"I'm just getting away. I think I'll go up north to the cottage and try to figure some things out."

"That's about a four hour drive, isn't it?"

"Yes," she meekly answered.

"*You will miss a whole week of classes!*"

"Yes, I know."

The building bell rang informing all that the time was 11:30 a.m.

"Richard, you better go to class now. I will talk to you next Monday," she smiled.

Richard didn't like it. The welts on her arm, the unexplained crying, the decision to be alone in a distant place, the acknowledgment of depression. He didn't like it.

"What is so special about this cottage?" he asked as if he did not hear her.

"Well, it's very serene. It's off the water. There is very little civilization and a lot of wildlife. It's a good place to think, read, and rest."

Richard was standing. His back was against the wall in the maintenance room. Valery was standing up facing him. He leaned down and softly kissed her lips. There was no resistance. She blushed. Richard locked the maintenance door and pulled Valery to him.

"Richard, go to class!" she whispered with her head on his shoulder.

"How do you feel about company, Valery?" he meekly asked.

"*What do you mean?!*" she asked, removing herself from his embrace while looking up at him in terror of the anticipated response.

"I mean, how do you feel about me going up to the cottage with you?"

"*Absolutely not!* That would be inappropriate. I just need to be alone!" she declared.

"Why do you need to be alone? Look, this could be a good opportunity for us to learn something about each other and find if we are compatible. I mean, you are the one who emphasized that we don't really know each other. Our spending a few days in isolation should resolve that issue."

She became irate,

"*No! No respectable man or woman would do that considering the short length of time of our association!*"

Richard continued, unimpressed with her position.

"Wouldn't do what? Spend uninterrupted time together despite the attraction and having interfaced over the last nine months? C'mon Valery, you're not that naïve. We are both curious to know how well we fit. This is an opportunity to find out. I promise, I will be the perfect gentleman."

She looked at him in disbelief. *He was serious!* Suddenly, the idea mutually excited and appalled her. He continued,

"What are you going to do for clothes? Were you planning to go home and pack?"

"No. I just now decided that I need to get away and felt that I would drive there immediately. Anyway, I have clothing at the cottage."

Richard was intrigued.

"Like, right now? Just walk off the campus and drive up North?"

"Yes."

"Have you ever done that before?"

"No."

"Okay, let's go! I can pick up some essentials on the way up there."

Valery continued to shake her head in disbelief at what was transpiring. Four days ago, June 23rd, she had the first conversation with Richard wherein she conveyed to him her opinions and attitudes of his social/economic inferiority. She is engaged to be married into one of the most affluent families in the country, and yet, today, Tuesday, June 27th, she's actually considering having Richard, in significant part, a stranger, accompany her to her father's isolated cottage... alone. But he excited her; he so much excited her.

"No, Richard, I don't think-"

Richard continued as if he was deaf to her objections,

"We only need to drive one automobile. We will take your Kurtis. I'll drive. Give me your keys," he assertively requested extending his hand.

She continued to be troubled and intrigued by the thought of this daring scenario.

"No, Richard! I-"

"Give me your keys," he softly insisted; his hand extended in anticipation of his request being met.

There was a silence...............Reluctantly, like an obedient child, Valery reached into her pocket and gave Richard her keys. She was mesmerized; curious to see if this impromptu unorthodox plan would actually move toward materialization. Richard took her books and they walked from the school building toward the parking lot. They got in Valery's 'Kurtis' sports car. She felt like a spectator watching this scene unfold from a play. Richard pulled Valery closer to him once inside the vehicle. Grudgingly, she moved closer and within minutes fell into a deep sleep on his shoulder as he began the drive north on Highway One.

CHAPTER XI

It was 4 o' clock p.m.

They were less than 40 miles from the cottage. Richard saw a full service store just outside of their destination. He awakened Valery and the two of them walked inside. Richard purchased two pair of khakis, essentials, undergarments, linen shirts, sandals, champagne, fruit, milk, cereal, salmon, bread, and a rotisserie chicken.

They arrived to the cottage at 4:45 p.m. The cottage was a 3000 square foot waterfront edifice. It was a contemporary ranch style property with three bedrooms, an open floor plan and a walkout lower level. There were three fireplaces; One in the great room, the family room and the master bedroom.

They walked toward the kitchen located on the northwest side of the interior with the bags of groceries. The kitchen was 20 feet by 20 feet in dimension with a large island in the middle closely aligned with the sink and counter space. Valery immediately began putting the groceries away. Richard took the clothing goods to the master bedroom and placed them on a side chair in the bedroom.

Richard was in awe by the size and magnificence of the estate. He walked out to the wood patio deck overlooking the river. A light wind played with the locks of his hair. Valery came out to the deck and stood next to him. He appeared calm, confident, very much at peace in his own skin.

She felt a shiver of fear. They were here alone. What were his expectations? She looked at him suspiciously. Richard was caught off guard by the way she leered at him.

"What is that look about?" he laughed.

"I hope you realize that you will have your own bedroom during this visit," she asserted.
He returned his eyes to the waves and waters and replied,

"I had not really thought about it but I assumed as much."

"Good thinking, Richard!" she sarcastically replied.

Valery left Richard on the deck and walked to the kitchen. She pulled out several cooking utensils in order to prepare a light dinner for them. Richard continued to stay on the deck and breathe in the beauty of the serene surroundings. Richard took a shower, shaved, combed his hair and put on the khaki pants, linen shirt and sandals he had recently purchased.

It was 5:45 p.m.

He walked into the kitchen and stood behind Valery as she was rinsing the assorted fruit and lettuce at the sink. He kissed the nape of her neck. She shivered.
Richard then offered,

"Hey, why don't you take your shower? I will finish dinner. We will have the rotisserie chicken, salad and fruit, agreed?"
Valery was pleased by the overture. She looked at him, surprised by the offer,

"Agreed," she answered as she turned and walked toward the master bath.
Valery showered and dried her hair. She put on flannel pajamas and her night silk robe anticipating same presentation would minimize any amorous ideas on Richard's mind relative to where the night was going.

It was 6:30 p.m.

Valery walked back to the kitchen. Richard was not there. She found him in the small quaint dining room. He had lit several small candles and found a station on the radio playing soft and easy listening music. The individual salad plates were prepared and accompanied with several variations of toasted breads. The chicken was sliced and warmed. The fruit dishes were prepared and refrigerated.

"Hi," she greeted."Looks interesting!"

"Hello", he answered back while assisting Valery into her chair. They quietly began to eat.

"How was your shower?"

"Good," she answered, looking at him with an air of distrust.

"Uh, oh, okay what suspect thoughts are you thinking now?"

"Nothing, I just hope you don't have any illusions of something sexual happening here because it's not going to happen, understand? I mean, we want to get to know each other, right?"

"Yes, Valery, nothing is going to happen that you don't want to happen."

"*Correction, Richard, nothing is going to happen, period!*" she stated as a matter of fact with her eyes firmly planted on his.

"Okay, already, can we eat and talk about something else other then sex? You seem to have a one track mind," he laughed.

"I'm not talking about sex! I just want to make it clear that-"

"Eat, Valery!" he laughed.

She continued eating, nervously looking at him in odd ways. After dinner, Richard poured them both a glass of champagne and they initiated in-depth small talk about his childhood, his parents, and the lunatic conduct and comedic behaviors of his younger brother, Leonard. When he told her about the early life antics of his younger brother, Leonard, particularly the day he set the baby sitter's dress on fire while playing cowboys and Indians, Valery laughed so hard that she literally began crying.

There was a brief silence.

"Richard, I have a small confession to make. I knew of you before you registered to State University."

"How is that, Valery?" he inquired while inquisitively looking at her.

"Well, Frank's father, Henry, and my father are on the University Board of Directors. There was a board meeting in my home about six months before you registered. The agenda for that meeting included the selection of prospective students for the G.I. Bill Supplemental Scholarship Program. Frank attended that meeting and gave a thorough and intense presentation of your military life and accomplishments in support of your scholarship petition. The acts of bravery he recounted on your behalf were amazing."

"Well, I'm sure his representations were exaggerated," Richard smiled.

"I don't think so, Richard. Frank is not typically one who exaggerates the performances of anyone other than himself," she laughed.

Richard laughed, "Well, I see you know Frank pretty well!"

Valery continued, "However, I never knew that the war hero they were talking about was you. Never in a thousand years would I have guessed that you were that war hero Frank was advocating for."

Richard was intrigued.

"Why is that, Valery?"

"Because you don't look like a war hero. One
normally expects a war hero to have a rugged,
rough outdoors look. I just recently connected
the dots."

Valery inquired further about Richard's military life and
experiences. Reluctantly, he discussed his four year tour of
military duty and deployment to France, Germany and various
parts of Europe. She was amazed to discover the level of
fluency he maintained of the French and German dialect.
Valery, having been tutored in French, challenged his cursory
mastery of the language and was impressed.

"You are so full of surprises! You really are a mysterious
fellow."

"No, not really. One of the strange benefits of the war is
that if you are deployed in a certain country long
enough, you pick up the language."

She looked at him, continuing to be baffled, and
continued,

" Richard, in some ways I feel sorry for you,"

"Sorry for me?" he questioned.

"Yes, sorry for you, Richard. You have seen or
experienced a lot of horror, pain and death for a
twenty-four year old."

"I have also experienced a lot of life as a result of those
same experiences, Valery," he smiled while looking into
her dark eyes.

Valery was jolted. She found his response to be
insightful. The level of his maturity astounded her. The
intellectual interaction of their conversation felt like foreplay.

It was nine-thirty p.m. They finished dinner and moved
into the family room. They sat on the oversized sofa in front of

the large gas fireplace. The carpeting within the family room was plush and accompanied by large jumbo pillows and blankets which were well placed around it.

At this point, the only music within the house was the sound and laughter of each other's voices. Valery's egotistical airs diminished with each glass of champagne Richard continued to pour into her half full glass.

> "Well Valery, what do you think? How are we doing so far?"

She looked at him from the corner of her eyes.

> "I don't know, Richard. One thing is for sure, we come from different worlds. In some ways, your world sounds more interesting than mine. However, I like the perks that come from wealth. I don't think I can give them up for a life style such as the one you have lived. I like the personal attendants who help me with dress and makeup. I like having access to beautiful pieces of jewelry. I like the one-of-a-kind tailored outfits I wear and availability to the new lines of weaves and wools."

Richard looked at her, stunned by her conclusions. He got up and walked from the sofa to the fireplace while Valery remained seated on the sofa with her legs crossed. Richard inquired,

> "*Do you think I'm asking you to give up those luxuries?*"

> "Well, yes, aren't you? I mean, *you have nothing!'*"

Richard appeared insulted and defensive.

> "Damien has nothing! Yet you seem to be enthralled with the idea of being his wife despite the fact that most people see the union of you two as a mixture of oil and water."

Valery was dismayed by the assertion.

"What do you mean he has nothing?! His family owns some of the most reputable oil refineries in this country. Their net worth is-"

"Give me a break, Valery!" Richard interrupted. "Damien doesn't have anything and he hasn't done anything other than conduct himself like an arrogant, pompous, airhead of a bully! He was simply blessed to have been born within a family of wealth. *Outside of what his mother and father gives him, he has nothing; not even two nickels to rub together!* He, like the bulk of those arrogant asses on that campus are wholly dependent on their families for their mere survival."

Valery was astounded by this perspective. She angrily got up and strutted toward him at the fireplace, confrontational, with her right hand on her waist.

"Well, Richard, in that case, your analogy would also apply to me! Consequently, you are inferring that I am one of those pompous-"

Richard sensed her anger but was not about to acquiesce his position.

"I don't want to talk about this anymore, Valery, *and we're not going to argue about this!"* he firmly asserted. "There is nothing weak or profound about my logic. Think about it!! *What has he done that is so deserving of this high regard you have for him?* However, let's get one thing straight! *I don't want you to give up anything!! I want the same wealth you want! If you are mine, I can assure you that we will have what you are accustomed to and more!* **I just want to be the one who gets it for you!** *I don't need my mother or father* to provide a job or a future for us. I want to get it for us. I just need time, Valery. Just stay with me until I graduate. **I'm going to be important. I'll buy you whatever you want!"**

She was speechless. She looked at him in a daze. Where did he come from? He was a walking contradiction. His soft, gorgeous, pretty boy looks were a masquerade. Tonight, she saw a man who is fiercely independent, intelligent, fearless, confident, assertive and focused.

Additionally, she was humbled by the level of allegiance he pledged to her; the things he wanted to do '*for us*'. This is crazy, she thought. *They barely know each other and yet, at this moment, tonight, she felt like she had known Richard all of her life.* She had never felt more comfortable or safe in the company of any man as she felt this moment with Richard.

Valery initiated a mental self examination of the substance and values of her affluent class and lifestyle. Her mind was in overload. She sat back on the sofa and pondered over their discussions.

Richard could see that Valery was lost in some sort of a meditational daydream. He walked toward her and squatted down to see where her eyes were focused and bring her back to the present.

"Valery,"

She returned to the present. Her mood and character had softened. She seemed more at peace.

"Yes, Richard"

"Where are you, Valery?"

"I'm here. I'm here with you. *I'm listening to you*," she softly replied.

He knelt in front of her and kissed her lips.

"Valery, it was not my intention to be insulting. I get a bit defensive sometimes when-"

"No! No need to apologize. Everything is fine, Richard. Some of the things you say make sense. However, those in my circle do not see ourselves or our lives in quite the way you have defined it. We might be a little more humble if we did. Most of us tend to look upon ourselves as royalty, silly, isn't it?"

Richard looked at her. She had the charms, grace, poise, mannerisms and class of a sovereign.

"In my eyes, Valery, you are royalty; *Princess Valery!*" *he declared.*

She laughed, "*Princess* Valery?"

"Yes," he smiled, "*Princess*, for short. Is that okay with you?"

"Yes," she smiled while tenderly looking at him and leaning over to kiss him on his forehead.

Richard, still kneeling, wrapped his arms around Valery's waist and brought her from the sofa to the blanket and pillow covering the plush carpeted flooring in front of the fireplace. Valery lay next to Richard as the dark monopolized the night and the light of the fireplace took over the interior of the room. Valery should have been tired and yet she was wide awake. It was an awakening that she had never previously experienced. Her perspectives on social class, values and entitlements were undergoing a metamorphosis.

Richard's arms held her body close to his and his right hand clasped the softness of her covered buttocks. They could feel the heat of their bodies longing for each other.

Richard kissed her soft lips that were now desirous to kiss him back. Valery unfastened the buttons on his white linen shirt. Richard pulled it off exposing a lean muscular upper anatomy.

He held her body closer and tighter to his. His right hand caressed the thighs and waist of her body as his left hand discreetly moved under the flannel pajamas and softly touched the wetness between her thighs. She was breathing heavily in his ear. He removed his left hand from the moistness and raised her legs in a fetal position. Richard gently yet assertively pulled the flannel pajama pants down from her waist and off of her legs.

The flames from the fireplace seemed to emulate the intensity of the fire that was raging between their bodies. Richard unfastened the three buttons of the flannel pajama top covering the fullness of Valery's breasts. She lie in his arms, nude, on the blanket before the fire. He turned over and got on his hands and knees in order to witness the whole of her. He visually inhaled the fullness of her beauty. She had more curves then a ski slope and each of those curves thrilled and excited him. Richard was drunk with desire.

Valery smiled at seeing the appreciation and longing in his eyes. He was hungry. He separated her legs to expose the treasure that he famished for. They were at the point of no return. Richard moved back to her face and kissed her lips as Valery cried out,

>*"Richard, we're moving too fast! We're moving too fast!!"*

He looked at her. Her eyes, confused, warm with innocence, doubt, desire, and whispered,

>*"No Valery. We're moving too slow...we're moving too slow!!"*

As they kissed each other's lips with warm tender hunger. In the dark, he could see both the want and the fear in her eyes.

"What is it, Valery?" he whispered.

She looked up at him, almost apologetically,

"I agree, Richard, we have moved too slow. *But please, don't take me tonight, Richard.* Let's be sure that it's not the champagne influencing how we feel tonight. Let me wake up in the morning and reminisce that tonight was real and not just a beautiful dream. You don't understand the misery I've lived. This morning, I felt border line suicidal and now I feel like a newborn. Please Richard, take me to bed and let me sleep and wake up. I promise that if you do that for me, then I will give you whatever you want."

 Richard smiled. He stood up and leaned down toward Valery's nude body and put his right arm under her legs and his left arm under her shoulders.

"Okay, Princess. Put your arms around my neck," he whispered.

As Valery wrapped her arms around his neck, Richard tenderly picked her up, kissed her lips, and gently carried her to the bedroom. His arms were strong. Her head lay on his shoulder during the short trip to the bedroom. Upon being placed in bed, she lie in his arms, under the blanket, and gradually fell into a deep restful sleep.

CHAPTER XII

It was Wednesday; 7:00 a.m.

Valery lie asleep nestled deep in Richard's shirtless arms. He softly kissed her lips and her eyes slightly parted,

"Richard...," she sighed.

"Go back to sleep, Princess," he whispered while subtly removing himself from bed as she fell into a deeper sleep on the fluffy down pillow. Richard walked down the hall to the guest bathroom and took his shower. He slipped on his khaki pants, a fresh linen shirt and sandals. He walked to the kitchen and began to prepare a pot of coffee. As the coffee was brewing, Richard stepped out of the sliding doors of the living room onto the front deck. He inhaled the fresh air while watching the ebb and flow of the river waves crashing toward the land. The waters always calmed him.

Meanwhile, the rich smell and aroma of the coffee ultimately made its way back to the bedroom. Valery's eyes awakened. She lay in bed, amazed by the mental and emotional peace she felt from within. There were no airs of depression; no feelings of discontent. She had not felt this kind of peace in years. She reminisced about the conversations she shared with Richard the night prior and the way her body responded to him. She recalled having mildly awakened twice during the night and being softly kissed back to sleep by Richard.

It was not a dream, it was real. It was not the champagne, *it was Richard*. He brought out a side of her that she had never seen before and yet she was never more comfortable with herself than with Richard. Valery arose from bed, showered, applied a light base of makeup and slipped on a white terry cloth robe. Richard was still outside meditating and taking in the strength and beauty of the surroundings. His back was to her when Valery walked out on the deck with a cup of coffee in her hand.

"Good morning, Richard" she greeted while extending the cup of coffee toward him.
Richard turned and smiled,

"Good morning, Valery", he replied, while accepting the cup of coffee.

He tasted it.

"Hey, this taste exactly like the way I would prepare it," he declared in surprise.

"Yes, I know, three sugars and two creams, right?" she questioned.

"Yes, how did you know that?"

"We just had coffee two days ago, Richard, or have you forgotten already?" she smiled.

"How could I forget? However, I am surprised that you observed how I like my coffee."

"Richard," she beamed, " I have always observed everything about you."

"Really?" he whispered, surprised by the revelation.

"Yes…Really!" she answered.

"Would you like some?" he inquired while extending the cup toward her.

"You don't mind sharing?" she asked.

"No. I like to share. I insist on it," he answered, continuing to extend the cup to Valery. She took the cup and drank from it while joining Richard at the railing and looking out into the waters. She then placed the cup on the deck table.

Valery turned to face Richard.

"Richard, I have never slept as well during the
night or felt more at peace in the morning as
I do today. Thank you, Richard."

Richard turned away from the aesthetics of their surroundings and focused on Valery. The morning wind played with her hair. He wrapped his arms around her body and held her tightly.

"So, it wasn't just a beautiful dream?" he asked.

"No," she coyly answered.

"It wasn't the champagne?" he asked, smiling even more broad.

"No," she smiled while tenderly looking at him.

"Good," he smiled.

There was a brief silence. Valery looked up at Richard and whispered,

"I made certain promises last night, Richard."

He looked at her and smiled,

"And?"

"I keep my promises, Richard. Are you still hungry?"

Richard held her tightly. It was obvious that there was no clothing between Valery and the terrycloth robe. He tenderly kissed her lips. She clung tightly to him and buried her head in his shoulder. The fresh clean sea smell of his body was invigorating.

"Starving," he answered.

She looked at him; excited by the hunger in his eyes that she had observed the night prior. Valery slowly removed herself from his embrace and took his hand and led him back to the bedroom. The clock on the end table read 9:45 a.m.

Once inside the bedroom, Valery unbuttoned Richard's shirt and helped him remove it. Richard took her into his arms, kissed her, and untied the belt to her robe. He visually inhaled the exciting nakedness of her body as the robe fell to the floor.

Richard picked up Valery and placed her in the center of the bed. He moved slow and deliberate. His hands, eyes and fingers visually explored and caressed the soft, tender, curvaceous architecture of her body. He hovered over her, tenderly, passionately, kissing her lips and tasting her neck, shoulders and breasts. Her breasts were works of art. He licked and sucked them wholly and slowly. They tasted sweet; maternal. The sight of her curvaceous petite body was driving him mad. Richard wanted more. However, he continued to move slow; methodical. He was intent to thoroughly feast upon and sexually exploit this blessed opportunity.

Richard kissed, licked, fondled and savored the delicate taste of her legs. Amidst Valery's nervous sighs and giggles, he sucked individually the detailed intricacies of each of her toes and gradually moved down to the fragrant soft tenderness of her thighs.

"More...more," she whispered.

He placed a pillow under her buttocks and spread her legs wide. His lips, mouth, tongue continued to travel until they reached the ultimate treasure between her legs. Richard's strong hands brought her body to his mouth as he began tasting, kissing, sucking, licking, relishing the sweet fruit juices of her orifice and inhaling the delicate scent of her inner thighs during his feeding. The more he feasted on her body, the more she flowed. The raw depth of his craving for her body both excited and terrified her. Valery's knees and legs quivered; spread wide in surrender and anticipation.

Valery tried to contain the uncivilized screams leaving her lips to no avail. She began to relate to how a lamb must feel when being taken by a lion. *Equally, however, Valery felt like she was being worshipped*. The pleasures she was receiving were corollary to the highest thrill and delight a queen could figuratively receive from a giving subject.

Richard's head came up high for air, his tongue and mouth relishing the flavor of the satiated fleshy liquid honey taken from her body. The loins of Richard's body were now aching to penetrate and feed from Valery's flesh.

During the course of his tastings and feedings, Richard had slowly, subtly edged out of his pants. He was naked, predatorily on all fours, leaning and leering over her. He had the lean muscular body of a god. Valery was aghast by the length of his erect manliness. Richard smiled. He had obviously seen that response to his nakedness before.

He hovered over her and kissed her softly. A small measure of worry crossed her eyes,

"*What do you think you're going to do with that?*" she asked, with a half smile.

"I don't know," he whispered in her ear, "We'll think of something."

She laughed and then pleaded in his ear,

"Richard, please don't hurt me."

"I won't hurt you, Valery," he promised as he lay over her; gently holding her head and tenderly kissing her lips.

Valery's body was flowing; wanting; full of anticipation as Richard began to take her. The head of Richard's erect manliness toyed with, rubbed and stroked Valery's pleasure while intermittently pushing for entry into her body.

The teasing began to drive her wild. Her body now hungered for him. His loins now demanded access to her flesh. She screamed as he entered her.

Richard was gently yet thoroughly plunging into the depths of Valery's wetness. His fingers wallowed in the pleasure and feel of her soft tender cheeks as he manhandled, moved, squeezed and manipulated her body in a manner that allowed him to totally engulf the length and fullness of his manliness into her body.

"Give it to me, Princess!" he whispered; kissing her softly, tenderly.

Valery complied, opening her legs wider and wider.

"Take it, Richard!" she whispered. "Take it!!" she cried, her body equally taking and wanting more and more of his sweet hard meat to feed her body.

Richard was greedily penetrating into Valery's flesh and she was uncharacteristically wantonly craving for and engulfing more of his substance to satisfy her. Valery's nails tore into Richard's back as she tried to deal with the unusual heights of sexual bliss her body and mind were now experiencing; experiences she had never had before. Valery felt that she might pass out.

"You're delicious," he whispered, "More

Princess..More!" he pleaded, while equally kissing her lips, her neck, as his loins greedily gyrated and fed from the depths of her body.

Richard was insatiable. *He did not want this dance to end.*

He was determined to enjoy every inch of this feast for as long as he could. They had waited so long!! Her body was more luscious than he had ever dared to imagine.

Richard wanted to see more, feel more, taste more, experience more. They were carnivores; taking and feasting from each other in order to counteract the hunger pains of the sexual famine that they had invoked upon each other for far too long. Their bodies were in rhythm; thrusting, engulfing, giving, taking, grinding, dancing. Richard and Valery were in a different dimension; ecstasy would be an understatement. She had brought out all of the bestial cravings, greed and hunger within him. He was voracious; moving into a dimension of gluttony.

Valery, an aristocrat, normally reserved, quiet; was screaming throughout the morning as she encountered one orgasm after another. They sounded like screams of terror yet they were screams of ecstasy.

They were both moving toward sexual exhaustion and yet still hungry for more of each other's body. He descended deeper and deeper, thrusting over and over, in order to completely take the last morsel of the soft pulpy tissues within her body until he felt there was nothing left. He was out of control. She was his obsession. Every part of her was like sweet candy.

"More, Princess," he whispered, "Give it to me!" he demanded, as his strong legs forced her limbs to spread wider and wider as he continued to plunge harder and harder, deeper and deeper, gorging himself in excess from that luscious orifice of meat in the center of her body; looking at her eyes, tasting her lips, kissing, sucking, feeling her breasts on his. Valery's legs and knees were spread high and wide as her body gyrated wildly while greedily grasping for more of the whole of his manliness within her.

"It's yours, baby!" she screamed, kissing his lips, biting his neck, "Honey!...Baby!...Take it!!!" she cried.

Richard's body finally exploded in climax. The milky juices of his orgasms voluminously flowed within and without Valery's body. They collapsed, sprawled on the bed like wounded warriors, totally exhausted, totally fed, totally satisfied.

Richard reached for Valery and brought her semi-conscious body next to his. Exhausted, she snuggled under him, breathlessly kissing his lips as they both fell off into a deep sensual sleep. The clock displayed 12 o'clock p.m.

****

The hands of the clock were moving to 5 o'clock p.m. Richard and Valery had slept for almost five hours. Richard lay still in a mild sleep. Valery had awakened but continued to lie enveloped in Richard's arms. She felt safe there. She rubbed the hairs on his arms while thinking about the passionate, sexual journey they had just shared.

Prior to Richard, Valery had little experience in love or love making. Damien had been the only real love or lover she had experienced. It was an experience that was sorely lacking in passion, satisfaction, commitment, excitement and sensuality. However, she had interfaced with her coed friends at the University in order to compare her love/life experiences with those of her female associates. Unfortunately, there was very little difference between her experiences and theirs. Valery had learned to believe and accept that these disappointments between the desired love fantasies and the real love/life experiences had to be compromised; *Until today*.

Richard had unmasked dormant sexual behaviors, cravings, feelings and wanton dimensions in Valery that she never knew existed. *The sexual journey she just shared was addictive*. Her body had never felt so completely taken and satisfied. Richard's professed love for her, his commitment, his integrity, patience and obsession for her were the traits she had dreamed about from her ideal lover.

Today, she realized that her dream lover had materialized and was lying next to her. Under no circumstances was she giving him up.

Valery had always been attracted to Richard and loved his physical look, his swagger, his sensuality. Over the last three days, she had challenged his intellect and values and witnessed the whole of his body and spirit. Richard is what she wanted.

She was engaged to marry the most affluent bachelor in the state. However, at this moment, Damien was no longer relevant. She was no longer willing to accept disharmony, discontent and abuse in exchange for status, affluence and material comforts. She deserved more.

The transition would be tricky. Those in her circle would never accept Richard. Valery didn't care. She wanted the freedom, respect, love, passion and peace of mind that Richard brought into her life. Additionally, she wanted to be owned and sexually possessed by this man. Richard had shown her a different dimension and perspective of life and love and she wasn't going back to the other side.

Richard's eyes slowly opened. Valery lifted her head to greet him as he awakened.

"Hello, Princess," he whispered.

"Hello, Lover," she smiled.

"What time is it, Valery?"

Valery leaned up from Richard's arms and looked at the clock on the night stand.

"It's after 5 o'clock, honey."

"Good grief," Richard replied, "that means we slept for over five hours."

"Yes, five wonderful hours."

Richard smiled at seeing the gaiety in Valery's face and smile.

"You seem rather awake and content, Princess."

"I am. Listen, I have a great idea. Why don't we spend some of my trust fund money on us? There is a great seafood restaurant less than five miles from here. Let me treat us to some dinner."

Richard appeared disinterested. There were other more pressing issues he wanted to discuss.

"I don't know. I think we need to talk, Valery. We need to pull some things together, baby."

Valery looked at Richard. He seemed concerned.

"Things like what, Richard?"

"Valery, I love you. I need to know where we're at."

"Richard, I'm in bed with you. I'm naked. I've just given myself to you in a manner that only you can have or take. How can you now be concerned about us?"

Richard had no desire to play any guessing games or conduct a verbose conversation on this subject. He needed direct answers.

"Where are we at, Valery?"

She looked at him, still stunned that he did not have the answers to these questions.

"Where do you want us to be, Richard?" she smiled teasingly.

"I want you to be mine!" he answered assertively.

"Okay, since you haven't figured it out! *I'm yours, Richard!*" she screamed. *"I'm yours lock, stock and barrel. I am totally in love with you! I've never been as happy in the company of any man as I am with you.*

I think I've loved you since the moment I saw you at Candle Light restaurant."

He kissed and hugged her tightly in his arms,

"Thank you. I'll be good to you Valery."

"You better be good to me," she grinned.

Richard laughed and turned her towards him. He kissed her again and nestled her tightly in his arms.

"I'll be better than good to you, Valery. Just stay with me. I'll be much better than good to you. You'll be happy."

Valery cried and kissed him hungrily over and over and over again.

****

Richard and Valery spent the balance of the week at the cottage. They shared six days and nights of planning, kissing, laughing, loving, living, and learning about each other; each day more happy than the last.

CHAPTER XIII

Damien, dumbfounded and acutely aware that Valery was drifting away from him, could not concretely answer why or to whom.

A rumor had been circulating around the private campus that something was developing between Richard and Valery; a rumor that they had become a discreetly steady couple. A confrontation was in order.

It was four o'clock Friday evening. Richard had just left Valery's home in route to laboring his evening shift at the garage. The doorbell rang. Valery answered it contemplating Richard having forgotten something.

"Damien!"

"You act surprised to see me. That reaction is not normal toward the man you're supposed to marry."

"Damien, we really must talk-I-"

"I've been trying to talk to you for over three weeks, Valery!" he interrupted in anger. You ignore and avoid me on the campus grounds, you are seldom home when I call nor ever available when I desire to see you. What in the hell is going on?!?"

"Damien, please . . . sit down."

"I don't want to sit down!" he exclaimed while nervously pacing the plush white living room carpet away from her.

"Tell me, Valery, is it true?" he asked in confused disbelief with his eyes leveled upon hers.

"Is what true?" she answered in softness, her eyes and head turned away from him.

"Don't play games with me, Valery! Not now! Are you involved with that poor grease monkey?"

"He's not a grease monkey!" she defended.

Damien was amazed by her aggressive defense of Richard.

"Then it's true!! If you think for one minute that you are going to leave me for that nobody then you are-"

"That's really what it is, isn't it, Damien?!!?" she interrupted in anger. "Giving me up doesn't bother you regardless of who initiates the break-up, you never really loved me anyway. But giving me up for someone who is socially or economically beneath you smothers your ego, your campus popularity. What's wrong, Damien?" she bitterly questioned, "Will your virile reputation be dampened if I become involved with Richard?"

"That doesn't have a damn thing to do with it!"

"*That has everything to do with it!*" she screamed.

"I loved you, Damien. I didn't love you because of your athletic ability or because of your campus popularity. Nor did I love you because your family's financial background is compatible with mine. Initially, I loved you for you, Damien. You forced me to love you for all of the irrelevant superficial reasons by not giving me anything else of you to love!"

Valery calmed herself and moved away from Damien. She peered out of the living room window and continued,

"I've found someone who cares, Damien. Someone who genuinely makes me feel special-something you could never do. I need that, Damien."

"Then I'll change."

"You can't! And even if you could it's too late."

"What does he have to offer you? He's nothing!!"

"What do you have to offer me, Damien?" she inquired.

Damien`s eyes widened in disbelief at her question. She was well aware of his family's wealth.

> "I'm asking what do *you,* not your family, have to offer me, Damien? Your family's status gives you status as my father's financial position enhances my social position. We are the fortunate few. But without their support you have no more to offer me than Richard. He has a strong, ambitious character which gives him strong potential. That's enough for me right now."

She was intelligent. Damien had never before bothered to evaluate that intelligence while realizing he now possessed too little time to appreciate it.

Flustered, unable to adversely respond to her logic, energy spent and speechless, Damien stormed from Valery's house and out of their intimate lives.

In anger, Damien drove to the corner of Eighth Street and Adams. He parked his two seat sports car outside of the entrance of Jim's Garage and walked within. Richard was not readily observant.

> "Richard!!"

He thundered amid the group of four mechanics working busily beneath the hoods of luxury automobiles. They peered away from the automobiles they were repairing as Damien's voice again screeched through the air,

> "Richard!!!"

Richard, face stained and hands covered with engine grease coupled with a white sweatband covering his forehead, as beads of sweat found passage room to cover small areas of his face, rose his busy eyes from beneath the hood of a green two-door Ford sedan.

"Over here, Damien!" he responded as Damien walked toward the back vicinity of the large garage where Richard's voice appeared to be coming from.

Richard, attired in dark green work coveralls, a black cotton work shirt and unorganized curly locks of hair trampling over his forehead, stepped his slim six-foot body into Damien's view. They were now less than four feet away from each other.

Had Jim, owner of the repair shop, been present within the garage, this showdown would never have transpired to its present point.

"You're living dangerously, Richard. She's going to be my wife!" Damien warned, his lips tight with anger.

"Is that what she told you?" Richard asked while wiping his hands clean of excessive engine grease on a garage towel while facing Damien.

"That's what I told you!" Damien bellowed.

"In regards to Valery, what you say to me means nothing, Damien!" Richard declared while looking into Damien's eyes, "It's what Valery tells me that counts. *Valery tells me that she is not going to marry you.*"

Damien closed the distance between them.

"I'm warning you, Richard, if-"

"Don't you warn me about anything!" responded Richard in anger, "You have no right to tell Valery who she loves or me whom I see. She loved you, Damien, and you blew it! Her love belongs to me now, as mine belongs to her, and there is nothing you can do about it. *Nothing*!"

Richard did not desire a violent physical battle with Damien but was prepared for one.

Damien, six-foot-four inches and of a heavier physical stature, was awed by Richard's show of confidence and composure.

"Go home, Damien," Richard advised as if understanding Damien's injured emotional plight.

 Damien, observing the audience of four mechanics now crowding around for a ringside view of an anticipated physical battle between these two, decided to leave the garage.

He realized that a fight with Richard over Valery would hamper his esteem, not enhance it; Valery was gone.

With pride still in his pocket, eyes centered upon the eyes of Richard, he retreated, turned, and walked-away.

****

Later that night, Richard and Valery sat and conversed upon her banister porch.

He grew disturbed behind her cool, quiet, solemn disposition.

"What's bothering you, Valery?"

"Ohh . .I don't know."

"I think you do, tell me, what is it?" he whispered.

"Damien came over today," she answered, her trance-like confused eyes gazing toward the stars that danced across the night skies.

"And?"

"We talked."

"And?"

"It's over."

"I guess now you have doubts??…. Second thoughts?"

"I don't know. . . perhaps . . . Richard, do you really love me?"

"Yes"

"How do you know, Richard? How do you really know?"

Richard placed his two hands tenderly around her delicate face and whispered,

"Valery, in my eyes there exists two distinct definitions of love and both are based upon need. Within one need lies a love which doesn't withstand the pressures of life nor the passage of time. Within the second need of love arises the foundation of a strong enduring relationship."

"What are those two definitions, Richard?" she inquisitively asked as if searching for direction.

"One definition says, 'I love you because I need you,"

"And the other?"

"The other whispers, I need you because I love you."

"And which need is your love for me based upon, Richard?" she whispered.

"I need you, Valery... because I love you."

And they kissed.

From that day forward their relationship ascended toward a pinnacle of involvement. Valery's presence was no longer entwined within the grasps of hungry, handsome males nor could Richard be found amid his group of academic peers.

They could only be found with each other.

CHAPTER XIV

Maybe it was a slow media day, but the news of the broken engagement between Valery and Damien hit the society pages of the town newspaper like an atom bomb. Valery's father, Clifford, challenged the logic of her decision.

The faculty and elitist student body were alarmed by the rumors that Valery had severed her relationship with Damien to be with Richard. The coeds within her social circle increasingly felt that she had lost her mind and gradually began distancing themselves from her.

The class schedules held by Richard and Valery grew to be one of conflict. Richard's daily class program normally ended at one o'clock p.m., whereas Valery's last class ceased after three. Richard would normally study in the campus library until her arrival and vice-versa when the circumstances warranted it. But the wait really didn't matter as long as the pot of gold was at the end of the rainbow. The awaited sight of each other grew to be their pot of gold.

Valery felt feminine with Richard; possessed, protected; loved. She had no intention of losing this newly discovered feeling of warmth. However, newfound discoveries of warmth and tenderness can create heightened feelings of insecurity. Insecurity bred by fear that a treasure found might tomorrow be a treasure lost.   An unexpected rainstorm hit the city. Richard and Valery were on campus without an umbrella. Consequently, they were forced to walk against the blowing rains upon Valery's release from class when she questioned,

"When will you stop loving me, Richard?"

"What kind of question is that, Valery?"

"An honest one, When will you stop loving me?"

"Never."

"Sure you will. Haven't you heard? Everything comes to an end, even love, doesn't it?"

"Only when there are boundaries which regulate the basis of that love," Richard smiled while pulling up

Valery's coat collar to give her greater protection from the chilling rains and cutting winds as they briskly walked hand in hand toward his car across the campus. "My love for you knows no boundaries, so it has no end."

She looked at him, pleased with his response, but she needed more.

"Then promise me, Richard,"

"Promise what?"

"Richard, promise me that you will never stop loving me."

Richard turned to her. Their walk slowly came to a stop. In the rain he took her into his arms and they embraced.

With their faces dripping the wetness of rain, they kissed.

"I promise, Valery, that I will never stop loving you," he whispered.

"I love you, Richard."

"I love you, Valery."

They then renewed their walk toward his car, now less than fifteen yards away.

****

This liaison was a communion of passion; strong, deep burning passion. Although each other's positive force, Richard and Valery could not keep their minds, hearts, nor hands away from each other during the initial six month period of their involvement. Consequently, they soon discovered a lack of time within a twenty-four hour day for each other.

After classes, Richard would normally drive Valery home before leaving for the garage where he worked evening hours from 4:30 until 9 p.m. daily and a full shift on the weekend. However, today was different. It was Thursday afternoon; Five o'clock p.m. Richard had taken a day off from the garage to study for a Friday morning Finance examination. He sat alone in the library, trying to concentrate on the subject matter, he couldn't. Thoughts of Valery crowded his mind. He wistfully got up from his seat, put on his jacket, and walked out of the library doors. The cool October winds gently blew against his body as he walked to his car, got in, and drove to Valery's residence.

Richard had become a constant guest within an environment of immense wealth. Charles, the butler, generally greeted him at the door and helped him with the removal of his coat. Richard would then be left in the large living room to relax and explore the uniqueness of the environment while awaiting Valery's appearance.   The plush bone white colored carpeting was so thick that at times he felt like a human pogo-stick when walking from space to space. A large white sofa with matching ottomans and chairs were positioned in the center of the room facing the large burning fireplace.

Above the mantle of the fireplace was Richard's favorite piece of art, a large wall-size still portrait of Valery Hall. It was an exact, exquisite, detailed painting which captured her soft sweet spirit and girlish charm. There were days when he would be so mesmerized by the larger-than-life painting that he would lose track of time while trying to explore every finite inch of its artistic realness. Valery walked into the living room and again saw him examining the portrait.

"Richard?"

He did not answer.

"Richard!"

Startled, he came out of the painting and turned to face her.

"Oh! Yes, Valery."

"C'mon in the kitchen, Richard," she smiled.

Richard walked into the large, modern kitchen. He was surprised to see her cooking.

"I didn't know you could cook, Valery," he initiated as she proceeded to prepare a salad.

"I always cook for my father, Richard. He likes my cooking. Says it tastes like my mother's."

"That's interesting, well, what do all of these maids do?"

"They cook for me. I can't stand my cooking," she laughed.

Valery took a large pot roast, flavored with carrots and cut potatoes, from the oven and placed it on top of the stove. The bread was still baking. Richard took a fork and tasted a piece of the tender, hot meat when Valery turned to the sink and rinsed her hands.

"Hey! This is delicious!!" he roared with approval, "Who taught you how to cook like this?!"

"I used to help and watch my mother cook when I was a child," she wistfully replied. "Even though we had all kinds of domestic help, she insisted on cooking dinner for my father and me. When my mother died, I decided to assume her responsibilities."

"Why, Valery?"

She looked at him as if he had asked an ignorant question.

"Why?? . . . What kind of question is that? In order to help my father, of course!!" she snapped.

Richard leaned against the kitchen counter and looked away from her. Valery took a deep breath, walked over to the counter, and kissed his lips.

"I didn't mean to snap at you, Richard. I . . . I've been so edgy lately. Look . . . Let me explain. When my mother died, my father fell apart. I tried to boost his spirit but nothing worked."

She paused, then continued,

"Anyway, one evening when I was nine years old, he stepped out of the house to attend a business meeting. The domestic help was off that day. I was hungry, so I cooked he and I a big dinner. The kitchen was a mess," she laughed, "but the dinner turned out pretty good. He was so pleased. I've been cooking his dinner ever since."

Valery walked to the stove and took the bread out of the oven. Richard casually walked behind her.

"You and your father really had a thing for your mother, didn't you?"

"Richard, I wish you could have met her. She was the sweetest, most caring, most beautiful woman I've ever known. . . I'm looking forward to having children. I'm looking forward to continuing the role she was not able to complete."

He was startled by her familial objective.

> "That doesn't fit, Valery. Your mother was not able to continue her role because she died. You cannot live her life nor continue her life within your space of time."

"It fits to me, Richard," she stubbornly replied while pulling a bottle of white wine from the refrigerator and pouring a glass for each of them.

Richard changed the subject as they both sat down at the kitchen table and sipped the wine.

> "Valery, you talk so much about your mother that I almost feel like I know her. Do you have a picture of her?"

> "I had a small portrait of her in my bedroom but I handled it so much that it became tattered and torn. However, there's the large painting of her in the living room."

Richard was surprised. He had explored every inch of that living room during his daily visits and never saw the portrait painting.

> "There is? Where??""

"Over the fireplace."

Richard was even more astounded.

> "Where?? The only portrait I've ever seen over the fireplace is that large painting of you."

He began to rise from his chair at the table, almost afraid of the declaration that was forthcoming.

"No, Richard, that's not me. That's my mother," she smiled. Shock and an unjustified terror filled his body. His eyes quickly examined Valery's face as he nervously paced, almost running, out of the kitchen toward the living room. He stopped in the middle of the large room and again dissected the large painting over the fireplace. His head was swimming. His eyes were in a daze. Valery quietly walked into the room and stood behind him. He continued to quietly look on at the portrait. She continued to stand a short distance behind him.

> "Tell me you are lying, Valery."

"I have never lied to you, lover, and I never will. That is my mother."

"That's incredible!" he wheezed. "It's utterly incredible! *You look exactly like your mother!*"

"So I've been told,'" she answered. "So I've been told," she repeated while walking back to the kitchen.

Richard, mesmerized, continued to look at the painting. The tumblers within the front door moved and Valery's father, Clifford Hall, walked in.

Clifford Hall was an extremely wealthy investment banker and the founder and Chief Executive officer of State Bank. Physically, Clifford Hall is six feet tall with hard yet attractive facial features and a beautiful head of black straight hair with scattered streaks of grey. Despite a magnetic and pleasing personality, he is feared and regarded as a ruthless and cunning business man who always gets what he wants. It is rumored that he has partnered with a discreet and growing criminal element to achieve his goals and ambitions. He considers himself a good Catholic with high morals despite his unsavory business practices to achieve financial goals and objectives.

Clifford Hall has two loves other than money; the memory of his deceased wife, Jennifer and his twenty year old daughter, Valery.

"Hello, Richard," he smiled while putting his briefcase down, taking off his trench coat, and hanging it in the front closet.

"Hello, Mr. Hall. How have you been?" he asked while walking toward him.

"Excellent! Excellent!" Clifford answered while looking through the daily mail.

The tailored, dapper dark blue pin-striped suit fit him beautifully.

"Well, how is school going, Richard?" he asked while stopping at the mini-bar in the right corner of the living room and pouring a glass of whisky.

"Fine, Mr. Hall. I think I'll make the Dean's List this semester."

"That's great, son. If those professors are half as happy with you as my daughter seems to be, *then I know you'll make the Dean's List.*" he smiled.

On the surface, Clifford was friendly and cordial towards Richard. However, the air and body language between them was not calm. Richard could easily sense that Clifford considered him subservient in class.

After a short dialogue, Richard joined Valery and her father at the long rich wood table in the large formal dining room for dinner. Clifford quickly ate and excused himself from their company.

Richard and Valery finished their dinner, freshened themselves, and strolled throughout the flowery landscaped gardens surrounding the property.
Time quickly slipped away.

The church bells informed them that it was eight o'clock p.m.   They walked back to the house and sat on her large front porch. A premature darkness covered the city. Valery rose from her chair, walked to the banister, and gazed at the bright stars adorning the clear sky.

"Isn't it beautiful out here?" she asked, looking for a confirming response.

"Yes . . . beautiful," he answered, looking intently into her eyes.

She blushed, smiled, and turned back to the skies. Richard gently turned her face toward his and kissed her lips.

"I have to go now, Valery."

"No, you don't!"

"Yes, I do Princess. I've got a big Finance examination tomorrow. I've got to review for it."

Valery walked with Richard to his car. Her eyes grew moist as she leaned against the driver's side of the vehicle.

"What's wrong, Valery?" he asked.

"I don't want you to leave. *I hate it when you leave me!*" she emphatically whispered with a lost look in her eyes.

"I hate it when I have to leave, Valery," he replied, gently taking her into his arms and kissing her forehead. She kissed his lips slowly, tenderly, desperately.

"Then stay here and study for the Finance examination."

"Where?"

"In my room," she replied.

Richard laughed, "*Yeah, I'm sure your father would love that!*" She became taut, intense, irritated, and turned her back and face away from him.

"It's not funny! This is not working!"

Richard sensed the intensity of her position. He walked to her and put his hand on the back of her right shoulder.

"What's wrong, Valery? What's not working?"

"We don't have enough time together, Richard. When you leave I feel empty. We need more time together, Richard. Between our classes, your time at the garage, and studying, we have little time left for each other. Time is robbing us of whatever it is we're supposed to have or supposed to be."

Richard was stunned to hear Valery declare her need for greater time and attention in the finite manner she did.

"Well, I can cut some of my hours at the garage and-"

"And then what?" she interrupted.

"Valery, let's be real. Your father tolerates me but he is not crazy about seeing me in his house with his daughter as much as I have been here lately. Additionally, it makes no sense for me to take you into my-"

"Your what?!" she interrupted.

"My slum urban apartment."

"Why shouldn't I go with you to your apartment?" she queried.

"Baby, because of where it is. It's not the safest area for-"

"I don't care about that!" she interrupted.

Richard sensed the intensity of her position. He was not going to persuade her on this issue.

"Okay, let's try it. Tomorrow after school, I will not go to the garage and we will spend the entire evening at my place until you are ready to go home. Is that good?"

"No! *Tomorrow and any other day I desire, I will spend whatever time I want at your apartment until I am good and ready to come home!*"

"Okay," he softly responded.

She was satisfied with that response.

"Okay," she softly replied with a discreet smile.

Richard opened up the car door, sat within, and started the engine.

"I will pick you up in the morning, around nine o'clock."

"Okay, Lover. Goodnight", she replied.

"Goodnight, Princess."

And he left.

CHAPTER XV

Richard had a flexible work schedule. The garage now closed by 8:00 p.m. Following the end of each working day, Richard would generally shower at the garage and visit Valery until 11:00 p.m. before departing from her home, alone. This schedule was inevitably altered wherein Richard would arrive at Valery's home after working hours and they would depart from her home to his apartment, together.

During the month of December, Valery expended extra time at Richard's apartment in an attempt to create a festive holiday home environment for him.

However, each day after class, Valery continued to prepare her father's dinner prior to Richard's arrival.

Clifford Hall, a staunch religious Catholic, was growing highly upset at finding less and less of his daughter's clothes within her closet and room without her presence. Consequently, his mild fondness for Richard was dissolving into an air of hostile indifference. His wife's death of cancer during Valery's childhood had thrust father and daughter into a co-dependent relationship with each other; a dependency which her father felt was vanishing since her relationship with Richard had appeared. He had complained to Valery about the impoverished location of Richard's apartment to no avail. Additionally, he felt it to be morally wrong for his daughter to be so obviously sexually involved with Richard. He assumed that they were not just conversing at his apartment on those multiple and continual nights that she did not return home.

It was a cold, snow-laid, December Friday afternoon, when Valery arrived home from class to prepare her father's dinner as she had done most days of her adolescent and adult life. She was surprised by the absence of domestic help within the home upon her arrival. After freshening herself, she looked for and found her normally warm and jubilant father in a silent, drunken stupor at the dining room table.

"Hello, Father," she cheerfully greeted.

He said nothing.

Observing the poor mood he was in, Valery decided to leave him in peace and commenced to prepare his evening dinner. Valery often wondered why her father had never remarried; he seemed so lonely at times. However, when she'd question his lackluster social life or desire for a wife, he would always side-step the issue or questions associated with it.

"Come here, Valery!" her father drunkenly bellowed.

Valery walked from the spacious, modern kitchen with her bright yellow apron still tied around her waist and approached her father, sitting in the same drunken stupor.

"I have seen very little of you in the last seven months, Valery. Where have you been?!?" he loudly questioned.

Confused by this question, Valery responded,

"Father, you know I have been with Richard."

"Why?" he questioned in anger.

"What do you mean by `why'?" she responded, irritated by the gist of this conversation.

"Why are you seeing so much of him?"

"Because I love him, Father," she whispered, "because I love him."

"Love?!?" he roared, "You're only a child, you don't even know the significance of the word!"

"It's baffling to hear you say that considering how recently you were in support of my being married to Damien!"

In a fit of rage, he demanded while pounding his fist upon the table,

"I forbid you to see him again!"

"*Why?*" she asked in shocked hysteria at this demand.

"I *don't* feel he's good enough for you."

"Father, I'm almost twenty-one, I must be the one who makes that decision. I don't understand you, Father. *I thought you liked Richard.*"

"I've changed my mind," he uttered. "Therefore, you will not see him again!" he imperatively stated.

"Father, I must!"

"Dammit, you will do as I say! You will not see him again!" he roared, highly exasperated, for his daughter had never before argued above his demands.

Valery began to cry but the tears did not subside her father's anger.

"Do you understand me?"

There was silence.

"Is that understood?!!" he demanded, in search of a positive response.

There was silence.

"Dammit, answer me!"He violently roared while rolling up the daily newspaper from the dining room table and standing over her.

Valery gained her composure. She was no longer crying, she was no longer in fear.

"No, Father."

"No Father, what?" he asked in shocked surprise and disbelief.

"No, Father, I will not stop seeing Richard," she calmly declared.

In a fit of drunken rage, Clifford began swinging the newspaper wildly upon his daughter with force. Valery, in shocked disbelief at the actions presently transpiring, tried to escape his blows but was pursued around the table, caught, knocked to the floor, and subjected to more of his violent attacks.

In his drunkenness, he missed her many times, and in the interim, Valery scrambled to her feet, ran to her room, and locked her bedroom door. Her father was in staggering pursuit of her and began attempting to forcefully gain entry. He was shouting vulgarities that she never previously heard from his mouth while attempting to force the door open.

"You fucking slut!! How dare you whore around with that nothing of a man!! Who do you think you are!! You can't hide in there forever you little bitch!"

His attempts to forcefully push the door open were appearing to be successful as the hinges of the door began to give way.

With tears falling from her eyes, Valery phoned her Aunt Earlene (sister of her deceased mother), and tried to explain the madness which was erupting.

"Earlene! Earlene! Come over quick! Help me! Help me!"

"What's wrong, child?" Earlene asked in puzzled panic.

"I don't know! My father! Something's wrong with him! He's trying to hurt me!"

Earlene, distinguishing something was dastardly wrong both by the fear and cries of her niece and the background verbal thunder of Valery's father, drove to her niece's house in haste. Upon entering the front unlocked door, Earlene found Clifford sprawled drunkenly asleep in front of Valery's bedroom door.

As Earlene entered Valery's room, she observed her niece's body bruised and suitcases packed. Valery's mind was obviously intent on vacating the abode she had always looked upon as home; and they both cried.

With suitcases in hand, Valery stepped over her drunk sleeping father, walked out of the front door, and with her aunt's assistance, packed her suitcases in the car-and departed. On this day, Valery knew she would never reside in her father's home again.

After reaching Earlene's home, Valery explained the domestic storm and in her recall of the incident, she cried. However, the sweet comfort of her aunt's shoulder was not enough. Valery thusly phoned Richard at the garage and tried to convey to him her present situation of fate.

Richard left the garage and sped to Valery's assistance, whereupon she fell into his arms upon his arrival. She desperately needed his shoulders, his strength... him! Earlene left Richard and Valery alone in the dining room area and initiated efforts to make room for Valery's anticipated residence. However, upon Earlene's return to them did she become quite aware that Valery would not be staying at her house that night nor any other night.

"Thank you," Richard whispered in sincerity to Earlene.

"Take care of her, Richard," Earlene pleaded.

"I will, Earlene," he promised, "I will," as he packed Valery's suitcases in his car and drove her to his apartment.

CHAPTER XVI

A bright early Saturday sun found a small crack of space between the drawn beige curtains in Richard's bedroom. A powerful, thin, vertical, almost mystic beam of light tenderly touched the peaceful sleeping face of Valery Hall. Richard, attired in the bottom half of his dark brown satin pajama pants, sat his slim, muscular body on the edge of his queen sized bed and examined the beauty of Valery's face. His gentle masculine hands touched the softness of her complexion as his fingers travelled the contoured oval construction of her face. Her full, seemingly fragile, tender lips multiplied and complemented the sensual sexuality of her unusually dark round bedroom eyes.

Richard pulled the loose bedroom covers tighter and more securely over the shoulders of his sleeping princess. He pondered over their future while stroking the long locks of her dark curls which flowed with life, bounce, and body below the center of her back.

Valery, sleeping soundly, altered the position of her body away from Richard toward the wall of his bedroom. As she slept, her small right hand searched for the body of her lover. Richard attentively examined Valery's unconscious actions as her fingers became frantic in their search for his protective sleeping body. The subconscious matter of Valery's mind became alarmed. Her eyes remained closed as she fought for consciousness. The upper portion of Valery's body, clad in Richard's pajama top, slowly arose to a sitting position on the bed. Valery's eyes fought to open themselves and her mouth took formation as she softly cried,

"Richard?... Richard!!"

"I'm here, Valery," he whispered, taking her upright body

into his arms. She laid her head heavily on his shoulders, closed her eyes, and seemingly fell back to sleep. Richard kissed her eyelids as the sun gradually disappeared behind the heavy gray overcast of the morning sky. He tried to lay her head back onto the thick, fluffy pillow but she clung tighter to his neck.

She opened her eyes.

"What time is it?" she asked while continuing to rest her head upright in his arms.

"Eight o'clock," he answered, kissing her forehead while his arms held her tighter to his body.

"What are we going to do, Richard?" she asked, perplexed by the present dilemma she found herself in.

"I don't know, Valery," he softly answered while caressing her shoulders as he held her tighter in his arms.

"What do you want to do, Valery?"

"I want to be with you, Richard; I just want to be with you." she whispered, her tired eyes looking up to her lover's face.

She kissed his lips and fell off into a mild sleep. Richard laid her tired head back on the pillow. He walked to the kitchen within his apartment and washed out the tarnished silver-colored coffee pot that was sitting on the old stove.   He poured the required tablespoons of coffee beads into the pot, turned on the stove to a light simmer, and let the coffee slowly boil. He walked to the old-fashioned, small, quaint, dark-wood bathroom and showered while waiting for the coffee to brew.

The rich aroma of the brewing coffee soothed Valery's sleeping nostrils. She arose from bed, brushed her hair, and walked barefoot and half-naked into the tiny kitchen.
She poured two cups of coffee and measured three teaspoons of sugar and cream into each cup. Valery carried the coffee into the living room and set one cup on the coffee table for Richard while commencing to drink from the cup she held in her hand.

She sipped the hot liquid while cuddling upon the living room sofa, waiting for Richard to emerge from his shower. As

Richard got out of the shower, he looked out of the bathroom window into the cold, white, snow-laid environment.

"I hate winter!" he whispered while drying his wet hair.

He walked out of the shower clad in a pair of black wool trousers while drying the wet locks of his curly hair. He was stunned and sexually stimulated by the obviously teasing pose of her near nude body as she nestled on his sofa.

"Good morning, Richard," she smiled while picking up the cup of coffee from the coffee table and giving it to him.

"Good morning, Valery," he smiled while taking the cup from her hands and sitting in the chair across from the sofa.

"Why are you sitting there?" she asked with an air of disappointment.

"Because I'm drying my hair, Valery. I don't want to get you wet."

"I don't care about getting wet. I have to take a shower anyway. Sit with me, Richard," she pleaded.

Richard sat next to her.

"Well, how do you feel, lover boy?" she smiled while pushing his wet head with her hand.

"Hey, you're going to boil me!" he laughed, sitting the cup of dripping hot liquid on the table and wiping his hand with a napkin.

"Do you always get up this early on Saturday, Richard?"

"Eight o'clock isn't so early, Valery. What time do you get up on Saturday?"

> "Eleven-thirty, maybe twelve, never eight o'clock, Richard. Getting up at eight o'clock on Saturday morning is ridiculous."

"Well, why don't you go back to bed, Valery?" he seriously replied.

> "I can't," she solemnly answered while taking another sip of her coffee.
>
> "Tell me, Richard, did yesterday really happen or was it a bad dream?"

"It really happened Valery," he quietly answered.

"I still don't understand it," she responded, her lips quivering with grief as she placed the cup on the table.

"Why? . . Why? . . .I don't understand it! As much as I loved him . . . as much as he professed to love me! Why would he turn on me like that? Richard, my Father has never hit me before, never! . . . I...I..don't understand it, I just don't understand it!!" she repeated as tiny tears began to rain down her face.

Richard took Valery into his arms and held her tightly as she cried upon his bare shoulder. She held him tightly as if her life depended upon the magnitude of their closeness.

"Don't think about it, Valery," he responded while kissing the tears as they slowly fell from her eyes.

"I can't help it!" she replied while burying her head deeper into Richard's shoulder, "Look at these bruises on my legs and arms, look at-"

"Valery," he softly interrupted.

"What, Richard!" she answered, angered at being cut off.

"Don't think about it, at least not today. Today let's concentrate on being happy."

She paused for a moment.

"Okay….maybe you're right. Let's concentrate on being happy. What is the first happy thing you'd like to do today?"

"Eat! I'm hungry, Valery."

"Okay, Richard. I'll make you some breakfast. What would you like?" she asked while rising from the sofa.

Richard held on to her arm as she was getting up.

"You don't have to cook, Valery. Let's go out for breakfast."

"But why waste the money, Richard? I don't mind cooking breakfast for you," she replied while again rising from the sofa and walking to the kitchen. She opened the doors of the chipped wood ice-box.

"Richard, there's no food in here!" she declared, surprised and disappointed.

"I know, Valery," he laughed, looking away from her. "I didn't have time to go to the market. C'mon, take your shower and let's go. I'm hungry."

Valery showered, dried and brushed her hair, and hurriedly pressed a black skirt and blouse from her suitcase. She leisurely sat on the sofa to put on her high-heeled shoes. She got her pink toothbrush out of the drawer and hurriedly went to the bathroom where she brushed her teeth and completed the application of her makeup.

Richard was standing by the front door, eager to leave his apartment, as Valery walked out of the bathroom. He helped her into her winter coat and knelt on one knee while putting her snow boots onto her feet as she put on her gloves.

"C'mon, Princess. Let's go," he petitioned.
She took his waiting hand and they strolled out of the apartment, down the stairs, and into his car. A light mist of snow flurries danced through the air amid temperature readings in the mid-twenties. Grey cloud overcast hung in the skies.

Richard drove to 'Lefty's Restaurant', located on the sands of the snow-covered beach and close to the harbor. A huge yellow and blue flame crackled from the large brick fireplace that covered the entire surface of the left wall. The fire warmed the light wood interior and provided a mellow cozy atmosphere for the patrons.   Shortly after being seated, a waitress arrived and took their order.

Richard tried to initiate small talk with Valery without success. She fell into a mood of silence while looking out the window at the snow covered lake. They finished breakfast and ordered more coffee for themselves.

"What is it, Valery?"

"Nothing. I just want to go home."

Richard was baffled and confused. She had made it clear the night prior that she never wanted to reside within her father's home again. He tried not to let his confusion show.

"Are you sure that you want to go back to your father's house, Valery," he quietly asked while looking directly into her eyes, searching for the truth, while placing the cup of hot coffee back on the saucer.

"I didn't say I wanted to go to my father's house, Richard," she smiled while extending her hand over the table and touching his fingers.

"I said I want to go home. *Home is with you, Richard.*"

Richard casually took her hand to his mouth and kissed the tips of her fingers.

"I love you, Valery," he whispered.

"I love you, Richard."

Richard motioned the waitress to bring the tab as Valery walked to the ladies room to freshen up. He put on his army fatigue jacket, brown scarf and gloves and waited for Valery to return to the table. Upon her return, he helped her with her garments and they walked out of the restaurant toward his car.

The cold air hit their faces as the fresh snow continued to fall to the ground. Temperatures began to plummet downward as the chilling winter wind blew gusts of frosty air around and against them. Richard's right arm securely circled Valery's body and brought her close to his as she held her coat collar tighter around her bare neck.

He opened the car door for Valery and quickly walked to the driver's side of his car, got in and drove to a supermarket prior to going home. They purchased the week's groceries.

It was one o'clock in the afternoon when they arrived to his apartment. Valery commenced to unpack the groceries and put them on appropriate cupboard shelves as Richard reviewed the mail he had received. He then began to clean his apartment.

Valery put on a pair of well-worn though tightly fitting denim jeans, a red sheer blouse, and commenced to help him clean the apartment. They worked quietly, content with the warmth and presence of each other's company. They completed the kitchen and living room. The smell of rich furniture polish captivated the air and filled it with fragrance as Valery continued to meticulously polish the oak wood furniture pieces through the apartment. Richard moved to the bedroom.

He stripped the bed of its thick cotton blankets and linen and fitted it with white fresh laundered sheets and seemingly pressed pillowcases.

Valery walked barefoot to the bedroom from the living room and leaned against the open bedroom door. As he worked, she coyly walked around the small room to the head of the bed. She grabbed a pillow from the bed and hit him in the face with it.

"Heyyyy!!!" he yelled, falling backward onto the mattress. She hit him again and again, laughing hysterically at his surprised defensiveness.   She screamed as he leaned from the bed and caught her around the waist. Valery continued screaming and whaling the pillow upon Richard's upper body as he lifted her petite body into the air and hurled her onto the center of the mattress. Richard dived upon her sprawled body but she hurriedly scrambled away from under him. She picked up another pillow and again proceeded to bombard him with pillow blows, laughing harder than before.

Richard was breathless. Valery was just beginning the battle.

He shielded his face from her pillow attacks with both hands and arms while trying to get up. Amid her laughing screams, he got out of bed and pulled the pillows from her hands. Richard lifted her body into his arms and carried her to bed. Valery was hitting his hard chest with her tiny fists rapidly, slowly-she stopped. He wasn't playing back.
He tenderly positioned her body on the bed while looking deep into her soft eyes,

"I love you, Valery," he whispered.

"I love you, Richard. I can't believe I'm loving a man as hard as I'm loving you," she replied while extending her arms around his neck and gently pulling his face and body down on the bed upon her.

She kissed his lips slow, long, easy, hard … soft.

"What are we going to do, Richard?" she asked, looking for direction from her present dilemma. "What are we going to do?" she repeated, her face worried and filled with uncertainty.

"I don't have any other family except my father and my Aunt Earlene."

"I don't know, Valery," he answered, looking away from her. "But let's not worry about it today, Princess. Today.. Let's be happy."

"Make love to me, Richard," she whispered. "I need the closeness."

Richard untied the arms that were securely fastened around his neck and lay them at her side. He knelt over her body on the bed and patiently removed the tailored sheer blouse from her shoulders. He unlocked the tight fitting bra which held her wild young supple bosom in place.

 The room was quiet; dark.

The zipper on her jeans screeched in the silence as Richard slowly pulled it down and gently removed the pants from her legs. There was no undergarment between the jeans and herself. Valery lay there. She smiled at seeing the pleasure and longing in Richard's face. He stepped away from the bed and took off his shirt. He walked to the bedroom window and pulled the rope that closed the blinds in order to divorce the sunny cold winter daylight from the privacy of the intimate encounter about to commence.

 Darkness covered the room. The long minute hand of the automatic clock made a loud "tick" and moved to the figure twelve, informing him that the time was four o'clock p.m.

 He pulled off his black wool trousers and briefs as Valery looked on with approval at the solid ruggedness of his slender body and the endowed eagerness of his manliness. With his right foot on the floor and his left knee on the bed, Richard stretched toward Valery's face and tenderly kissed her lips.

"More!" she whispered, wet, eager and impatient while kissing his lips and pulling his body upon hers.

Their lovemaking was slow, sensuous, pounding, intense, hugging, kissing, sucking, caressing ventures of sensitivity; greedy, demanding, gasping voyages and journeys of oneness. Her body was his meal and he ate, stroked and took every morsel of flesh his loins could take from her body. He was addicted. Her body was his drug and she was his generous supplier. The penetrations were long, sensual, and intensive. Their daily excursions of feeding each other's sexual hungers concluded when exhausted within the captivity of each other's climax.

Valery felt weak, peaceful, and relaxed. She lay her head upon Richard's shoulder as his arms held her tightly against his body. They wandered off into a deep, peaceful, sleep.

CHAPTER XVII

The phone rocked and rang like a fire truck speeding to a violent fire. Richard looked at the clock while reaching for the phone. It read seven o'clock.

He assumed it was seven o'clock Sunday morning because of the deep restful sleep that he and Valery had shared. The voice on the other end of the line informed him otherwise.

"Hello," he sleepily greeted.

"Hello. Richard? It's Frank."

" Oh! Hi, Frank. How are you doing?"

"Fine, Richard. Hey, listen, friend- I've got two extra tickets for the alumnae ball tonight. Would you like to go?"

"I don't know, Frank," he answered unimpressed.

"You know how I feel about those elite affairs on State's campus".

"Ahh, c'mon, man. You're almost in your junior year. You've got to come out of that! There are going to be some influential businessmen there. It's time to start making some contacts."

Richard grew silent. Frank continued.

"Look, Richard. *Valery has always attended the Alumnae Ball.*"

"She has?"

"Yeah, as a matter of fact-"

"Hold the line for a minute, Frank."

Richard held the mouthpiece of the phone and nudged Valery, resting in a semi-conscious state.

"Valery, would you like to go to the Alumnae Ball?"

Startled, she gained consciousness. Her eyes widened.

"When?" she replied while turning over in bed and leaning on her elbows to face him.

"Tonight."

"That's right! It is tonight! I completely forgot to bring my tickets," she responded, excited and disappointed.

"Franks got two extra tickets. Do you want to go?"

"Of course I want to go, Richard... Don't you, Richard?" she asked, hoping for a positive response.

"Sure! ... Sure!" he replied while returning to the phone.

"Okay, Frank. I want to go."

"That a boy, Rich. Look, my date and I will stop by your apartment on the way to the campus ballroom and we can all go together ... say around nine o'clock?"

"Okay, Frank... And Frank,..."

"Yeah?"

"Thanks."

"No problem, Rich. That's what friends are for. See you shortly."

They hung up.

Before Richard could hang up the phone, Valery had gotten out of bed and was in the shower. She was obviously excited about attending the ball.

Richard got out of bed, pulled on a pair of trousers and walked to the small kitchen wherein he poured himself a small glass of white wine.

Valery stepped out of the bathroom wearing a flowery lace beige robe. He watched her as she walked into the bedroom and opened up her expensive leather luggage. She pulled out a long beige semi-formal knit dress coupled with a beige knit shawl. She pulled the iron out of the hall cabinets and began to iron the wrinkles that had formed in the dress as a result of it being in the suitcase overnight.

Amid light conversation, Richard shaved and showered. Clad in a white terrycloth robe, he walked to his bedroom closet and pulled out his black suit, white shirt and pleated tie. Valery dressed herself in the bedroom. Richard dressed himself in the bathroom in order to give Valery more space and privacy. Time was galloping away.

Richard was examining his face in the bathroom mirror when the doorbell rang. It was Frank and his date, Rita. Frank introduced Rita to Richard and Valery and gave them their tickets. Richard and Frank drove their own cars to the student ballroom located in the center of the campus grounds.

The Alumnae Ball was a populated yet intimate affair. A massive chandelier of white crystal adorned the center of the sculptured ceiling. The lights were dim, vibrations soft, and an air of elitist sophistication emanated through the room. A small orchestra played contemporary and easy listening music for the patrons.

Valery and Richard found a small corner table, away from the crowd, in order to share a degree of semi-privacy. Frank and Rita walked around the ballroom greeting and networking with various local businessmen attending the affair and ultimately retreated to sit with Richard and Valery. Valery and Rita went to the ladies' room to freshen up. Frank moved his chair closer to Richard,

"I've known Valery for a lot of years, Richard, and I've never seen her as happy or relaxed with anyone as she is with you. She's like a different person. You're working some good magic, Richard."

"Thanks, Frank," he   smiled, while modestly looking away from him.

The size of the crowd grew and the music was more raw and urban. Richard could sense Frank's desire to intermingle with the professional businessmen attending the affair.

"Look, Richard, this is one hell of an opportunity for you to meet some strong corporate contacts. I mean, there are people here who can put you on the map after graduation."

"Hell, Frank. I've got plenty of time. Anyway, Valery's dealing with some domestic issues. I think I should stay close to her tonight. You and Rita go ahead and enjoy yourselves."

"Sure you don't mind, Rich?"

"No, not at all. . . and by the way, Frank, thanks again."

Frank and Rita left the small table shortly after the girls returned from the powder room. Richard and Valery sat at the table, absorbed in each other's company. They walked over to the refreshment table and ordered two glasses of champagne. The champagne's effect on Valery was subtle yet immediate. She became more verbal and demonstrative. She gently grabbed Richard's arm and pulled it around her waist and turned to him,

"I have to tell you something", she whispered looking intently into his eyes.

"What is that, Valery?"

"I was lost until the day you found me. Thank you for finding me, Richard."

Richard was humbled and in awe by the sincerity of her position. He softly kissed her lips.

It was a grand affair. A pop band replaced the orchestra as the evening progressed and Richard and Valery danced and laughed the balance of the night.

As the affair came to a close, the band played slow and easy listening music. As they danced, Richard held Valery's soft perfumed body close to his and whispered,

"I've been meaning to tell you how good you look tonight, Val," while kissing her on her forehead.

"Thank you, Richard!" she replied cheerfully, barely moving her feet on the waxed wood floor.

"You look quite handsome yourself, lover boy," she smiled while looking intently into his eyes.

"Would you say that we're a handsome couple, Richard?"

"I believe I would," he smiled as they continued to dance.

"As a matter of fact, I'd say we're a very handsome couple. As a matter of fact, thanks to you, I'd say we're the most handsome couple at this ball."

"Is that right?" she teased, breaking their closeness in order to look at him.

"Absolutely!"

"I don't believe you!" she replied playfully, pouting her lips and raising her head toward the ceiling.

"You don't?... Okay, I'll prove it," he replied as the band concluded the social.

A student member of the Alumnae board was walking in their direction and about to pass them when Richard gently grabbed his arm.

"Sir, wouldn't you say that this beautiful woman and I are the most attractive couple at this ball?"

Valery was embarrassed.

"Richard!"

Startled, the young man replied and nodded approvingly while looking at Valery,

"Why. . . uh . .looking at her... yeah! Sure!"

"What did I tell you, Valery!" he laughed while taking her hand and moving toward their table.

"You're crazy!" she laughed, "That poor guy is still trying to figure out what happened to him."

"Well, that makes two of us "he replied while helping her into her chair and seating himself, "Since I met you, I'm still trying to figure out what happened to me."

Valery blushed. She placed her polished manicured fingers in Richard's hand on the top of their table. The evening progressed. It was moving toward twelve-thirty a.m. Valery leaned her soft head on Richard's shoulder as he stood and talked to Frank, peers and various alumnae businessmen at the refreshment table.

"I want to go home, Richard," she whispered in his ear amidst male conversation.

Richard gracefully excused himself from the group and walked with Valery to the coat check room where they received their winter garments.

He helped Valery button her knee-length fur coat and secured the collar tightly around her neck. They walked in unison, within each other's arms, out of the ballroom doors.

The winter air was mild, clean, and peaceful. The dark skies were contrasted by multiple scores of burning street lamps adorning the open spaces of the large campus grounds coupled with literally hundreds of bare trees landscaping the outside area.

They sleepily walked down the path leading to the campus parking lot.

"Richard," she whispered.

"Yes, Valery," he answered, looking more at the icy ground than towards her as they cautiously continued their snow covered walk.

> "Every day of my life was a living nightmare of depression before you found me. I was miserable and persuaded to believe that the basement of misery I lived in was to be the height of my happiness. Thank you for finding and saving me, Richard. Thank you for giving me, you, and this beautiful dream."

They reached the car, located in an isolated dark area of the parking grounds. Richard turned her toward him and looked into her sleepy bedroom eyes.

> "Every day of my life has been a beautiful dream since the day I met you. Thank you for the dream, Valery."

Richard unlocked the passenger side of the car and assisted Valery within. She sat close beside him and fell asleep on his shoulder as he drove them-home.

****

Three weeks quickly passed since the confrontation and domestic battle between Clifford Hall and Valery. Neither had called either during same passage of time.

Richard and Valery celebrated Christmas and New Years Day together alone in the solitary confinement of his apartment.

Wednesday, January 7, 1948

They returned to the second semester of classes and became aware that stories were being circulated throughout the University by unnamed sources that Valery no longer lived at her father's home.

Tuesday, January 13, 1948

Richard and Valery initiated efforts to find her an apartment in order to quash innuendo about her private life. They were well aware that Camden is a small city town with big moral based values.

Thursday January 15, 1948

Valery signed a lease for an upscale studio apartment in the city and wrote a check from her trust account to secure the apartment lease.

Monday, January 19, 1948

Valery was advised by the lease manager that the check she provided was returned unpaid by her bank. Valery immediately drove to her bank branch office to inquire on the reasons for same denial and was advised that her bank account had been closed and terminated due to court challenges against her trust account by her father, Clifford Hall.

Richard did not earn enough money to pay the leases for two apartments. They decided that they would discreetly continue to live together until their financial picture changed. They removed themselves from the company of their friends and relatives in an effort to minimize third parties from becoming aware that they were cohabitating together.

CHAPTER XVIII

It was Saturday, February 21, 1948. Over two months had passed since the night of that domestic storm between Valery and her father, Clifford Hall. They were two months of sensual bliss for Valery. They were two months of guilt and loneliness for her father, Clifford Hall.

Valery enjoyed falling asleep and waking up in Richard's warm arms. Each day was a continuing story of an intimate experience that Valery had never even dared to hope for. They drove to school together, walked the campus corridors and grounds within the spheres of each other's company, and shared a frugal or homemade lunch on the college grounds.

Each night was a romantic journey of love. Valery would generally prepare an elaborate candlelight dinner for Richard as he worked at Jim's Garage. Richard would shower and shave prior to leaving the garage and pick up a cold bottle of wine or champagne at the town's winery. Once home, they would settle within the small dinette and share the intimacy of soft music, gentle conversation, eclipsed with the passion and intense excitement of feeding the appetite and sexual hunger they now harbored for each other's body.

Tonight, however, was going to be different. It was Valery's twenty first birthday. Plans were made to celebrate the occasion with Frank and Rita at a posh restaurant called the 'Towering Top', located in the center of town. The 'Towering Top' was a modern glass encased structure located forty-three stories high above the city. It provided a breathtaking view of the city.

Richard and Valery arrived at the restaurant at seven o'clock. Frank and Rita had not yet arrived. Richard requested and received a corner window table. They ordered a light cocktail while waiting for Frank's arrival.

Valery was immaculately dressed. She wore a black velvet gown that seemingly hugged her in the right places. Assorted simplistic pieces of gold and diamond jewelry covered her neck and arms and accentuated her appearance. Valery looked down upon the night lamps landscaping the streets of the city.

"I love this view", she whispered while continuing the trance-like gaze over the city.

"So do I," replied Richard while looking directly into Valery's eyes.

A small smile crossed her lips.

"Happy Birthday, Princess."

"Thank you, Richard," she replied while taking the cold glass of Chablis wine to her lips.

"How does it feel to be twenty-one years old, Valery?"

"Well, no different. It's kind of nice to know that I can now drink my favorite wines *legally*," she laughed.

"Do I look any older to you, Richard?" she asked while examining his face.

"No, but you appear to be more confident in your old age," he smiled.

"Thanks to you, Richard," she replied while sliding her fingers on the top of the table and into his hand.

At that point, Frank and Rita walked inside the restaurant's door. Richard saw Frank requesting information from the hosting waitress of Richard's table location.

Richard stood up, caught Frank's attention, and motioned them toward the table. He remained standing until Frank and Rita were seated.

"Hello, Rich!" Frank greeted while giving him a firm handshake.

"Hello, Val! Happy Birthday" he greeted with a smile while leaning over and kissing her on the cheek.

"Hey, you guys remember Rita, right?"

"Sure. How are you, Rita?" greeted Richard and Valery in unison.

"Fine," she answered with a warm smile.

"How long have you guys been here? Have you ordered already?" asked Frank while quickly browsing through the menu.

"No, Frank," answered Richard, "We haven't ordered yet. We just got here about twenty minutes ago."

"Great! I'm starved!!"

The men ordered a steak dinner, salad, and beverage. Valery and Rita requested baked lobster. Frank provided the humor that kept the group laughing through dinner. Nevertheless, Richard could sense that something was amiss. He detected that a very quiet anger within Frank was simmering toward a rapid boiling point.

Valery and Rita went to the ladies room to freshen up after dinner, leaving the two men alone.   Frank's eyes grew cold while he eased back on the legs of his chair, bringing the cup of hot coffee to his lips. He looked at Richard long and hard. He examined his face as if he was examining spit.

Richard grew disturbed and defensive.

"*What does that stupid look mean, Frank*?" he asked while taking his own cup of coffee into his hands and bringing it to his lips.

Richard was calm; patient. Frank was growing anxious. Richard looked out of the window as the church bells began to ring. It was nine o'clock. The streets were dark yet peaceful. The halo of the night lamps provided a dreamy picturesque glow that flourished through the city.

The soft lights of the restaurant were lowered. The waitresses walked around to each table and lit the bone-white candles standing tall in the sterling silver candle holders. Frank initiated conversation.

"Richard, today I was told by a somewhat reliable source that Valery is living with you on Bond Street. I want you to look at me and tell me that it isn't true."

"Who told you that, Frank?" he quizzed, shaken by the disclosure.

"Don't worry about that, Richard! Just tell me that it isn't true."

"Is that what you want me to say, Frank?" he asked, while looking up from his coffee cup as he placed it on the saucer.

"Yes!" asserted Frank.

"Valery is not living with me."

"Whew!" smiled Frank; relieved by the declaration. "I didn't believe it was true but I had to be sure. It's amazing how rumors can-"

"I didn't say the rumor wasn't true, Frank," interrupted Richard while looking intently into his eyes.

"What?!! Why! I mean… You just said-"

"I just said what you wanted me to say! Now do you want to know the truth?"

Frank was jarred.

Richard continued without waiting for an answer.

"Yes! Valery is living with me!"

"On Bond Street?!"

"Yes, Frank. She's living with me on Bond Street."

Richard sat back in his chair, tired and flustered. Frank became the verbal aggressor.

"Richard, have you lost your mind? You have the daughter of one of this country's wealthiest men *living with you in the slums! Wake up, Richard!!!*"

Richard was growing upset. He had felt like an impoverished outsider for most of the last two years of his attendance at State University. He had heard the cutting whispers of his social/economic inferiority throughout his tenure there. However, he had not expected Frank to convey those same subservient airs.

"I'm awake, Frank! I'm awake to you and every other two-bit elite in this town! Now you listen to me!! She's living with me because her father beat her up for seeing me! What other choice does she have?!!"

"Well, she has an aunt! She can live with her!!" Frank snapped, his lips growing tighter with anger.

"Dammit, Frank! Her aunt has a husband, two teenage daughters and a son. There's no room for her at Earlene's three bedroom house!"

"Well, she has money, Richard! She can-"

"She has nothing, Frank! Her father froze her trust and

148

terminated her charge privileges!"
Patrons sitting at surrounding tables were disturbed by the volume of Richard's voice.

"Sshhh, do you want everyone to know what we're talking about?" asked Frank while leaning over the table and motioning with his finger over his mouth for Richard to quiet down. Richard suddenly became aware of the audience of angry spectators observing their argument. He was embarrassed. He threw his cloth napkin on the table and began nervously leaning on the back legs of his chair.

"I don't want to talk about this anymore!" declared Richard.

Frank angrily continued,

"This is 1948, Richard! You're courting trouble. Now you can play 'house' as much as you want but believe me, this is a dilemma you're going to have to deal with! I know Clifford Hall, Once he finds out-"

"The girls are coming, Frank. We'll talk about it later!" he interrupted, motioning Frank to lower his voice as the girls approached the table.

Richard got up and helped Valery to her seat.
Frank remained sitting at the table with his head buried in his hands as Rita sat down next to him.

"What's wrong, Frank?" asked Rita while pulling his hands from his face and trying to create eye contact. Frank would not look at her. He continued to look down on the table; perplexed.

"Nothing's wrong, Rita. I just don't feel very well."

"You probably ate too much, Frank," she smiled. "Here, honey. I'll order you some seltzer and water."

"No! Don't bother, Rita," he replied while abruptly getting out of his seat, "It's time to go. I have an early appointment in the morning."

Frank put on his coat and helped Rita with her coat.

The folk singer continued to strum his guitar as his rich nasal voice filled the dark spaces. Rita was surprised by the sudden change in events.

"Well . . . it was nice seeing you again, Richard and Valery," smiled Rita with a puzzled look on her face.

"It was nice seeing you, Rita," they replied.

"Happy Birthday again, kid," smiled Frank while leaning across the table and kissing Valery on her cheek.

"Thanks for coming, Frank," she replied with a confused smile of appreciation.

Frank and Rita hurriedly left the restaurant.

Valery turned to Richard. His arms were crossed on the table. The white of his eyes glowed in the candlelight.

"What was that all about?" she asked.

"What was what all about?"

"Don't play coy, Richard. You know what I mean. Why did he leave so quickly? Rita and I were just beginning to enjoy each other's company."

"I have no idea, Valery."

Valery looked hard into his eyes.

"Are you telling me the truth, Richard?"

He didn't answer.

"Come over here and sit close to me, Richard."

Richard did not move. With his elbows standing on the table, he buried his head into his hands.   Valery moved her chair closer to him.

"What is it, honey?" she asked while holding his arm.

"It's not important, Valery."

"Let me be the judge of that, Richard," she petitioned.

Richard paused. He looked momentarily into her eyes. He looked out the window. He looked back into her eyes.

"Someone told Frank that we're living together."

She was alarmed.

"How??! . . . We've been discreet... I know Earlene wouldn't have told a soul...How??"

"I don't know, Valery."

"Would I be correct to assume that Frank doesn't approve?"

"You would be *very correct*, Valery."

150

"Did you tell him of the circumstances surrounding my move, Richard?"

"I did"

"And??"

"He feels there should be other alternatives."

"Like what, Richard?"

"Like living with your aunt Earl-"

"Besides that, Richard," she interrupted.

"He didn't say, Valery."

Valery was growing nervous. Her mood became solemn.

"Are there any other alternatives, Richard?" she asked while quietly looking down at their table. She began playing with her fingers.

"There is one, Valery."

"Which is?"

"*Marriage, let's get married.*"

"No!" she adamantly responded while looking intently into his eyes. "*I love you more than life but I wouldn't marry anyone under these circumstances.*"

She began to sit back on her chair and casually bite the knuckles on her right hand.

"Don't think about it, Valery."

"I can't help but think about it, Richard. What do you think we should do!?!" she whispered. Her face conveyed worry.

Richard pulled her chair closer to him.

"What do you want to do, Valery?"

She looked at him. The folk singer was humming the melody of that same soft love song. Small tears began falling from her eyes as she nervously pulled on his arm.

"Richard, the last eight weeks have been the most beautiful days of my life. I have never felt as loved, comforted, peaceful, and happy with any one person as I have felt with you, but-"

"But nothing, Valery!" he asserted. He turned her tear-stained face toward him,

"Are you happy living with me, Valery? . . .I mean really happy?" he intently asked while looking into her soft dark eyes.

"Yes, Richard. I'm really happy," she smiled as the tears continued to fall.

"Then it's settled! You're staying with me and no one is going to pull us apart! Okay? No one!!...okay?"

"Okay, Richard," she laughed while leaning on his shoulders and kissing his lips. "No one!!" she emphatically exclaimed ...."No one!!!"

Chapter XIX

It was a Sunday morning. Another month had passed.

Clifford Hall decided that the stalemate between he and Valery had gone on long enough. Clifford had closed access to all of her financial vehicles, including her trust account, and cancelled all of her charge privileges. Clifford assumed that Valery was now a financially broken woman who would welcome returning to the luxurious life style she had prior to their battles. Clifford drove to Earlene's house at eleven o'clock that Sunday morning to initiate peace efforts and overtures with his daughter. Clifford assumed that Valery was staying with Earlene predicated upon prior misleading conversations he'd shared with Earlene relative to the residence of his daughter. He also knew that Earlene's lower middle class life style were contrary to what Valery was accustomed to. Clifford rang the doorbell of Earlene's small brick house. Earlene opened the door. She was shaken to see Clifford standing at the entrance.

"Good morning, Clifford." She greeted with a forced smile while opening the door for his entry.

"Good morning, Earlene." He replied while walking inside and kissing her on the cheek.

"Well, how have you been, Sister-in-law?" he smiled, trying to cover up the apparent nervousness filling up within him.

"Fine! Real fine!" she answered while locking the screen door and pushing the heavy wood door shut. She helped him take off his trench coat and hung it up in the front closet.

"C'mon to the kitchen with me. You're just in time for coffee."

"Where are Harold and the kids?"he inquired.

"He had to work today. Valery and my daughters went to a late mass."

Clifford walked behind her lead. He seated himself at the quaint kitchen table. Earlene pulled out two saucers and two cups and placed them on the table. She took the coffee pot from the stove and poured the coffee. She sat down with him at the table.

"I haven't seen you in quite a while, Clifford," she smiled, while seating herself and bringing the cup to her mouth.

"Well. . . I've been very busy, Earlene."

"You've been very busy and very embarrassed, right, Clifford?"

He grew silent.

"I imagine that Valery told you about our little argument?" he asked while picking a piece of imaginary lint from his black wool suit coat.

"Better than that, Clifford. I was there that night...I saw you drunkenly asleep at her door. Her bedroom door was cracked and broken in five places; the hinges had nearly been torn off the frame. I saw those bruises and welts on her legs, face, and arms!"

"Well, that's over now!" he asserted while looking away from Earlene.

"Over? Really?! I shudder to think what would have happen to Valery had you been able to get into her room that night."

"Like I said, Earlene, that's over now!" he impatiently declared.

"Clifford, you don't seem to understand. Valery is afraid of you. You can't initiate such a dramatic, painful experience on such a sensitive child like Valery and expect her to easily get over it!"

"Well, I think that once she comes back home, she'll realize-"

"I don't think you understand, Clifford. She's made it clear to me that she is not going back home."

Clifford's temper snapped.

"Dammit, Earlene!!" he roared while shoving the cup of hot coffee off of the table with the back of his hand,

154

"Will you stop trying to outtalk me! I didn't come over here for this! What are you trying to do? Drive my daughter away from me?!" he abruptly inquired while standing up and nervously walking around the kitchen. Earlene looked at the broken white cup and saucer on the floor. The splattered hot liquid continued to display a mist of vapor in the air.

"No, Clifford," she patiently answered while continuing to sit and drink her coffee. "I'm not trying to drive your daughter away from you. You're doing a good enough job of that. However, I would be afraid for her safety and well-being if she was to go back into that house. The fact of the matter is that you never really want Valery to leave. You always want her with you in that house irrespective of your declarations to the contrary. You're trying to live an unreal life!!" she continued, trying to control her anger and the volume of her voice. Clifford's back was against Earlene as he stood by the stove. His body became taut as his strong, dark, handsome face slowly turned toward Earlene.

"What are you saying?" he growled. His eyes were cold with anger. Earlene got up from the table. She walked toward him. The love Earlene felt for her brother-in-law overshadowed the fear in her heart. She reached up and placed her soft hand on his angry face.

"Brother-in-law," she whispered, "My sister Jennifer is dead!! Your wife, Jennifer, is dead!! Stop pretending that Valery is Jennifer!" Clifford quickly removed himself away from her.

"You're sick!!" he bellowed while hastily walking to the living room and getting his coat out of the front closet.

"Am I, Clifford?" she asked while walking toward him.

"You tell Valery to call me the moment she gets back from church!" he demanded while opening the front door.

"There is an alternative, Clifford!" she responded while continuing to walk toward him.

"What kind of alternative?!?" he angrily inquired while standing at the open door.

Earlene was not enthused about Valery living with Richard. She felt that such a living arrangement would eventually hurt her reputation and cause Clifford embarrassment. It was a small town. Rumors spread fast. In addition, Earlene feared for Valery's safety in the impoverished area of Richard's residence.

"She needs money, Clifford. Restore her trust account or give her a living allowance so that she can sustain herself until she graduates from-"

"I'll not give her a red cent!" he vindictively asserted. "You just tell her to call me the minute she gets back from church! Goodbye, Earlene!"

Clifford walked out of the door, into his car, and sped away.

That same Sunday evening, Earlene called Valery and informed her of Clifford's disturbing visit. Earlene recommended to Valery that she call Clifford in order to avoid any suspicions regarding her place of residence.

Valery did not inform Richard of the conversation she shared with Earlene. For whatever reasons-Valery did not call her father.

CHAPTER XX

It was a Saturday afternoon, March 27, 1948. Richard was studying in the bedroom and Valery was taking a shower when the doorbell rang. Richard, clad in a pair of khakis and a white sport shirt, answered the door. His eyes sprang wide with surprise, his mouth opened, and his speech became slightly slurred.

" Da..da..Dad!!.. Mother!..Leonard!?"

"Close your mouth, son, before a fly gets in it," smiled Tina while walking into his apartment.

"How are you doin', Son?!" greeted his father, with a robust hearty smile and a firm handshake while walking past him. Leonard patted Richard on his shoulder and quickly walked in.

Everyone was inside the apartment and yet Richard was still standing at the open door. He returned from his state of shock and shut the door. He walked into the living room.

"I mean . . . ah...you know... It's really great seeing you?" he initiated while walking to his mother, sitting on his sofa, and kissing her on the cheek.

Fear touched his heart. Valery had unlocked the bathroom door and was brushing her hair. The only clothing she wore was a bra and panties. A small front entrance hallway separated the bathroom from the living room.

"Excuse me, please," Richard quickly requested while hastily walking to the bathroom door and pulling it shut.

Richard had previously told his parents of his love for and involvement with Valery. However, they had not previously met her. Additionally, they did not know of the domestic fight between she and her father nor that she was living with Richard.

"He seems kind of nervous about something, doesn't he, William?" asked Tina, growing anxious by her son's unsettled behavior.

"No," defended William. "He's just surprised and excited to see us! He's fine!"

Leonard walked into the kitchen.

"Hey, Richard? What have you got to eat?" he yelled while opening the ice-box. Richard walked to the kitchen. He forced a broad superficial smile at his mother and father as he walked toward Leonard.

"Hey, Ma! Dad! Richard has learned how to cook!! I can't believe this ice-box!" Leonard roared as if he had discovered a gold mine.

"Look at all this baked chicken, pasta, and look at this pie... I can't believe it! Look at this!!" he excitedly petitioned while pulling all the pans and bowls out of the ice box.

Richard tried to focus their attention on the cooked dishes Valery had prepared. He needed time. His memory bank searched for the proper introduction to present his live-in lover to his parents. Leonard was warming the chicken in the oven. William, Richard, and Tina were looking over the pasta and vegetables.

Half of Richard's mind was involved with the warm jovial conversation he shared with his parents. The other half of Richard's mind was engrossed with the most delicate manner of introducing Valery and promoting a good impression of a questionable situation. Consequently, he did not see Leonard walk out of the kitchen toward the bathroom to wash his hands.

Valery was unaware that Richard's family was in their apartment. Leonard was unaware of the existence of Valery Hall. Leonard opened up the bathroom door. He gasped at the sensual encounter of their first meeting. Her back was turned against him as she leaned over to place a thick yellow towel on the rack over the tub. The perfumed smell of her well-shaped body, covered only by a bra and sheer black lace panties, drunken his senses.

Leonard quickly stepped out of the bathroom and shut the door before she could notice him. The bathroom door was slightly ajar. He continued to peek at Valery as she looked into the bathroom mirror to examine her face. She leaned over the bathroom sink with a pair of tweezers in her hand and commenced to arch her eyebrows. Leonard's eyes widened disproportionately. He breathed fast and heavy as his eyes took sordid liberties observing her beauty. The encounter had happened too fast. He backed away and leaned against the hallway wall, literally clutching his heart, trying to calm himself down.

The food was in the oven. William and Tina were complementing their son for his supposed newly acquired culinary skills. He was humbly accepting those undeserved praises while tossing a green salad in a large wooden salad bowl.

Suddenly, he dropped the wood fork and wood spoon into the bowl. He looked at his parents. They were standing across the table and drinking white wine.

"Where's Leonard?!" he blurted.

"Why, I think he went to the bathroom to wash his hands, Richard," answered his mother. They were both jarred by Richard's sudden change of mood.

Richard sensed that he was creating suspicion and tension. He settled down.

"Well, I'll be right back, Mom and Dad. I have to get a towel for Leonard to dry his hands with."

Richard put his hands into his pocket and casually walked toward the bathroom. As he turned the corner separating the living room from the hallway, he looked over his shoulder and saw his parents eyeing him suspiciously.

Leonard, still clutching his heart, had moved back to the cracked opening of the door.

Richard walked into the hallway. Leonard's back was against him. Richard was angry. Leonard was conducting acts of voyeurism toward Valery's near nude body. Richard was less than two feet from Leonard.

"Leonard!...Leonard!!" he whispered.

Leonard quickly turned his head around toward Richard. A huge embarrassed grin covered his face. Richard's eyes projected intense anger. Leonard walked over to Richard and patted him on the back.

"So this is what you call a 'steak and potato' woman, huh, Richard?"

"Shut up!" he quietly growled.

Leonard continued,

"Man, this isn't just steak, Richard. You've got the whole cow, brother, and every bit of that cow is USDA grade 'A' choice filet mignon meat. *I'm really proud of you, Richard,"* he chuckled. "I knew you had it in you. I'll say one thing for you, Rich, you've made a convert out of me. Hell, if I could find me some 'steak and potatoes' like that I'd-"

"I said,' shut up', Leonard!!"

Richard's anger subsided. He slumped to the floor of the narrow hallway. With his back against the wall, his head ached realizing that he would have to come clean and reveal the details and dilemmas of his life and Valery to his parents.

At that moment, Tina and William walked into the small hallway. Tina turned on the light of the hallway. She saw Richard sitting on the floor with his head buried in his hands. Leonard was standing erect with both hands in the pockets of his brown corduroy pants. A wide grin remained planted on Leonard's oval handsome face.

William spoke up first.

"Richard, your mother and I think that you're not quite yourself tonight. Is something bothering you, Son?"

"Well...uh...Yeah, Dad," he replied while taking his eyes from the floor and looking hard and seriously into the eyes of his parents, "I would like you and Mother to please have a seat on the sofa. I need to talk to you about something."

William and Tina were puzzled. They heard movement in the bathroom. They walked into the living room and sat on the sofa. Richard got up from the floor. He and Leonard proceeded to walk into the living room to join them.

As they were walking, Leonard leaned over, grinned, and whispered,

"*I'm really proud of you, Richard.*"

"I can't stand you, Leonard!" Richard whispered, while rolling his eyes away from him.

Richard joined his parents and briefly explained the domestic storm that had taken place between Valery and her father. In addition, he expounded upon the reasons why she had little choice but to stay with him at the present time. Tina and William knew their son. They believed him.

Richard excused himself and informed Valery that his parents made a surprise visit to their home. Valery quickly put on her robe and exited from the bathroom to the bedroom and dressed. She emerged immaculately dressed in a white knit skirt and blouse.

Richard introduced her to his parents. They immediately took a liking to Valery's soft character and feminine charm. Valery and Tina set the table. Prior to eating, William blessed the table and included a special prayer that the problems between Valery and her father be resolved. Valery loved him for it.

During and after dinner, they all interacted and enjoyed the pleasure, humor, and warmth of each other's company. Leonard's comical behaviors and stories kept them amused.

At seven-thirty p-m., Valery and Richard escorted William, Tina, and Leonard to the family car. Leonard, Valery, and Tina walked ahead of Richard and William. William put his arm around his son's shoulder.

"That's a very beautiful and charming girl you have there, son," beamed William.

"Thanks, Dad," he smiled in appreciation.

Their walk continued toward the car. William's head slowly turned toward his son.

"You say her name is Valery Hall, right?"

"Yes, Dad."

"Son, would she at all be related to that there wealthy banker with the last name of Hall?"

161

Richard looked away from his father.

"Yes, Dad. Clifford Hall is her father."

It was a cool spring night. Richard had not bothered to put on a coat.

"Look at me, Son."

Richard looked at his father. The streets were quiet except for the girlish talk and laughter being exchanged between Valery and Tina.

"Are you sure you know what you're doing, Son? I mean. . . is everything under control?"

"Yeah, Dad. Everything is under control", he smiled.

"Good!" replied William while patting his son on his back.

They all reached William's car and exchanged kisses, handshakes, and said their goodbyes. Leonard was driving. He opened the door for his parents and walked around to the driver's side of the car. Richard walked with him.

"Drive back carefully, Leonard."

"I will, Big Brother. You guys take care of each other, okay?" he smiled.

"Yeah, we will. You take care of yourself, too, Leonard."

"Oh, I intend to big brother," he grinned. "The first thing tomorrow morning I'm going shopping for some steak and potatoes!"

Richard and Valery stood by the curb and watched the car disappear in the darkness. Richard put his hands into his pocket and began to walk back to his apartment building with Valery's arm entwined securely around his.

****

The following week, Valery obtained a part-time job in the campus library in order to help Richard with their living expenses. The head librarian thought that it was peculiar for the daughter of the town's wealthiest businessman to labor as a clerk in the library. However, she was not going to question the motives of Clifford and Valery Hall.

CHAPTER XXI

It was Wednesday, March 31, 1948. Twelve weeks had passed and Clifford had not yet heard from his daughter. Gerald McDaniel, a business associate, informed Clifford during a late evening business board meeting that he saw and spoke to Valery the night prior at State's library. Gerald went on to question Clifford's reasoning for allowing Valery to work late hours clerking as a Librarian's assistant. Clifford was startled by the communication.

After lunch, he went back to his office and called Earlene. Earlene was not in. Her son, Jerry, answered the phone. Jerry disavowed any knowledge of Valery's job in the library. Clifford questioned Jerry further. It was obvious during the midst of their conversation that Earlene had not briefed Jerry about the fabricated story of Valery's residence with their family.

Clifford was in shock. He sat alone at his massive desk and looked out of the large picture window of his luxurious twenty-ninth floor office. He abruptly requested his secretary to immediately phone for the company's chauffeur-driven automobile. He grabbed his trench coat from his closet and was driven to State's campus.

Valery was pushing a grey, steel book cart down the back aisle of the library's main floor. The cart was filled with books which had to be returned to their appropriate shelves. While pushing the cart, she looked up at the large, dark wood antique clock adorning the center back wall of the library. It read 5:45 p.m. She hastened her pace. Richard would soon arrive to take her home and she wanted to freshen up before his arrival.

Valery continued to work along the back aisles of the almost empty library.
She knelt in front of the cart and read the inside cover of various books in order to determine which reference shelves they were to be placed. A hand firmly grabbed her shoulder. She was startled and turned.

"Father!" she exclaimed while looking up into his hard eyes. She was visibly shaken.

"What are you doing?!?" he angrily asked as his eyes narrowed and his mouth pouted with disapproval.

Valery tried to force a smile,

"I'm working, Father," she answered while getting up and walking around him to place three books on the shelf in the center back aisle.

"You don't have to do that. Why are you humiliating yourself in such a manner?"

"Work is not demeaning, Father," she answered, while walking back to the cart and picking up three more books to place on the upper left rear shelf.

It was obvious by Valery's demeanor that she was uncomfortable with his presence.

Clifford tried a softer approach. He placed his right hand tenderly upon her shoulder as she reached toward the top shelf to place a book. Her body quivered. The clock read 5:55 p.m. No one was in the back aisles, only Valery and her father.

"I want you to come home, Valery," he requested with his hands behind his back. They were inches from each other. He touched her hair and tried to create the contact and closeness they once shared.

Valery turned to her father. Her clear, large eyes looked up toward him. She wanted to talk to him. She wanted to be honest without hurting him. She wanted to explain how much he had physically and emotionally hurt her the last time they were together. She wanted to explain her fear of him; her love for him. She wanted to discuss the abnormal closeness of their relationship and the void it had left in her life.

Above all, she wanted to discuss the deep love she had for Richard and how that love had awakened her from a darkness she no longer wanted to revisit. These were topics she wanted to discuss, but she didn't. He wouldn't understand.

"I'm not coming home, Father."

Clifford was stunned by the strength and confidence of her declaration.

"Why not, daughter? Look, I know I overreacted but-"

"I'm just not happy there, Daddy!" she interrupted.

Clifford was growing angry. He always got what he wanted. He could not deal with her newfound air of independence. He nervously paced back and forth down the short back aisle.

"Where are you staying now?" he bitterly questioned.

"With a friend," she answered with her eyes lowered. The negative vibrations being projected by her father persuaded her to move away from him.

"What friend, Valery? Who is she? I know you're not staying with your Aunt Earlene!!" he stammered.

Valery began to back away from her father.

The sudden flash in his eyes and the painful look on his face informed her that he had answered his own question. She could feel the internal conflict going on in his head. He did not want to accept what suddenly appeared to be the obvious. He leaned against the wall. His eyes widened as he turned and looked at his daughter in disgust. His voice was almost hoarse.

"Are you living with Richard?!!"

"Yes," she answered, "but it's not what you think, I mean it's-"

"What do you mean it's not what I think? .... Are you sleeping in his bed?!"

"Why, yes but-"

"You slut!" he sneered. "You dirty, ungrateful slut!"

Clifford began approaching Valery in an aggressive hostile manner. Valery began to back away from him. She could see the anger and hostility in his eyes. She panicked and began to yell,

"*Don't you touch me! Don't you touch me!!*" she screamed.

Her cry filled the confines of the library walls.

Most of the students and visitors of the library ran in the direction of her screams to determine the conflict. Richard had arrived to the library and was standing at the front library desk where he normally picked up Valery at shift change time. He

165

ran to the back of the library accompanied by the head librarian and saw Valery speedily backing away from her father. Amidst the chatter of the crowd, Richard ran to Valery's side. Clifford continued to approach Valery as if Richard wasn't there. Richard shielded her body behind his own and forced Clifford Hall to acknowledge his presence. The crowd continued to look on as if they were witnessing a playground brawl.

"What are you doing to my daughter, boy?!!" he sneered while trying to grab Valery from around Richard's physical shield.

"I'm loving her, Mr. Hall," he answered while gently yet firmly pushing Clifford's leaning body and overreaching arms off of him as he continued to reach for his daughter.

"I'll bet you are!!!" he sneered. "Dammit, Valery! Don't you see what he's doing to you?!!!?"

Valery appeared shaken by the question. The librarian who had accompanied Richard to the back of the library continued to look on.

"No!" she answered. "I don't know what you're talking about... What is Richard doing to me?"

Clifford continued trying to grab his daughter. His attempts to physically grab her were getting desperate.

"He's making a whore out of you!!" he emphatically declared.

The crowd of onlookers grew noisy and unsettled when he made this allegation.

Richard was shaken by the accusation.

"That's not true!" he firmly replied. "That's not true at all!!"

Clifford stopped wrestling with Richard for Valery's submission. He was breathing hard. He looked intently into Richard's eyes while trying to catch his breath.

"You're out of your league, boy!!" he bellowed, "and I'm not going to play this cat and mouse game with you for my daughter any longer. You see to it boy, that my daughter is in my house by ten o'clock tonight."

"And what if she isn't, Mr. Hall?"

"If she isn't home by ten o'clock tonight, then you will regret the day that you ever laid eyes on her," he warned. "Ten o'clock!!" Clifford repeated while straightening his tie and coat and walking toward the front door of the library. "Ten o'clock!" he repeated. The head librarian looked at Valery and Richard in disgust. The male members of the crowd walked pass Richard and purposely bumped hard into him and Valery during their stride.

****

Richard did not return Valery to her father's house. The following Friday afternoon, Valery was discharged from her position with the library.

CHAPTER XXII

One week had passed since the heated library confrontation between Valery, Richard, and her father Clifford Hall. News of the confrontation had spread throughout the university like a wild fire.

It was Wednesday morning. The clear April skies were royal blue and the air was unusually warm as Richard walked the campus sidewalk toward his Economics lecture. Approaching him on the same walk was a group of six business students moving in the direction of the Finance building. Richard knew them well. He had shared lunch with a few of them on numerous occasions. As the distance between them began to close, his senses determined that something was wrong. They appeared hostile. They were bunched together in such a way that Richard did not have any room to walk on the concrete path.

Richard's slim body was casually attired in his pea-green Army trousers and a maroon colored turtleneck sweater. His clear complexion appeared more soft and handsome in the bright morning sunlight. He tried to pass by David, the biggest of the six males blocking his path.

"Hello, David," he smiled. "Will you pardon me, please?"

David and his peers stood rigid in their path and uncompromising to render room for Richard to pass. They looked at Richard as if he was a convicted felon.

"No, Richard. I don't think that I will pardon you. Why don't you walk around us?" he replied with a firm paternal voice. Dave's colleagues snickered and sneered at Richard during the confrontation.

Richard was puzzled by Dave's response. The two of them had associated well in the past.

"There's no room for me to walk around you fellows, Dave." he diplomatically replied while looking into his eyes.

"Then walk in the street, Richard!!" he responded, projecting an air of anger.

Richard was relaxed, cool, and unafraid. Dave and his colleagues moved in closer toward Richard. Richard stepped back away from them. They stopped. He glanced at his watch which read 9:15 a.m. He'd have to hurry to reach his 9:20 class on time.

"I don't know what this is all about Dave, but I'm not walking in the street. If there's something on your mind, say it! Likewise, I recommend that you and your friends get out of my way before someone gets hurt."

The sneers and smiles vanished from their faces. A few of them were visibly afraid by his stance. David was not surprised. He was well aware of Richard's heroic exploits during the war.

"Yeah, Washington. I have something to say!" he bellowed. "We don't appreciate you coming into our town and ruining the lives of our women!"

"*Your women*?? This is ridiculous! Get out of my way, David!" he replied while trying to push his way through. They merged together and pushed back. Richard could not pass. His growing frustration was apparent.

"Get out of my way!" he demanded.

"We will, Richard. After you hear us out!" replied David.

"If what you have to say has anything to do with Valery, then you have nothing to say!" he roared.

In a fit of anger, David lunged at Richard, grabbed him by his left arm and threw him to the ground. Richard got up, turned, and knocked David to the ground. Two of the remaining three male business students hurriedly scampered from the immediate area upon viewing Dave's condition as Richard approached them. The remaining male walked back to David's semi-conscious body and helped him to his feet. Dave took out a white handkerchief and wiped the blood appearing from a cut on the corner of his mouth. He initiated a lone scolding.

"You're playing with fire, Richard. You'll never get away with it!"

Richard was baffled and puzzled by the warning.

"Get away with what?! I don't understand you and the rest of this crazy city.   What Valery and I do is our business!"

"No, Richard. In this town, what you and Valery do is everyone's business," he replied while dusting the dirt from his pants and brown tweed sport coat.

Richard looked at his watch. It read 9:35 am. He was late for class.

"See you later, Dave," he quietly replied while hurriedly walking toward the Finance Building.

∗∗∗∗∗∗∗∗∗∗∗∗∗∗∗∗∗∗∗∗∗∗∗∗∗

Valery was the president of the Phi Beta Kappa Sorority. It was a position Valery was finding increasingly harder to hold. The elite campus community clicks were initially jarred upon learning that Valery had broken off from Damien.

However, they were flabbergasted to learn that she was involved with Richard. To further compound things, gossip of the library encounter between she and her powerful father had spread through the campus like a wild fire. It was no longer an isolated secret that Valery was living in the slum part of the city with Richard. Her social life and good name had been critically damaged.

During the first three years of her collegiate life, she had been regarded as the most beautiful, intellectual and charming coed on campus. Today, she was regarded as a confused wealthy tramp. Prior to Valery's involvement with Richard, she was always pursued and surrounded by men of promise and wealth.

Today, when not within the company of Richard, she generally walked the campus grounds-alone.

In the recent past, whenever she spoke her sorority sisters would intently listen. In the tenure of three short weeks however, she felt that she was being ignored.

Valery was increasingly becoming a president without power; a leader without followers.

It was Friday April 9, 1948. State's basketball team had again won the division championship. The Phi Beta Kappa sorority was responsible for coordinating the Championship Ball. Valery arranged a five-thirty p.m. sorority meeting to be held in the Student Activities Center in order to expediently resolve the finishing issues for this event. She arrived thirty minutes early for the meeting and assembled her notes in the middle of the long oval table. Next, she filled the large coffee brewer with water and the appropriate measures of coffee.

As the coffee brewed, she reviewed her notes and the agenda of issues to be addressed. The clock read 5:30 p.m. The Student Activities Room was a large conference room with an Eiffel Tower type glass ceiling. A rich dark wood paneling covered the interior walls. A tall, large, antique grandfather clock with bold roman numerals on its face grabbed one's attention upon entering the room.

Valery loved this room. She had spent many isolated moments here to study or meditate on her future. It provided her an aura of warmth, serenity and safety.

The bold clock now read 5:45 p.m. and not one of her sorority sisters had yet arrived. The coffee pot was rapidly percolating and emanating the rich smell of fresh brewed coffee. She got up from the large oak chair, walked to the coffee pot and poured a cup of coffee for herself. She walked back to the table while sipping the hot coffee. She appeared relaxed and confident. She wondered how Richard was doing and pondered upon how much she loved him.

Valery looked at the clock. It read 6 p.m. and her sorority sisters had not yet arrived. She was concerned. She reviewed her notes again. The clock read 6:15 p.m.

The members of the sorority trickled in together. Some of them took seats upon entering the room while others nonchalantly poured a cup of coffee and casually talked to each other prior to taking their seats. Very few of them spoke to Valery. None of them offered an apology for being late.

This was no common group of women. Their dress, sophistication, mannerisms, and hard-boiled snobbishness were all denominators of their families' wealth. They took their seats at the conference table.

The room was warm prior to their entrance. Upon their entrance, the room felt icy cold. Most of the coldness was directed toward Valery. Valery was strong in her softness. She ignored their cold stares and opened up the meeting. She turned to Margaret, the secretary of the sorority, and requested her to read the minutes of the last meeting. Margaret looked at Lillian, the tall, prissy, vice-president of the sorority. Lillian nodded approval. Margaret then read the minutes of the last meeting.

Valery was puzzled. She could not understand why Margaret sought Lillian's approval to her simple request. Valery then turned to Annette, the treasurer of the sorority and requested her to report the monies deposited in their account. Annette turned to Lillian. Lillian nodded approval. Annette read the monies on account in the treasury.

Valery was bewildered. Lillian slowly turned her head toward Valery and smirked at Valery's apparent impotence.

Lillian, though every bit as attractive as Valery, always envied Valery's grace, charm, and internal beauty. Lillian flaunted her sexual attributes. Everything about her was exaggerated. She was regarded as cold, spoiled, and uncompromising. She radiated a warm, friendly rehearsed smile that beckoned for attention and a response. Many men considered her a challenge. Mature men considered her a problem to be avoided.

Lillian could no longer tolerate Valery's presence. Valery was a constant reminder to her that she was only second best. That fact had been emphasized over and over again. Lillian desired Richard. Valery had him. Lillian wanted Damien. She got him on the rebound after Valery left him-for Richard. Lillian was the vice-president of the sorority and Valery was the president. She was tired of being second best.

Valery commenced the meeting. She smiled while straightening up her notes. No one smiled back.

"Good evening, Sisters. As you are aware, the purpose of this meeting is to discuss our role as coordinators of the Division One Championship Dance. This affair will be held in the Student Ball Room. For the last three years our boys have excelled on the court and won the division championship. I know that we're all proud of them. In addition, I'm grateful that the faculty had enough faith in our sorority to appoint us to chair this event. I've prepared a few notes on the subject. I kind of think that if we all compare our notes and ideas, that we can derive a good strategy towards making this event a big success."

Margaret politely   raised her hand. Valery acknowledged Margaret with a smile.

"Yes, Margaret?"

"Valery, I think there is another topic we should discuss first"

"Okay, Margaret. What subject is that?"

"*Your Presidency!!*"

Valery was stunned. Her face paled.

"What…..what about my presidency?" she asked while looking at Margaret.

"Valery, there's a wildfire of a rumor going on around campus that you're shacking up with this junior named Richard Washington. Is there any truth to this rumor?"

"That's irrelevant, Margaret. My personal life is my business."

"That's right, Valery," interceded Lillian, "your personal life is your business, but the image of our sorority is predicated in great part by the image of our president. Please answer the question, Valery. Are you living with Richard?"

Valery felt like a prisoner on trial. She blushed with embarrassment.

"Well . . . yes. Right now I'm living with Richard."

The members of the sorority gasped in shock and disgust. The room became noisy as they busily talked amongst themselves about the confessed admission. Valery tried to talk above the extraneous chatter.

"However, there are certain personal reasons for this situation. I-"

"Valery, darling," interrupted Margaret with a sadistic smile, "we are not concerned with the reasons for your unladylike behaviors. However, we do not feel that you represent the image we desire of our president. We don't want a president whose 'shackin' around, " she asserted with the demeanor of a small town county prosecutor.

"It's deeper than that, Margaret."

"*I'll bet it is,*" snickered Lillian. All of the women robustly laughed. They were laughing at Valery.

Valery realized that their ears were closed. She was mentally and emotionally distressed. They had all once claimed to be her closest friend and now they were figuratively and intentionally hurling stones of abuse towards her.

"Well, what are you proposing, Margaret?" she inquired, looking more at the table than towards Margaret. She felt like she had been convicted and about to be sentenced.

"We've appointed Lillian to be our new president, Valery. You can contest this but I would suggest that you not do so. I don't think the additional notoriety in conducting such an appeal will do you any good. Furthermore, you can remain a member of the sorority if you like, Valery, however, we'd prefer it if you wouldn't."

The room grew silent. Valery sat in her chair in a state of shock. Her external appearance was calm. Her insides were caving in.

Lillian pulled out a pocket mirror, examined her face, and teased her hair with her fingers. Valery looked at her. Lillian, sitting in the chair to Valery's left, stopped looking into the mirror and rolled her eyes toward her. She had figuratively beaten Valery Hall and she was enjoying it. A sarcastic victory smile danced across her lips.

"I'm sure no one would object if you were to excuse yourself from this meeting, Valery," asserted Lillian.

Valery felt weak; hurt; beaten. The pressures of the last eight weeks were too heavy. She wanted to speak but didn't from fear that if she opened her mouth, tears would flow from her eyes. She had to appear strong. She could not give them proof of how badly they had hurt her. She wanted to walk out with some resemblance of pride.

Valery patiently gathered her notes from the table and put them into her briefcase. She gracefully pushed her chair from the conference table and got out of her seat. She turned to Lillian and extended her hand to her. Lillian was jarred by the act but felt it wise to take and shake Valery's hand.

"Lillian, I wish you a presidency of luck and success," she sincerely declared while standing with her briefcase in hand.

They were impressed with her seemingly calm mannerisms and grace in an environment of hostility. She continued,

"If there are any questions you need answered regarding the organization of the filing system, the policy and procedures of the school board governing our sorority, or the present work-in-progress to be completed, please feel free to call me."

"Thank you, Valery," Lillian softly replied, spellbound and attentive.

Valery walked to the door, opened it, and walked out of the room. Once on the streets, she hailed a cab. As the cab travelled through the streets, she sat in the backseat of the cab's drab interior-and she cried.

CHAPTER XXIII

Another week had passed. Richard was involved in an early evening conference meeting with his Marketing professor, Mr. Charles Griffin.

Richard was leaning over the professor's desk, highly upset about a failing grade he had received on a research project. He had worked on this project and supporting papers for two months. This research and the accommodating papers constituted twenty-five percent of his semester grade. Charles Griffin was an early fiftyish, lean, polished gentleman with a head full of unruly hair and full beard incorporating streaks of gray throughout.

"Professor Griffin, I don't understand it. How could you give me a failing grade on a one hundred page typewritten research paper!! I posted the references which support my conclusions. I ... I have typed in all of the proper footnotes. There are no grammatical errors. I don't understand!!!"

He was angry. The more he pleaded his case the more he leaned and leered over the desk toward Professor Griffin.

Professor Griffin's arms were wrapped behind his head as he leaned backward further and further on the back legs of his chair as Richard continued to petition for a more fair judgment of his work. Prior to today, Professor Griffin was one of Richard's favorite teachers. Richard enjoyed the objective manner by which this teacher educated his students. He would always persuade his students to see and argue both sides of a Marketing or Financial issue in order to promote independent thinking and judgment.   Richard had received excellent marks from Griffin in various marketing courses over the last two years. He couldn't understand the change in grading behavior that had taken place in the last three weeks. If the present trend continued, he would ultimately fail all of his classes.

"I just don't agree with your conclusions, Richard. I feel there is nothing wrong with the marketing strategies of monopolies in this country!" he replied while leaning further back on his chair.

Richard's eyes widened in anger and his lips got tight.

"I don't believe you're saying this! You've been preaching the whole semester about how monopolistic type corporations tend to produce those goods providing the highest unit of marginal profits in contrast to those goods desired by the consumer with smaller marginal returns."

"Now wait a minute, Son. I've also given some strong arguments supporting the good features of monopolies!"

"Yes Sir, you have! But I've written a good paper supporting the former argument! I've provided all data and 3rd party documents supporting my position. How can you give me a failing grade simply because you don't agree with the conclusion despite the intrinsic and extrinsic evidence to the contrary?"

"Because I'm the teacher, Richard," he smiled, "Because I'm the teacher!"

Richard could sense that this discussion was fruitless. He stopped leaning
his towering body over Griffin's desk. Griffin stopped leaning backward on his chair away from Richard. Richard sat down in the chair across from the professor's desk. He rubbed his right hand over his forehead as if he was trying to massage the pressure of the past few weeks from his mind.

"What's going on?" he asked while looking into Griffin's eyes. "Why are you guys trying to bury me?"

"You're trying to bury yourself, Richard," the professor nonchalantly declared while cleaning his clean fingernails with a fingernail file.

"How?"

"Think about it, Richard...think about it."

"No! You tell me! What's the reason for this conspiracy?"

"I've told you too much already, Richard. Listen, you're a bright boy. Think about it. Is it really worth it?"

"Is what worth it?" he asked, puzzled by Griffin's line of questioning.

"Richard, I have to end this meeting. Another student conference is pending. You're going to have to leave now."

Richard got up from the chair and walked out of the professor's small office. He was in a daze. He walked through the corridors, out of the business building, and into the sunny streets in a drunken state of stupor.

Frank was walking toward Richard in- route to his evening class. His intention was to ignore Richard. They had not spoken to each other since the night of Valery's birthday dinner some six weeks prior. He was still upset about their live-in relationship. However, he could readily observe by the uncoordinated manner Richard was walking the campus grounds that something was wrong . . . very wrong.

Frank walked past Richard. Richard did not see him. He did not appear sober and continued to walk in an uncoordinated fashion. Frank turned around and called Richard by name,

"Richard!"

He did not answer. Frank called his name again.

"Richard!"

Again he did not respond to his name. Frank ran in front of Richard and shook him,

"Richard, what's wrong with you?"

He came out of his daze.

"Oh, Frank! How are you? I didn't even see you" he greeted with a faint smile.

"Hey, fella, what's wrong with you? Have you been drinking?"

The smile quickly faded from Richard's mouth,

"What the hell's it to you?!! You're just like all the rest of them'" he sneered.

Frank couldn't detect any alcohol on Richard's breath. It was obvious that something was wrong. Frank decided to skip class and find the cause for Richard's taciturn behavior.

"Look, Richard. Let's stop at the coffee shop and get something to eat," he requested while putting his arm around Richard's shoulder.

Richard pushed Frank's arm off of his shoulder.

"I'm too upset to eat! I want to do something productive."

"Like what, Richard?" he asked while grabbing his arm and making him stop.

Frank tried to force eye contact but Richard would not look at him. He was hyper and upset. His head and eyes darted across the ground and skies in a circular motion.

"Like what, Richard??" Frank again asked.

"I think I want to kill somebody," Richard answered.

Frank laughed. His laughter relaxed Richard as a broad smile crossed his tight, tense lips.

"C'mon, what's wrong, friend?" asked Frank as a mild gust of wind blew against them.

"Friend?? Hell I haven't seen you since the night you walked out on Valery's birthday dinner, that was six weeks ago. You don't know the meaning of the word."

"Sure I do," Frank replied. "As a matter of fact, the concerns I expressed about this living arrangement gives credibility to my friendship."

"How?" Richard asked, rolling his pupils out of the corner of his eyes to look at Frank as they continued to walk the campus grounds.

"Because I know the serious complications which can result in your life if you cross Clifford Hall! How are you and he doing, anyway?"

Richard turned away and looked into the distance.

"Well, Frank, I guess you heard about that library scene, right?'

They stood on a street corner waiting for the red light to change.

"Yeah, Richard. The whole school has heard about it,"

"Well, neither I nor Valery have seen nor heard from the guy since, Maybe he's given up."

179

"No, Rich. Clifford Hall doesn't give up on anything Clifford Hall wants. But anyway, if he isn't bothering you, what is the problem?"

The light turned green and they renewed their walk through the crowded campus streets.

"I don't know, Frank. It seems to me that all of my teachers are trying to fail me!"

"What? How?? Why?!?"

"Beats the hell out of me, Frank. Three weeks ago I had excellent marks in all four of my business classes. Recently, however, I have received poor or failing grades on every test and every paper I have submitted. I don't understand it."

The intensity left Frank's face. They walked past his parked sports car.

"Rich, let's get in my car for a minute."

"For what, Frank?"

"Well, I've got a good bottle of Scotch under the seat and I think we both could use a stiff drink."

Frank walked over to the driver's side of his car, opened the door, took off his suit jacket and threw it in the back compartment of the small two-seat vehicle. He got into his car, leaned over and opened the passenger side of the car. Richard got in. Frank reached under his seat and pulled out the bottle of Scotch, opened up his glove compartment, and pulled out two plastic cups. While pouring them both a cup of the spirits, he commenced conversation.

"Richard, the reason for the sudden change in your professor's behavior is obvious."

"I guess you're going to say that their actions are triggered by Clifford Hall's desire to see me fail," replied Richard while taking the cup to his mouth.

"Exactly."

"I've thought about that, Frank. But I don't believe that's really the reason. I don't believe that one man could influence decent men to conspire to program my failure."

Frank was floored by Richard's response.

"Richard, you really don't understand the leverage of wealth and power!" he snapped. "Clifford Hall built this town. He's a senior board member on just about every chief institution here. In addition, his bank holds the mortgages of about seventy percent of the teaching staff at the University."

"Okay . . . okay! Let's say I'm ready to accept what you're saying as true. What can he possibly get out of seeing me fail my classes?" he asked in a state of exasperation.

"Dammit, Richard. Think!! Think! He can get your scholarship!"

Richard was shocked. The cup of Scotch shook in his hand.

"How?"

"The conditions of the scholarship are that you must have better than average grades each semester you're in school. If you have a failing semester then the scholarship may be rescinded. Once he flunks you out of school, he can easily rid you from the community and away from his daughter."

Richard turned the cup of Scotch up and swallowed the liquor down his throat. Frank refilled his cup. Richard looked out of the passenger window.

"This is a rather long-winded back door method of getting me, isn't it Frank?

"It's one of several planned maneuvers, I'm sure", replied Frank.

"What am I going to do, Frank?" he asked in a barely audible frustrated tone.

Frank was concerned. He shared Richard's fears.

"Richard, listen to me. Life is like a good game of poker. You've got to know when to keep a good hand and when to throw your cards in. Right now, the whole deck is against you, Richard. If you throw your losing hand in early, then you won't lose too much. If you keep that bad hand too long then you can lose everything."

Richard turned his head toward Frank and timidly looked into his eyes,

> "Yeah, Frank. I think that makes sense. But if I throw my hand in, I lose Valery."

Frank's eyes conveyed sympathy. He could see the conflict, worry and pressure on Richard's young face.

> "But at least you keep the scholarship, Richard. *After all, that's the reason you came up here, remember?* If you continue along the present path, you will lose the scholarship and Valery. It's inevitable."

Richard looked at his watch. It read 3:45 p.m.

> "Well, I have to go to work, Frank. Thanks for the advice," he meekly smiled while opening the door.

> "You're welcome, Rich. But tell me, what are you going to do?" he asked while grabbing Richard's arm and keeping him in the car as he tried to get out of the passenger seat.

> "Nothing!" Richard asserted while shaking Frank's arm loose and getting out of the car.

> "What?!!!? In other words you haven't listened to a damn word I said!" he angrily responded.

> "Frank, my father always told me that when you don't know what to do, don't do nothin'. But there is one thing that I do know, Frank. I'm not giving up Valery! I'm not giving up Valery for anyone!" and Richard got out of the car.

Frank jumped out of the car, shielding his eyes from the bright sun with his hand as Richard walked across the hilly landscaped greenery toward the student parking lot.

> "Now listen, Richard-!"

> "I'm keeping' my hand, Frank! He's going to have to show me the whole deck!" Richard declared while looking back at Frank and gradually disappearing over the hill from view.

CHAPTER XXIV

Saturday morning, April 17, 1948

Valery snuggled her sleeping body closer to Richard's as the daylight slowly stretched its arms and began to rise over the small city of Camden. Richard heard two happy bluebirds cheerfully singing crisp melodies of music as they pursued each other through the heavily clothed branches of the white oak tree outside of his bedroom window.

Richard tenderly kissed Valery's sleeping lips and freed himself from her embrace. He got out of bed and walked to the bathroom wherein he showered and shaved. He put on his dark blue work overalls and black oxfords. He walked to the kitchen and brewed a pot of black coffee prior to sitting at the kitchen table. His insides were uneasy. His elbows were standing on the table and his head was buried into his hands when Valery sleepily walked into the kitchen. She pulled his hands down from his head.

Startled, Richard's head snapped to attention.

"Oh! . . . Valery. Good morning," he greeted with a half-smile.

She sat in the chair next to him while trying to keep her eyelids open.

"Richard . . . why are you up at six o'clock in the morning?" she asked as her head wavered back and forth in an attempt to remain conscious.

"I have an early shift at the garage," he answered while watching her almost futile attempt to remain awake.

"But why, Richard? You don't go to the garage until 12:00 p.m. on Saturday,"

"Yeah, yeah, I know," he impatiently replied, "but extra hours mean extra dollars . . . God in heaven knows that we need all the extra money we can get."

The academic and financial pressures were beginning to affect him. He got up, poured a cup of coffee for Valery and himself, and walked back to the kitchen table. Valery took the large cup in both of her small hands. She drank the hot coffee while trying to ease into a mild conversation.

"What`s wrong, Richard?"

"Nothing," he answered, looking away from her.

"Yes there is. Tell me. Is it too much pressure for you?" she asked gently touching his arm.

"Nothing I can't handle," he arrogantly replied while getting out of his chair and walking to the living room window.

Valery remained seated at the kitchen table and continued to drink her coffee. Richard looked out of the window and pondered upon their present financial situation. He walked back to the kitchen and stood by the sink.

"Aren't you worried?" he asked.

"About what?"

"About how we're going to make it."

"I don't see any problems, Richard. We have a roof over our head, a car, clothes, and we're getting our education. We're doing okay."

"How can you say that, Valery? I'm barely able to give you fifteen dollars a week spending money. You haven't bought any clothes since you've been here, and you are living in this old one bed-room apartment in the slums instead of your twenty-two room marble home. This entire area is a low income slum district compared to what you've been accustomed to. It's not even very safe over here. The only reason you haven't been harassed is because these residents haven't yet figured out who you are."

Valery walked to Richard and tenderly kissed his cheek.

"A twenty-two room house is no longer of interest to me. I like this apartment. It's warm here. Its okay for now, I'm sure we'll be able to move in time," she replied.

"With what, Valery? I'm doing the best I can on the money we have now."

"Well, things will improve, Richard. Won't they?"

184

"Ohhhh . . . I don't know!" he sighed. "Little money. . . shit professors."

"What about the professors?" She inquired, puzzled by his impulsive tangent change in topics. Richard had not informed Valery of the apparent conspiracy to fail him from the university. He also felt that this was not the time to discuss it.

"Nothing!" He emphatically answered while walking to the closet and getting his jacket. She walked behind him, shaken by his erratic, hard behavior.

"I have to go Valery. See you tonight," he replied while quickly kissing her lips and walking out of their apartment.

The time at the garage quickly passed. It was a productive and laborious day. The clock read 5:45 p.m. Richard had tuned up two station wagons, rebuilt one carburetor, and was helping a fellow employee overhaul a public streetcar engine when Jim paged him over the loudspeaker.

Richard walked to Jim's office at the front of the garage. Jim's desk was cluttered with business papers and an outdated adding machine. A low wattage light bulb burned as Jim tallied the service sales of the day.

"You wanted to see me, Jim?" he inquired while attempting to wipe his hands clean of the axle grease with a towel. Subtle traces of dirt and oil appeared on his cheeks, forehead, and bridge of his nose.

A broad smile appeared on Jim's round face as he looked up to acknowledge Richard's presence. A bond of love had developed between Jim and Richard over the two years of Richard's employment.
Jim, as others, was awed by Richard's mechanical talents and amused by Richard's wit and good humor. The business revenue at the garage had doubled over the last two years. Jim attributed much of the increase in business activity to Richard's employment.

"Yes, Richard. I do want to see you. Have a seat."

"Sure, Jim. What's on your mind?"

"You, Richard," he answered. He leaned back in his chair and paused as if searching for the right words to begin the conversation.

"Son, because of you, I'm making more money today than I've ever made at this garage."

"That's good, Jim. I'm happy to hear that. You've been a big help to me too,"

"Well . . . anyway, Rich, to make a long story short, I'm giving you a raise."

Richard's eyes widened. He was happy; excited. Suddenly he appeared sad; depressed.

"Jim, you're paying me fifty dollars a week for twenty six hours of labor. That's more money than a lot of veteran mechanics are making on a full-time shift. I mean . . . I know you're a good friend of my father's but-"

"Richard," he interrupted, "This has nothing to do with my relationship with your father. If the present trend continues, I'm going to net fifty thousand dollars this year. That's twenty thousand dollars more than this garage grossed last year. You are largely responsible for our success. Believe me, boy, your Father has nothing to do with this. I could be a millionaire if I could figure out a way to clone you, " he laughed.

Jim leaned over his desk and handed Richard his pay envelope.

"Keep up the good work, Richard. There's more where that came from."

"Thanks, Jim," he smiled while taking the envelope and getting out of his chair.

He shook Jim's hand and walked out of the office. Richard walked toward the shower room while opening the envelope. He pulled out his check and stopped dead in his tracks. Richard hurriedly walked back to Jim's office and opened the door. He was inflamed with excitement.

"Hey, Jim! Jim!! I think you made a mistake! There's too much money in here!"

Jim turned from his file cabinet, smiled, and shook his head in disagreement.

"No, Rich. You deserve every dollar of it!!"

"But Jim, *there's five hundred dollars here!!*"

"That's right, Richard! Furthermore, your salary is being doubled" he smiled.

"I don't understand, Jim," he continued, "Are you saying that I'll be earning over a hundred dollars a week?!!?"

"Yes, Richard," replied Jim while laughing and shaking his head affirmatively to convince Richard that he understood him correctly.

Richard began walking around in circles in the tiny office; talking recklessly.

"Well, now I can finally get us a decent apartment, buy her some clothes, damn!! There must be a God!"

"Her?" Jim inquired, "Are you getting married, Richard?"

Richard realized he was talking too much. Jim wasn't aware of Richard's present dilemma and he saw little reason to inform him of it now. "No, Jim. I'm just talking out of my head. Thanks again, Jim." he smiled while walking out of the office.

Richard hurriedly walked to the garage pay phone and called Valery.

"Hello," she greeted.

"Hello, Valery! Honey, it's me. Did you cook dinner?"

"Of course I cooked dinner. It's getting cold! Why are you working so late? Are you coming home now?"

"Yes, but listen. Whatever you cooked, wrap it up and put it in the icebox. We're going out for dinner tonight."

"Richard, you know we can't afford-"

"Oh yes we can!!!"

"But how?"

"I'll tell you when I get home. Put on your best 'going out' clothes honey. Tonight we're celebrating."

Richard hung up the phone and walked to the locker room. He showered, paid special attention to how he combed his hair and put on his clothes.

In route home, he stopped at a winery for a bottle of expensive champagne. Tonight, the world was theirs.

Richard drove up to the front of his apartment building at 7:15 p.m. The sun had set early that spring evening and a light darkness hovered over the city. He got out of his car and walked toward the front door of his apartment complex.

A muscular figure of about six feet three inches tall in stature was leaning on the pole of a street lamp, approximately thirty yards from the building. As Richard opened the front door of the apartment building, the large burly figure called his name.

"Richard! Richard Washington!"

Richard could not recognize the voice or the physique of the man approaching him. He was curious. He stopped at the front door as the large mysterious stranger approached him.

"Did you call my name?" he asked, puzzled by the nature of this unfamiliar person's inquiry.

"Yeah, I've got a message for you," the stranger replied. His eyes were cold and calculating. His broad facial features were hard and unattractive. A large scar adorned his right cheek and a painted smile danced across his otherwise emotionless face. The stranger wore expensive casual clothing that did not fit his street character and a pair of black leather driving gloves was locked under his right arm.

"A message from whom?" Richard asked.

"A message from Clifford Hall," he answered with the smile growing broader across his cold face.

The vibrations in the air turned violent. Richard's senses warned him of the danger this stranger posed against his physical well-being. He looked around to see if there were any more like him in the immediate area.

"It's just me, Washington," the stranger smiled.

"Well, what's the message?"

"Do you mind if I come in?"

"Well, yes I do. Strangers aren't allowed in this building."

"It will only take a minute, Washington."

Richard was intrigued by the mysterious nature of this visit. He wanted to hear the supposed message from Clifford Hall. He opened the door and allowed the stranger entrance into the building. They walked side by side toward the elevator. His spirit alarmed his body to protect himself. Richard turned away from the elevator and faced the eerie stranger.

"Okay, buddy. This is as far as you and this game are going. Now what's the message??!?" he questioned in anger.

At that precise point, the doors of the elevator opened. The stranger abruptly knocked Richard into the open elevator door, causing the bottle of champagne to fall from his arm and splatter on the granite facing of the main floor. Two other bullish strangers of the same height and stature of the first were already standing in the elevator. This drill had been rehearsed.

Two of them grabbed both of Richard's arms as the third one closed the doors and pressed the basement button. Richard was struggling to free himself from the brutal grip exerted on his arms and shoulders by his captors. They began talking amongst themselves as the elevator began moving toward the basement. Richard was struggling harder and more desperately to free himself from the eminent danger. One of the two who held his arms yelled to the third,

"Eric, I think we have a wild one here. Why don't you calm him down?"

At that point, the stranger called Eric began battering Richard's face, eyes, and stomach with his fist until his fists bled. The elevator stopped in the dark basement.
Richard was near unconsciousness and yet the barbaric intruders dragged his limp body out of the elevators as Eric continued to beat him while lecturing him between intermittent pauses,

"Like I said, Washington, I have a message for you!" he exclaimed while continuing to hammer Richard's crumbling body.

"Stop making a whore out of Clifford Hall's daughter! Stop sleeping with her! Stop holding her!! Take her home!!"

Richard was beaten unconscious. The two men restraining him realized that if Eric continued to pummel him, Richard would not survive. They could literally hear the bones of Richard's upper body breaking throughout this beating.

"Okay, Eric! That's enough," one of the thugs yelled.
They all hopped back into the elevator with Richard's scarecrow-like limp body and pressed the button to the third floor. They propped Richard's brutally beaten body in front of theirs in order to avoid direct attention.

A small crowd of residents, waiting for the elevator on the first floor, were terrified by the grotesque bloody mess of a man that stood propped in front of his oppressors.
In fear, they ran in various directions hoping to avoid the fate that had fallen upon him.

The elevator doors closed and moved to the third floor. The three barbarians undraped Richard's body and hurriedly dragged him down the hallway to his apartment unit. Once they reached his unit, they kicked him relentlessly as Eric knocked on the apartment door. Eric could hear Valery walking toward the door. They hurriedly walked away.

"Who is it?" Valery cheerfully asked while rubbing lotion on her hands as she walked toward the door. She was expecting to hear Richard's reply.

Valery was dressed in a clinging white skirt, heels and white silk top blouse.
Her glowing dark hair was fashionably combed up and away from her face, emphasizing her distinctive high cheek bones and large eyes. She was stunning, happy; content.

"Who is it??" she again repeated.
Richard had taught her never to open the door without being able to acknowledge the person on the other side. Valery looked out of the peephole and couldn't see anyone.
A sliver of fear streaked through her body. She pulled open the door, looked, and screamed with horror at the bloody condition of Richard's body coiled in a fetal position on the floor. She bent down and shook his shoulders but he would not awaken.

Valery ran to the apartment unit to the right of her and banged on the door. No one answered. She banged on the door again until the elderly couple named 'Cunningham', hesitantly opened their door.

"Mr. Cunningham, please help me! Richard's been hurt!" Cunningham looked out of his door and saw the bloody mess just yards away from him. Fear covered his face. He quickly muttered a few incoherent words about not getting involved and closed the door on Valery's face.

Valery was shocked. Anger filled her body. She violently pounded and cried on Cunningham's door until her hands ached but he would not answer. Valery ran from unit to unit of their third floor complex but the residents would not answer the door. A few residents were curious about the commotion she was emanating in the hallway. They looked out of their door, saw Richard bloodily sprawled on the floor and Valery pounding on doors for help. They would therein step back inside of their unit when she would begin approaching and petitioning them for help.

Valery realized that she was not going to get any help from the residents and ran back to Richard. She stopped crying. She regained her calm demeanor. She knelt beside Richard and put his right arm over her shoulder and tried to lift him up. He groaned. His flimsy arm tangled. She could detect that his right arm was broken and any pressure on it would injure him more severely. Her white attire was becoming heavily soaked in blood. She moved over to Richard's left side. She knelt on her knees and placed his left arm over her shoulder. Three times she tried to lift his heavy body up in order to move him into their apartment, three times she failed.

She knelt by his side, exhausted and frustrated by the lack of progress she was making. She sobbed. Valery tried a fourth time to lift him up on her tiny petite shoulders. She was adamant. The dead weight of his unconscious body crushed her. Nevertheless, she was able to make small steady steps from the entrance door of their apartment to their bedroom.

Valery fell on top of him while laying the top half of his body on the edge of the bed. She quickly lifted his knees and legs upon the bed before their dead weight caused the top half of his body to fall from the bed's edge. Valery sat on the bed next to him. She picked up the phone and attempted to call an ambulance.

"Operator! Operator!? Please send an ambulance to-"
  Valery jumped when she felt a group of fingers creeping on her back. It was Richard. He was semiconscious.

"Hang up the phone, Valery," he whispered in pain.

"Hang up the phone? Are you crazy, Richard, who did this to you??"

"Hello??... Hello???" repeated the operator.

"Oh, yes! I'm sorry, operator, Please quickly send an ambulance to-"
  With the last ounce of strength within him, Richard swatted the phone from Valery's hand. It fell hard to the floor.

"I said hang up the phone, Valery!" he repeated. His eyes were a glassy weak.
  She became hysterically confused.

"I don't understand! What do you want me to do? Let you die??!"

"I'm not going to die," he whispered. "Now hang up the phone and call Frank. Tell him to bring his doctor over here as quickly as possible."

"Hello? . . . Hello?" again questioned the operator.

Valery was in a daze. She cut the connection between herself and the operator and called Frank. She informed Frank of the present situation. Within thirty minutes, Frank and his doctor were in Richard's bedroom. Frank turned away in horror at the sight of Richard's battered body. He and Valery therein helped the doctor to disrobe Richard for the examination.

Frank took Valery into the living room and sat on the sofa as the doctor conducted the examination. Frank was filled with anger.

"What happened to him?"

"I don't know, Frank. I heard a knock on the door, opened it, and found Richard on the floor as you see him now."

"You realize who's responsible for this, don't you?" Valery answered as tears began to erupt from her eyes.

"Yes. I realize that my father's responsible for this."

Frank got up from the sofa and walked around the small living room in anger. Valery continued to sit on the couch. Frank stopped pacing the living room floor. He turned toward Valery with his hands clinching the side of his waist.

" Well, what are you going to do about it, Valery?" Valery would not look at him. She looked aimlessly at the floor.

"I don't know," she cried. "I don't know. I'll figure out something. What do you think I should do?"

He did not answer.

"Let's go see how Richard is doing," he coldly requested while walking toward the bedroom.

Valery meekly followed his lead.

The doctor was walking out of the bedroom as Frank opened the door.

"Well, how is he, Doc?"

"He's in bad condition, Frank. He's got a broken arm, broken jaw, couple of fractured or broken ribs, but it's still not as bad as it looks. Against his protests, I'm checking him into the hospital. He will need some surgery and we must do the appropriate tests to confirm that there isn't any internal bleeding."

Valery looked at the doctor; puzzled, and asked,

"Why doesn't he want to be admitted into the hospital?"

"He doesn't want anyone to know how badly he was beaten up. He's a proud man; too proud."

Frank made a quick decision.

"Okay, let's put him into that private clinic just outside of town. We need to admit him under an alias name just in case the party responsible for his condition decides that they want to finish him off. We need to have a private ambulance absent of the sirens with medical personnel to transport him there. Is there any way we can do this in a manner that guarantees his anonymity?" The doctor nodded affirmatively and made the appropriate calls to achieve Frank's requirements.

****

 Richard was admitted into the hospital at 9:14 p.m. Fourteen days later he was released from the hospital in good health. Outside of a cast covering his left arm, Richard's physical appearance had not been disfigured.

Chapter XXV

Richard was discharged from the hospital on a Tuesday morning at 11:23 a.m. Hospital regulations required that all released patients sit in a wheelchair while being escorted out of the hospital by the presiding nurse. Valery obtained permission to push Richard's wheelchair while escorting him, with a nurse, out of the small hospital.

"This is ludicrous," he muttered as he sat in the chair and Valery wheeled him down the second floor corridor toward the elevator.

"A rules a rule, Richard. Just hold on. We'll be out of here in a moment," she smiled while leaning over and kissing his forehead as the doors of the elevator opened. She wheeled him within the elevator doors.

"Well, what would you like to do today, lover?" she asked as the elevator moved to the main floor.

"Anything except go to school, I feel good today. I don't feel like being depressed."

The doors of the elevator opened to the lobby floor. Valery pushed the chair onto the lobby quarters.

"Richard, I don't think you've been quite straight with me. How come you didn't tell me that some members of the college faculty are trying to fail you?" she asked while pushing the wheelchair down the corridor toward the front hospital doors.

"Who told you, Valery?"

"Never mind who told me, Richard. You seem to have forgotten that we're in this thing together."

"I'll bet Frank told you. Yeah, it was Frank."

The hospital personnel opened the door as Valery wheeled Richard out of the hospital. It was an unusually warm May day. The temperatures ranged near the high eighty degree mark. Richard got out of the chair and walked toward their car parked in front of the hospital door. Valery walked to the driver's side of the vehicle.

"I can't believe how warm it is today!" he exclaimed, looking at the blue sky and deep green grass while standing at the street curb.

"Yeah, I know," she smiled, "The last few May days have been unusually warm. The temperatures are supposed to reach mid-nineties by late afternoon. C'mon, Richard. Get in the car!"

Richard got into the passenger side of the car. Valery turned on the ignition and whisked them away from the hospital. The both of them were unusually quiet as Valery drove out of the city toward the more distant suburbs of the county. She had been driving for over thirty-five minutes along scenic Highway one.

Richard was seemingly lost in a daydream when Valery initiated conversation.

"What are you thinking about, Richard?"

"I don't know. I guess I'm trying to figure out where we're going."

"I'm sorry," she teased. "Didn't I tell you where we're going?"

"No, Valery," he answered. "You didn't tell me where we're going. Where are we going, Valery?"

"We're going on a picnic!" she beamed.

"That sounds good. But why are we driving so far, Valery? There are some nice beaches in the city."

"Yes, I know, Richard. But they're all crowded. I want you to myself today. We need to talk."

"Talk about what, Valery?"

"Talk about us . . . talk about that violent beating that almost cost you your life."

"You mean the *accident?*"

"Accident?"

"Yeah… accident. I don't want to talk about that today, Valery," he replied, looking out of the passenger window.

"Honey, we must!" she pleaded.

Richard appeared anxious and agitated. Valery, observing his discomfort and tension tried to appease him.

"Look, honey. Forget it for now. Just sit back, relax, and enjoy the view."

Richard sat back in his seat and looked at Valery.

"Yeah . . . nice view!" he smiled.

She blushed.

Valery continued to drive until she reached a large oak tree near the center of the street. She turned right from the street and drove down a desolate dirt road. Towering wicked trees without character, standing tall two hundred feet in stature, hovered all around them. In addition, untamed, uncut vegetation, baby deer, and hostile crickets, were loud and seemingly upset by the intrusion of trespassers.

They continued to journey down the bumpy forest road for fifteen long minutes.

"Are you sure you know where you're going?" Richard asked as he and Valery bobbed, weaved, and bounced in the car as she sped on.

"Yes, Love, I know where I'm going," she answered while alertly watching the narrow dirt road.

Several, 'no trespassing' signs appeared in the immediate darkness.

In a matter of seconds, the eerie darkness of the wooded area was broken by a large sun-filled opening. Valery stopped on the embankment. She and Richard got out of the car. Richard was astonished. He had never seen sands more white or water so clean and blue. A man-made waterfall flourished below. Fruit trees adorned the hills. Richard was amazed. Valery leaned against the car and absorbed his appreciation.

"This place is beautiful. It must be the Garden of Eden."

"It's funny you should say that, Richard. My mother named this place `Eden'. She used to love going on picnics when I was a child. However, my father detested crowds and feared for her safety on the public beaches and so-"

"So he made his own private beach," interrupted Richard while shaking his head in disbelief.

"Yes, Richard," she timidly confirmed. They took off their socks and shoes and walked down a narrow brick path to the beach's foundation. Richard spread the blanket across the warm sands. Valery pulled the salad, steak, bread, and wine out of the picnic basket. Within moments, light laughter filled the air midst Richard's sharp wit and warm conversation.

"Richard, I really missed you while you were in the hospital," Valery declared while looking into his eyes, cutting a piece of the tender steak with a fork and placing it into Richard's mouth.

"How could you have missed me, Valery? You were at the hospital practically 24 hours a day."

"I know . . . but it's not the same as seeing and having you home with me."

"Yeah, I know what you mean, Valery. But you really didn't have to come every day. I was beginning to feel guilty about your expending all of your time on me."

"Sure, Richard. Now what would you have done if I'd missed just one day?" she laughingly inquired.

"Oh . . . nothing much. Just knocked off a few doctors.... blow up the hospital…. ..You know…typical average things a man does if he hasn't seen his woman in 24 hours."

"I'll bet you would have done just that!" she laughed.

They ate a very light dinner. Richard and Valery then quietly walked the warm sands while taking in the beauty of 'Eden'.

"Okay, Lover. Let's talk," she initiated as the cool sea winds softly blew the locks of her dark flowing hair.

"What would you like to talk about, Valery?"

"Your 'accident', 'she assertively replied.

"Let's talk about something else," he replied, looking away from her.

"No, Richard! Let's talk about your 'accident'. First of all, Richard, I know that my father had you beat up. I also know my father! What you're experiencing is just the beginning."

"He can't do much more, Valery. He's failing me out of school and he's had me beat up. What else can he do?!"

"Richard!" she screamed while stopping and grabbing his arms, "I don't think you heard me! I know my father!! I've seen how he operates in business! I know how he deals with people who stand in his way! Believe me, Richard! This is just the beginning!"

"I don't know, Valery. What else can he possibly do?"

She was angered by his bullheadedness. She stopped walking, turned him around, and angrily grabbed him by the front of his shirt collar. She brought his head down to hers.

"He can make you disappear, Richard! He will have you killed, Richard!!! Richard, we're going to have to move!!"

Richard's face lit up in surprise. He moved Valery's tight grip away from his shirt collar and wrapped his arms around her shaking body bringing it close to his while looking deeper into her eyes.

"Move?? . . . Would you go away with me?" he quietly asked.

"Of course I would, Richard! What kind of a question is that?!? Don't you believe I love you?" she asked, surprised by his question.

He looked away from her.

"Yes, Valery. I believe you love me. But if you run away with me. . . well. . You will be giving up so much."

"Giving up what, Richard?" she asked, disappointed with his reply, "You mean giving up the prestige of being recognized as Clifford Hall's daughter? . . . Giving up the option of arbitrarily walking into a department store and buying expensive clothes or jewelry?!?"

Richard replied assertively,

"Well, yes. Doesn't that life beat this frugal life you're living with me? C'mon, Valery! Let's be for real!! This running away thing sounds romantic, man, but that's it!! You're used to a good life of beautiful things. You will get tired of-"

"Yes, Richard, *things!!*" she screamed, cutting him off. "One *thing* I have learned about this so-called good life is that clothes wear out, cars quickly depreciate and stop running, houses burn down, silver tarnishes … believe me, Richard, *I have had more than my fill of things! I have learned that you can't build your life and happiness on things. Things can't fill the void in your emotional life. I need love, Richard! I need your love. We've got to move!*" she cried.

He was jarred and appreciative by the intensity and allegiance she professed to him at this moment. They continued to walk barefoot in the sands as the small waves crept in and washed their feet. He quietly looked at the blue water and turned back toward Valery.

"You know, in a way, I'm kinda glad your father had me beat up."

A smile crossed her lips as she looked away from him.

"I've got a confession to make, Valery. I've already considered moving. As a matter of fact, I called a number of universities and colleges in a few states that we might consider moving to."

"And?" she inquired.

"And it's not as easy as it seems, Princess. Listen, if you stay at State University you will have your degree in about two months. However, if we immediately move to another state and attend another university, *you will have to repeat your entire senior year.*"

"Why, Richard?"

"Because every college or university I contacted has got this rule that the last twenty-five hours of undergraduate study must be completed at the university awarding the degree."

"I think that's crazy," she snapped.

"Well, crazy or not, that's the way it is."

They continued walking on the beach as new waves crashed higher against their bare feet. Valery turned to Richard for answers.

"Well, what are we going to do, Richard?"

He looked at her, still surprised by the sincerity and intensity of her desire to leave Camden.

"I feel we have two options, Valery."

"Okay, let's hear them," she eagerly requested.

"Well, I read the regulations covering my scholarship."

"And...?"

"Well, this scholarship is transferable. So I could drop these classes before these professors have a chance to fail me. If they can't fail me then my grade point average will not be affected and I can use the balance of the scholarship at another university without any prejudice."

Valery's eyes beamed with excitement. A broad smile covered her face. She was excited. She clapped her hands.

"*That's great!...good! Sounds great so far, Richard!!!... Go on.*"

"Well, then I could move to the state of our choice, find a job, and set up housekeeping while you finish the last two months of your education."

She became silent. Her mood grew cold; angry.

"You mean... separate?"

"Yes," he answered. "But it would only be for two months."

"And you say you love me!! How can you be so much in love with me and talk about separating?!!"

"But it would only be for two months, Valery. I could work and send you the money to rent a nice place and you wouldn't lose your last year of education and be denied your degree. *You deserve that! You've worked hard for it! It makes no sense for you to have to start the last year all over again at a different university!*"

"No, Richard! That wouldn't work! I couldn't deal with this pressure alone. I also couldn't bear with the thought of being without you for so long. You mentioned two options, what's the next option?"

"I could go to your father's office and try to explain that-"

"*That's no option, Richard!* You have to go through a series of security personnel to reach him. He wouldn't even allow you up into his office. *We have to move, Richard! I'll just repeat my senior year."*

Richard was literally in pain by what Valery was prepared to sacrifice for him.

"No!..No!..We can't be too hasty, Valery. How much do we have left in our savings account?"

"About ninety-three dollars, most of that five hundred dollar bonus you received went to pay doctor bills."

Richard's face dropped. His head moved in a negative direction.

"That's not enough for the kind of move we're talking about, Valery! That's not enough for *any kind* of a move!!"

Valery was shaking angrily with fear. She turned away from him, covered her face with her hands and began to sob uncontrollably. Richard walked in front of her, removed her hands, and caressed her tightly within his arms.

"I couldn't bear to see you beaten up like that again, Richard. We've got to move! You're trying to be logical and practical with a narcissistic man who wants to ruin your health and take your life. *It's going to get worse! I know it!!"* she cried.

Richard continued to hold her tightly. He thought about the credence of her argument.

"Okay, we'll move," he softly declared.

The tears began to subside from Valery's eyes. She moved away from him and looked intently into his eyes.

"When?"

"This weekend. That gives us five days. We need at least that time to wrap up our business here and decide where we're going. I think I should go to the garage tonight. We can use all the money we can get."

"That's a good strategy, Richard. What we will do is drop out of our classes at the university this Friday evening. That way, we will only have a withdrawal on our transcript and no failing grades. We can then leave the city Saturday morning before the administration and my father are aware of our strategy and relocation. We must keep this plan to ourselves, Richard, so no one can interfere with us in the interim, okay?"

"Okay, Valery"

They slowly gathered up their picnic basket and blankets and traveled back to the city.

Valery dropped Richard off at the garage and drove his car to their apartment.

CHAPTER XXVI

Richard walked into the locker room of the garage at five-thirty p.m. He pulled off his white sport shirt, took off his shoes, and was sitting on the bench next to his locker when Jim walked into the room. Jim was startled to see Richard back and ready for work.

"Richard! Richard!! Good to see you!" he greeted with a smile while shaking his right hand.

"Thanks, Jim. It's good to be back"

"What really happened to you anyway, Rich?"

"Just a small accident Jim."

"Well, you've got me intrigued. I still don't understand why you told me not to tell your father that you were in the hospital."

The smile slowly faded from Jim's face. He looked concerned.

"What kind of accident, Rich?"

Richard stood up and pulled his work clothes out of his locker.

"Just a small accident, Jim. It was nothing to worry about," he answered nonchalantly while grabbing a sweatband from the top compartment of his locker. They were in the locker room alone.

"Son, some of these two-bit mechanics are spreading some gossip about Clifford Hall being after you for something. Are you in any trouble, Rich?"

"No, not at all," he answered as he closed his locker door and put on a fresh work shirt.

"Then why are the police after you?"

Richard was stunned. He stood frozen and motionless.

"Police??"

"Yeah, Rich. They've been looking for you for about three days. They say you've broken some law."

"That's ridiculous!" Richard responded in disbelief.

"That's what I told them, Richard. Look, son, walk on up to the office with me. I need to talk to you in private for a minute."

They walked side by side out of the locker room into the noisy garage and toward Jim's office. Jim walked around his desk and sat down. Richard sat in a chair across from the desk.

"Ohhh . . . this is too formal," Jim muttered with a smile as he picked up his chair and walked around his desk with it. He placed his chair next to Richard and they sat in a small huddle.

Richard sat patiently in his chair with his legs crossed as Jim opened up discussion.

"Son, I want you to tell me the truth. Are you in any trouble?. . . Now before you answer just keep in mind that I've known your father since he and I were six-year-old kids. I was there when you got baptized. In the early years, I lived in your neighborhood and watched you grow up. We've always gotten along well together. You've got a lot going for you. I'm on your side. But I can't help you unless-"

"Jim, I love you like a member of the family and I'm not in any trouble. Why do you feel so convinced that I am?"

"Well, the police were here today and .. and-"

"And what? C'mon Jim, spill it!!"

Jim got out of his chair and walked to the window of his office. He informed Richard that the bank had threatened to revoke his lease on the garage.

"But why, Jim?" he asked, getting out of his seat and walking over to him.

"They say because the lease was not renewed before the expiration date."

"Is that true?"

"Yeah, it's true. But the lease on this building expired nine years ago!! Hell, I was told by the banker at that time that I didn't need to sign a lease agreement, that I would be allowed to operate this place as long as I wanted it."

Jim's anxiety was apparent. He sat back down.

"Did you get that in writing, Jim?"

"No. I assumed that I was dealing with honorable men. I guess I haven't been much of a businessman in the past. Anyway, they're using that technicality to manipulate me."

"There must be something you can do, Jim. Have you spoken to any bank officials?"

"Yes."

"And?"

"Well.....Rich. There is something I can do, Rich. They tell me that if I discharge you from my organization, then I can continue to operate here."

Richard was silent. His eyes darted nervously across the linoleum grease-stained floor.

"I told them that I was not going to discharge you, Rich. I told them that I would not be manipulated, but then the police came around and said that if you come to this garage then I should call them immediately or face prosecution for harboring a criminal. Of course I'm not calling anyone! But I am worried, Rich."

Richard lifted his soft face and eyes toward Jim.

"You're backed against the wall, Jim," he quietly responded.

"I will not be manipulated!!" Jim roared.

"You don't have any choice Jim. If you don't release me you will be ruined. I'm sure that this two- bit banking organization will see to it that you won't be able to operate in this city again if you fight them. You're only one man. It's going to take a united revolt to make some changes here, Jim."

Richard got up and walked toward the door.

"Wait, Richard! I've got an idea! Maybe I could piece meal the work to you at some different location."

"For how long, Jim? Three days? A week? Two weeks? And what kind of repercussions would you suffer once they found out that you really hadn't discharged nor reported me to the authorities?"

Jim grew solemn; quiet; sad.

206

"Don't worry about me, Jim. I'll be alright... I'll be alright."

Richard extended his hand toward Jim. They warmly clasped each other's hand. Richard opened the door and proceeded to walk out when Jim offered some farewell advice.

"Call your father, Richard. He'll know what to do, call your father."

Richard felt that his parents had worried enough about him during his tenure in the military services.
Just weeks ago he had told his father that he had everything under control.

"Don't call my father!" Richard emphatically requested in reply to Jim's advice. *"If you're really a friend, Jim, don't call my father!!"*

Richard walked to the locker room after exiting Jim's office. He changed back into his pedestrian clothes, combed his hair, and walked out of the garage. He glanced at his watch. It read six-thirty p.m.

Richard nonchalantly walked the wide city streets and tried to strategize how expediently he could pursue a better life for him and Valery. He was stressed. He was standing in front of a jewelry store, looking at the display window of women's rings and watches when Frank drove past him.

Frank made a u-turn and drove back to the jewelry store. He honked his horn and awakened Richard from his daydream. Richard walked toward the car as Frank leaned across the seat and opened up the passenger door of his vehicle.

"Hey, Rich. How are you doing?!" he greeted exuberantly with a broad smile as Richard walked over to the car, got in, and shut the door.

"I'm doing okay, Frank," he smiled back. "It's good to see you, Frank. I haven't seen you in two whole days!"

"It's good to see you, Rich!" he replied while patting Richard's left shoulder. "When did they discharge you from the hospital?"

"Today . . . today at about eleven o'clock this morning. By the way, I want to thank you again for everything you've done for me. You really are a good friend."

"Hey, don't mention it, good buddy. Well, what have you been doing since you got out?"

"Well, Valery and I went on a picnic this-"

"No, wait!" Frank interrupted while shifting his car into gear, "Tell me about it over a good dinner and a stiff drink. This is something to celebrate about. I know a fantastic place less than six blocks from here."

"No! No thanks, Frank. I'm really not hungry," Richard declared as the smile on his face slowly disappeared as Frank zoomed through the streets.

"C'mon, Rich. Snap out of it!" Frank cheerfully demanded as he turned into the rear lot of the restaurant.

Frank and Richard got out of the car and walked from the back lot toward the front door of the restaurant. Frank's arms were wrapped around Richard's shoulder. Richard turned to Frank while trying to force a smile.

"You're sure in a good mood today, Frank."

"You're darn right I am. I just landed a big contract for my father's agency, my best friend is out of the hospital, and to further complicate my life, I think I'm in love! Life's great!!!"

"You?!! You're in love? C'mon, don't kid me, Frank. In love with who?" Richard asked as he opened the front door for them.

"Rita! You know Rita, the one I brought with me when we celebrated Valery's birthday."

"Yeah! Well, she must be a pretty heavy lady to soften up a hardnosed capitalist like you, Frank," he laughed as they were escorted by a young waitress to a corner booth.

"Yeah ...she is. I'm thinking about marrying that girl, Rich. I don't even know how it happened. One day I'm thinking about what a nice, sweet girl she is and the next day I woke up and realized that I don't want to live without her. It's amazing! This kind of thing has never happened to me before!" he excitedly continued.

"How are things going with you and Valery, Richard?" he asked as the waitress placed the menus on their table and filled their cups with coffee.

"We're doing fine, Frank."

Frank slowed down the tempo of their conversation.

"I've got some good and bad news for you, Richard. . . Are you aware that the police are after you?" he asked while taking the cup of hot coffee to his lips.

"Yeah. What in the hell for?"

"Well, seems like that asshole Clifford Hall found some old idiotic state statute that makes cohabitation a criminal offense. The guy's really flipped!" he smirked.

"Is that the good news or the bad news?"

"That's the bad news. The good news is that the tide is turning in your favor."

"Meaning?"

"Meaning that as a result of more detailed information having been revealed, that more and more people are beginning to support your position, Richard. The townspeople, guys at school, even my father tells me that if he was in your shoes, he probably would have done the same thing. More and more, people feel that it was most natural for Valery to go to you after being beaten up by her father for seeing you."

Richard grew silent.

"Go ahead, Rich. Order anything you want, I'm treating."

"Listen, Frank. I appreciate what you're doing but I really don't feel like eating or talking. I think I should leave," he replied while getting out of his chair.

Frank was baffled and hurt by Richard's response.

"C'mon, Rich. Have a drink if you're not hungry," he petitioned while holding Richard's arm and pulling him back down.

Richard pushed Frank's hand from his arm, his anger was apparent.

"Hey, what did I do?!"

"Nothing, Frank, It's just hard to have a conversation when you've lost your job, are running from the cops, got a hospital bill you can't pay. . . . I need some time to think."

"You lost your job?!"

Richard walked out of the front door of the restaurant. Frank rallied behind him.

"You need to talk about it, Rich. You keep too much inside yourself."

"You're a friend, Frank. Thanks! I'll talk to you later," he replied while walking across the large street.

Richard was half-way across the empty street when a police car zoomed around the corner toward him. Richard was lost in thought. Frank happened to look over his left shoulder prior to opening the front door of the restaurant and saw the eminent danger.

"*Richard! Richard!! The cops! The cops!!*"

The patrol car quickly drove in front of Richard as he stood motionless and bewildered in the middle of the street. He made a move to run. The two officers jumped out of the car and quickly withdrew their revolvers from their holsters. Realizing it was fruitless to resist, Richard froze in his tracks.

The officers threw Richard against the patrol car, roughly handcuffed his hands behind his back, and pushed him into the back seat of their vehicle.

Frank drove to Richard's apartment and informed Valery of the actions that had transpired. She said nothing. Her face projected an intense fit of rage. She requested Frank to drive her to her father's banking quarters. Once there, she got out of the car, thanked Frank, and requested him to leave.

Valery walked up the long, large brick steps leading to the glass door entrance of the stone tower complex that kissed the clouds. Frank drove away.

****

The police vehicles arrived to the main precinct. The officers got out of the police car and bullied and pushed Richard into the station. They removed the handcuffs, performed the routine finger print procedure, confiscated his personal belongings and against his protests, pushed him into a large cell.

Richard was depressed. He lay on a small uncomfortable cot in the back left corner of the cage and fell-asleep.

CHAPTER XXVII

Four hours had passed before Richard awakened from his sleep. He walked around the dark dingy solitary cell and pondered upon why he had been segregated from the other prisoners.

The loud chimes of the church bells rang in the air, informing him that it was midnight. He had been detained in jail for five hours without any formal charges being levied against him.

"What a joke!" he whispered to himself.

He had not eaten since the picnic venture with Valery at two o'clock p.m.

At that point, the sound of heavy footsteps and the dangling of keys were becoming more audible to his ears. It was the jailer. He unlocked Richard's cell door and rolled in a cart filled with hot food.

Richard was baffled. The dinner plates held warm baked turkey, an assortment of pastas, vegetables and coconut cream pie.

The jailer was a stocky built officer of less than average height. His face bore little expression as he proceeded to set up the tray of food in front of Richard. He was totally flabbergasted as he continued to sit on the jail cot with his elbow resting on his leg and his head resting on his hand.

"What is this?" he asked with his eyes rolling up toward the eyes of the jailer.

"It's dinner. Eat!" the jailer emphatically replied while turning around and pushing the empty cart toward the open cell door.

Richard continued to look at the hot food sending a well-prepared aroma through the air.

"Hey, wait a minute!" Richard demanded to the jailer. The jailer was at the door. He turned around just prior to walking out of the cell.

"Yeah, what is it?" he indifferently responded.

"I know prisoners don't eat this good. What's goin' on?"

"I've learned not to ask too many questions in this town, boy. It might be to your advantage to learn the same." The jailer pushed the empty cart out of the cell and locked the door.

Richard continued to smell the rich aroma of the food. He picked up a fork and tasted a piece of the turkey. It was good. Thirty minutes had passed. Richard was continuing to taste and nibble the food tray when the sounds of more than a dozen footsteps thundered through the walkway of the cell block.

An entourage of men, including the jailer, finally stopped outside of Richard's lone solitary cell door. The men broke their circle and Clifford Hall emanated from their midst.

The jailer opened Richard's cell door, placed a small backless chair within, and locked the door after Mr. Hall had entered. Clifford motioned to his bodyguards and the jailer to leave the immediate area.

Richard was unimpressed by this presentation. He continued to bite into the piece of turkey lingering on the fork as Clifford quietly walked around the large dimly lit cell while looking at Richard from the corner of his eye. Richard continued to sit on the cot and eat from the tray of food while guardedly watching Clifford walk around the cell.

"Hello, Mr. Hall," he solemnly greeted while wiping his hands with the damp cloth napkin on his tray. Clifford did not acknowledge Richard's greeting. He stopped walking and leaned his back against the wall adjacent to Richard's cot. The full light of the moon covered the interior of Richard's cell.

"Mr. Hall, will you please tell me why I've been arrested?" he requested while looking across the cell room toward him.

"I have no idea," he muttered.

"I think you do, *Mr. Hall*. I think you're responsible for my arrest. By the way, thanks for the meal. That wasn't a bad parade, either."

Richard sat back on the cot and leaned his back on the cold brick wall. Clifford walked to the small wood chair, lifted it up, and walked over to Richard's cot. He was growing convinced that brute power alone would not be a persuasive factor in dealing with Richard Washington. He began to sit down on the chair when Richard angrily continued.

> "I think you're responsible for persuading the University to fail me out of school! You're responsible for paying hoodlums to beat me up! You're responsible for having Valery and I discharged from our jobs! . . I don't think I like you very much, *Mr. Hall.*"

Clifford was shaken by the intense direct anger of Richard's words and the cold, watery rage reflected in his eyes. Clifford slowly sat dawn on the chair with his legs spread and his elbows resting on his knees. His steady hands loosely joined each other.

Everything about Clifford Hall conveyed polish, class, and wealth. He was a traditional aristocrat. His styled black hair, dapper pin-stripe wool blue suit, manicured hands and clear rugged face projected success. Above all, he was a businessman. He was here to discuss a business proposition.

A warm plastic smile covered his face.

"I've checked out your background, Son. You come from a rather poor family. My sources inform me that you're very close to your family. Is that true?"

Richard was startled by this line of questioning. He sat up straight on the cot. He and Clifford were less than a foot away from each other.

> "Poor? I don't think my family is poor. Compared to what? My brother and I always ate well and dressed well…Yes, I'm very close to my family."

Clifford continued,

> "Well, I'm sure you'd like to help them if you could, wouldn't you?"

> "Of course I would. What are you getting at?"

Clifford's demeanor became more businesslike. His hands were tightly entwined together.

"I'm a man of few words, Richard. I don't believe in playing games. Some so-called businessmen offer the least for a desired objective and negotiate upward. I make my initial offer my best offer and walk away if the person I'm dealing with isn't intelligent enough to accept my generous proposal. Do you understand what I am saying, Richard?"

" I understand."

"Good!" he replied. After a brief pause, Clifford continued.

"Richard, I've learned that your father's net income for the last twelve years has been less than seventy-five thousand dollars. I will match that sum today and have it incorporated within a portfolio of blue chip investments in such a way that your parents can immediately retire into a life of luxury. In addition, I will give you a personal check in the amount of one hundred thousand dollars. I will also arrange to have you finish your formal education at another university of equal stature as State University."

Richard was amazed by the way Clifford Hall casually discussed such high dollar denominations.

"Let me see if I understand you correctly," he replied. "You will give me a check for one-hundred thousand dollars and deposit seventy five thousand dollars into my father's account. You will also see to it that I am accepted into a university of the same status as State University. Is that what you just said?" he asked with his eyes wide in disbelief.

"That's what I said," Clifford confirmed with the continuing superficial grin.

"The money sounds good. Transferring to another university sounds good too. But what about my grades here? My professors are *failing me.* I don't want those kinds of marks on my transcript!"

"Your marks will be corrected. If you adhere to my proposal, you will have the B+ average you were maintaining before our... misunderstanding."

215

Richard was jarred,

"When? How?"

"Immediately.   Don't worry about how. My chauffeur will stop off at the University and pick up a certified copy of your transcript for your records."

Richard's head was swimming. He paused and looked hard into Clifford Halls face. His senses informed him that Clifford was serious, very serious.

"I don't think I'd want you to deposit that money into my father's account. You just give me a check for an agreed amount of, let's say…two hundred thousand dollars and I'll take care of the distribution."

"Fine," he replied in an effort to quickly close the deal. "I figured you would say that. I'm prepared to pay you now!!'"

Richard sat back on the cot and leaned his back and head against the wall.

"Now, what have I got to do for this instant wealth? … Or is that a silly question?"

Clifford Hall's lips tightened. His eyes grew cold and hard. He was stern and exact about the desired objective.

"I want you *out* of my daughter's life! I never want her to talk to, see, or hear from you again!"

Richard grew silent. He tried to digest the gist of this proposal. He was calm; patient; soft.

"I expected that....why?"

"Why what? " Clifford angrily snapped.

"Why are you so intent on getting me out of Valery's life?"

"You come from a different world, Richard. Your values, your environment, your training, your questionable ethnicity, everything about you is foreign or contrary to the way I have groomed my daughter. You are out of your class."

Richard replied,

"What you're saying is that I'm not good enough for Valery."

"I have said what I have to say," Clifford replied.

Richard paused.

"If I agree to your proposal, when will I be released from jail?"

"Immediately! I will have the police escort you to the airport."

"Well, that's fine. But first I have to go to my apartment and pack my clothes. I also want my car. Maybe I should drive out of-"

Clifford was growing impatient and angry.

"No! With the money you receive you can buy all the clothes and cars you want. You will be driven to State University for your transcript and chauffeured to the airport. I want you out of my daughter's life *today!* You will *rot* in this jail if you refuse. I can see to it!!"

His anger and frustration was escalating.

"Well, boy? Do you accept my offer?"

Richard was not intimidated by Clifford Hall's anger. He again studied his face.

"Well, where's the check?"

Clifford was relieved. He went into his inner suit coat pocket and took out an envelope. He handed the envelope to Richard containing a cashier's check for two hundred thousand dollars. Richard had never seen so many zeroes on any one check in his life. He looked at Clifford. Clifford appeared genuinely warm and relaxed.

"Son, don't worry about that hospital bill. I'll take care of it. I want you to know that it was never my intention to have you beaten as badly as you were. I was very sorry when I heard the news of your condition. I . . I guess they got a little carried away. I'll also-"

At that precise second, Richard held the check between his legs and began tearing it up into tiny pieces. Clifford was startled. His eyes widened with anger.

"*Hey!! What are you doing*??!"

"I'm tearing up your check. *There aren't enough zeros you can put on this check to persuade me to give up*

217

Valery," Richard answered while looking at him as the torn pieces of the once negotiable instrument fluttered to the floor.

Clifford Hall was asserting violent vibrations in the air. Richard could sense a physical attack pending so he stood up from his cot and walked toward the corner of the large cell. Richard's back was facing Clifford. Clifford was fixated with anger. He ran behind Richard and knocked him to the floor.

"You fool!!" Clifford bellowed. "How dare you oppose me. I tried to be generous! *I tried to be fair! You're a fool and you'll die a fool's death,*" he exclaimed while angrily swinging at Richard's face as he lay stunned on the floor.

Richard put up his arms to shield himself from Clifford's fists. Clifford grew more angry and flustered by the wasted energy he was expending. He commenced kicking Richard's body wherever he could penetrate.

Richard caught Clifford's right foot and forcefully pushed him hard into the corner of the cell floor and he fell to his knees.

"Guard! Guard!!" yelled Clifford in fear and intense shock as he lay on the floor.

Richard sprang upright standing over Clifford's fallen body.

"Well, what's next, Mr. Hall!?!? I guess you plan to have me killed next, right!?!" Richard bellowed as Clifford meekly retreated on his knees in fear.

The jailer and bodyguards ran to the cell and saw Richard ranting and raving over Clifford Hall's body. Expecting the worse, the jailer quickly unlocked the door. Mr. Hall's bodyguards ran to the corner of the cell and hurled Richard to the ground while nervously attending to Clifford Hall and talking amongst themselves,

"Are you okay, Mr. Hall?"

"Did he hurt you, Mr. Hall?"

"I don't know why he'd insist on talking alone with that trash."

"What should we do, Mr. Hall?" each inquired while lifting him up on his feet and dusting off his suit with their hands.

Richard backed away as two overzealous bodyguards ran toward him. They quickly caught him and began pummeling him around the cell. The prisoners in the other cell blocks jeered their disapproval at the way Richard was being mauled.

"No!!" roared Clifford. "Don't get him here. The last thing we need is a witnessed police brutality charge."

Richard slowly got up from the floor. He walked over to the front bars of his cell and acknowledged to the other prisoners that he was okay.

The jailer opened the cell block door and Mr. Hall and his hired thugs walked out. Clifford stood outside the cell door and looked at Richard with a cold, biting stare.

"Get used to that cage, boy. It's going to be your home for a long, long time. When I get finished with you, you're going to regret the day you ever laid eyes on this beautiful city."

Richard's eyes were cold. A wide sarcastic smile danced across his mouth.

"Beautiful city???! Beautiful city??!? . . . You call this a beautiful city?!!? I've got my own name for this city.... Shit!!! Yeah ... *Shit City!!!"*

"Now you wait a minute, boy-"

At that point Richard began to scream in defiance,

"*Nawwww!!! Yeahhh!!! Shit!!! Shit City!!!!!* Because only the citizens of a *Shit City* would allow one man to manipulate and fornicate with their lives the way you do here!!"

A futile expression covered Clifford Hall's face. He was momentarily speechless. Everything in his body told him that Richard Washington would not be persuaded to give up Valery.

"You're hopeless," he muttered as he and the others walked away from Richard's cell and out of the prisoner's quarters.

Richard walked to the small cot in the back of his cell, lay down, and fell into a mild sleep.

CHAPTER XXVIII

Three hours had passed. Richard, having fallen asleep, was brought back into semi-consciousness by the sound of approaching footsteps. The footsteps stopped outside of his cell. Richard continued to lie on his cot while trying to wipe the sleep from his eyes. The jailer unlocked the door.

Clifford Hall walked within. He was alone. He motioned for the jailer to leave the immediate vicinity.

>"Good grief!! " Richard whispered out loud while turning his face and body back to the wall.

Clifford continued to stand by the cell door. A handsome tan felt hat with a small red feather adorned his head. A beige trench coat loosely wrapped his body.

Clifford said nothing; he just stood by the front of the cell door.

Richard tried to fall asleep. He couldn't. He turned back around, hoping Clifford Hall would not be there. Clifford continued to stand by the front of the cell door. His back was facing Richard.

Clifford broke the fifteen minute silence.

>"It's not easy being a parent, Richard. You buy your daughter the best clothes, send her to the best schools, feed her the best foods, raise her in the richest environment, hire the finest doctors to remedy her pains, introduce her to the wealthiest men, change her diapers, awaken her from nightmares, ballet lessons, piano lessons, French tutors, braces, *and what does she do!??!*" he angrily asked while slapping the jail bars with his hand.

Richard answered,

>"*She runs off and lives with a poor grease monkey in the slums.*"

Clifford turned his head toward Richard. A heavy look of disappointment covered his face.

>"Yeah," he confirmed,

"She runs off and lives with a poor grease monkey in the slums."

There was silence.

Clifford continued to stand by the front of the cell. He had the look of a beaten man. He stood still as in a state of deep trepidation. Richard continued to lie on the hard cot.

"I was thinking about having you killed, Richard."

"Why didn't you?" Richard asked while turning on his side to look at him.

Clifford turned his head toward the cot.

"I would lose my daughter forever if I had you killed. I've got to keep you alive. She'll come to her senses eventually."

There was silence. Clifford did not move. Richard remained lying on the cot.

"How would you like to work for me, Richard?" I'll pay you twice whatever you're-"

"No thanks!" he abruptly interrupted.

Clifford continued as if he didn't hear Richard's rejection.

"There wouldn't be any games or pressure, Richard. You could learn the banking business and afford to live in a more desirable-"

"No thanks!"

Again there was silence. Clifford slowly turned back toward the cot.

"Why is my daughter *living with you*? If you love my daughter so much, why didn't you marry her?"

"She won't marry me, Mr. Hall. She said that she doesn't want to be married under these circumstances."

Clifford slowly walked from the front of the cell to the small chair next to Richard's cot. He sat on the chair and took a long hard look at Richard's face. Richard continued to lie on his back.

"You don't like me very much, do you, Richard?"

Richard began laughing.

"You're funny," he replied.

"How am I so damn funny!" Clifford angrily asked.

"Mr. Hall, can you think of one good reason why I should like you?"

Clifford did not answer. He began to cover and rub his face and forehead with his hands in an attempt to remove the tensions and frustrations from his mind.

>"My daughter came to my office today, Richard. I've never seen her so violent or so angry. I tried to calm her down but it didn't work very well."

Richard was intrigued. Valery did…what? He stopped lying on his back and sat up on the cot with his back against the wall.

"What's on your mind, Mr. Hall?"

A brief silence transpired.

>"I . . . I've decided to let this thing run its course. She'll come to her senses faster that way."

Richard sat up closer toward Clifford Hall; *Negotiation time.*

>"Well, what about my grades? I don't want to lose my scholarship…or should we leave town?"

>"Your marks will reflect your true classroom performance. I'll see to it! I'll also pay the hospital bill for that, uh, little mishap that occurred. The monies you previously expended for your hospital care have been deposited into your account."

They sat up closer to each other. They were less than a foot apart.

>"I want my daughter out of that neighborhood, Richard. *I want her out now!!!"*

>"We're going to move."

"When?"

>"Mr. Hall, I was prepared to move two weeks ago. We would have moved by now if your gorillas had not put me in the hospital."

Clifford appeared satisfied by Richard's response.

"Mr. Hall, what about my job at the garage?"

" I . . . I'll take the pressure off Jim. You can go back to work tomorrow."

Clifford looked deep into Richard's eyes and explored his handsome face. He got out of the chair and walked toward the front of the cell. Richard remained seated on the cot.

"Is there anything else?" Clifford asked while looking outside the bars of the locked cell.

"Yes," Richard seriously answered. "I would like to have the personal addresses of those three goons who beat me up."

A small smile crossed the corner of Clifford's lips as he slowly turned around and looked at Richard.

"I can't do that. However, I give you my word that they will never cross your path again."

It was 4:57 am. Clifford called the jailer. As the jailer arrived, Clifford motioned for Richard to get up. They both walked out of the cell block.

Clifford proceeded directly out of the precinct office. The jailing officer gave Richard back his wallet and personal belongings and had him sign the release forms indicative of same.

Richard then walked out of the jail precinct office. He inhaled a large dose of the clean morning air and began walking toward Main Street to catch a cab.

Clifford's black chauffeur-driven limousine drove beside Richard and sounded its horn. Richard walked over to the corner of the curb as the rear windows descended. Clifford, was sitting deep in the back seat of the vehicle.

"Can I give you a ride home, Richard?"

"Ahhh, no sir. I don't think so."

Clifford looked disappointed.

" I hope there are no bad feelings, Richard."

"Nothing that time won't cure, Mr. Hall."

"Take care or my daughter, Richard. She's all I've got."

Richard looked into the eyes of Clifford Hall.

"I will, Mr. Hall," he sincerely promised. "*Believe me, I will take care of Valery!*" he repeated.

They shook each other's hand. The limousine drove off. Richard walked up to Main Street, hailed a cab, and was driven home. Richard unlocked the door of his apartment at 6:03 a.m. He walked into his bedroom. Valery was not there. He walked into the living room.

Valery was fully clothed, lying asleep on the sofa. A worn, blue cotton blanket loosely covered the lower portion of her body. It was obvious that she had been crying.

Richard sat next to her sleeping body and whispered,

"*Valery. . . Valery.*" She began to wake up.

"Richard. . . Richard! Are you home, Richard?"

"I'm here, Princess," he confirmed. "I'm home."

They kissed each other's lips long and tenderly as Richard lifted her body up into his arms and carried her to the bedroom. He was free. He was home.

CHAPTER XXIX

Their lives were good together.

Richard and Valery immediately commenced their quest to relocate to a more affluent and safe sector of the city. Valery independently found what she regarded as the perfect place for them in the Northern Heights section of the city. She scheduled a Saturday afternoon showing of the property for Richard.

The building and surrounding property was breathtaking. It was a forty story beautifully landscaped high-rise with extensive security personnel and security measures. The unit Valery desired was located on the twenty-fifth floor. It encompassed a cozy living room with natural fireplace, cathedral ceilings, an intimate dining area, family room, a master bedroom, library, kitchen with modern appliances and conveniences, and an ultimate scenic view of the city.

Richard was in awe by its majestic presentation.

"It's beautiful, isn't it, Richard?"

"Yes...something you deserve, Valery." He then turned toward the manager of the exclusive complex and asked,

"When can we move in, sir?"

"In approximately two weeks."

"And what is the monthly rent payment, sir?"

"Four hundred and seventy-five dollars a month. Of course, you realize that a security fee of-"

Richard was in shock and momentarily lost his voice. Upon catching his, voice he yelled,

"Four hundred and seventy-five dollars?!? "

"Yes sir," the short, mannerly mustached manager confirmed.

Richard then turned to Valery, composure gone, eyes widening,

"*Four hundred and seventy-five dollars*?!?"

Valery turned to the manager and requested,

> "Will you give us a brief moment alone, sir, please? We need a little privacy to talk."

She then took Richard by the hand and led him from the living room to the kitchen for a conference.

> "Richard, how much did you think an apartment like this rented for?" she asked with a smile of tenderness on her lips.

> " I certainly did not know they rented for such high fees," he stuttered. "Princess, where am I going to get that kind of money?"

Valery reasoned with Richard that the increased expense would only be a burden on him for a three month period of time considering that she would be graduating from the university at such time. She further advised him that she had been assured a teaching position at a local school after graduation and she could assist him with their living expenses.

That night, Richard calculated that if he cut trivia expenses and labored additional hours at the garage, then he could reasonably afford the increased expense. They rented the apartment.

On August 15, 1948, Valery received her degree as expected and obtained employment within an elementary school in the center of town. Economically they were now moving. They were each other's stimuli. They were in love.

There was laughter, so much laughter. Like the time they went canoeing at the beach…

> "Richard we're not moving fast enough, let me help," Valery requested while picking up the extra oar in the boat.

> "No, Valery, you'll tip the boat."

> "No, I won't, Richard. Let me help you!"

> "I don't need help, Valery!! . . . Paddle the other way, Valery. Paddle the other way!!! No, Valery! Stop! No! Wait! Other way! VALERY!!!"

> SPLASH!

The boat tipped over. As they swam to the surface, they laughed, they laughed, how they did laugh.

************************** *

Richard, now twenty-five years of age, had advanced to his senior year as a result of the exhaustive accelerated academic pace he scheduled at State University. He studied hard; he studied very hard.

Richard decided to remove himself from the rumors and campus politics of the university by attending late afternoon and night classes. He also decided to increase his class load in order to expedite his graduation. Consequently, he labored a day shift schedule at the garage and attended his classes from late afternoon until the early evening hours of the night.

Between six thirty and seven o'clock in the evening he would arrive home to Valery's home cooking which he could smell emanating from their apartment the moment the elevator doors opened.

After dinner, Richard would then try to study. He would really try to study. However, there now existed another daily hunger pain which demanded to be fed. Only Valery was capable of feeding that hunger-and she did.

Around ten o'clock p.m., Richard could be observed crawling out of bed and staggering to their kitchen table to study until the early hours of the morning. Regardless of their hunger pains, sexual or otherwise, they were intent on achieving higher levels of success.

On those nights when he desired to be lazy about his study routine, Valery would remind him of his promise.

"What promise?" he'd sleepily ask.

"The promise of having lots of love and my name on the social register."

"Oh," he'd mutter quietly.

"Yes, Richard, *Oh*," she'd simile. "Now get up and study." And Richard would get up and Richard would study.

They were a different couple. It was magic. They were even able to buy the snazzy yellow foreign sports car Valery desired.

"We're moving up in the world," he'd whisper to her,
"and nothing or no one will stop us."

Richard, now two months away from his Marketing degree, was subject to many on-campus pre-employment interviews coupled with many rejections of employment for whatever reasons. However, rejection literally strengthened his resolve to be successful. He had learned from his life experiences that with effort came progress, but that progress was sometimes so slow.

Three weeks prior to graduation, Richard's patience paid off. Tandem Incorporated, a growing recognized computer industry, was interviewing potential graduates for placement within their marketing department.

Richard wanted this position. He found the computer industry to be innovative, fascinating and a futuristic necessity among middle and large corporate structures to control their complex financial programs and cash-flow systems. Additionally, Richard desired to be employed with a cash rich industry that provided its sales and marketing executives the ability to earn significant incomes.

On a cool Thursday afternoon of May 8th, 1949, Andrew Anderson, the personnel director for Tadem Industries, was on campus to interview Richard, among other applicants. Richard had taken off from the garage that day to prepare for the interview. He wore his best black conservative wool suit, his black and white silk tie, and white heavily starched shirt.

He arrived early for the interview and seated himself among the other male applicants. At 12:15 p.m. his interview was about to commence.

"Mr. Richard Washington," called Mr. Anderson's secretary. Richard rose and walked confidently to her desk.

"Mr. Anderson will see you now, Mr. Washington," she stated matter-of-factly.

She then escorted Richard to Mr. Anderson's cubicle and after formally introducing the two men to each other; she departed, closing the door behind her.

Anderson was a late fortyish, five-foot-eight-inch muscular man with hard, serious, businesslike features.

"Have a seat, Richard," requested Anderson politely while reviewing Richard's resume and work application.

"Why do you want to be involved with the computer market industry, Richard?" asked Mr. Anderson, still scanning through the resume.

"For the money, sir," Richard affirmatively answered.

"What?!!?" replied Anderson in bewilderment at this response. He stopped reviewing the resume.

"For the money, sir," repeated Richard.

"Exactly what do you mean?" Asked Anderson, obviously taken ajar by Richard's continued response. He had interviewed a countless number of young men who purportedly desired computer marketing for supposed other reasons, such as challenge, excitement, being involved in a frontier kind of industry, job enrichment, and so forth. No candidate had answered as honestly as this man.

"Sir" continued Richard, "I feel that computers are a necessary and viable force within the paper-flow systems of American industry today. For this reason, they are anticipated to be in strong demand by businessmen who seek some level of simplicity within their otherwise complex business structure. Where there is need, there is demand; and where there is demand, there is money, and I need money, sir-lots of it."

"Why do you need so much money?" Anderson inquisitively asked.

"I'm getting married, sir," answered Richard, "and I want to give my wife the best. As you know, sir, a man can't do these things without money."

"Yes, I know, Richard," smiled Anderson, "How well I do know."

Andrew Anderson was impressed. He visualized in Richard the high level of motivation, aggressiveness, and honesty required within the competitive field of computer marketing. After more questioning on a less substantive scale, Anderson informed Richard that a second interview would be arranged within three days' time, and they parted company. The interview had been a success.

With the interview behind him, Richard's mind was now dominated with someone of more importance- Valery. Questions regarding their relationship had been filtering through his mind like an infected sore and this sore was now beginning to bleed.
He needed answers and was intent towards obtaining those answers today.

Valery and Richard had been living together for over a one-year period of time and yet she had never mentioned marriage to him. Why? Did she discreetly think that he wasn't good enough for her as he and others once thought? Was she planning to leave him eventually? Was this just a game to her? Did she even think he could let her leave now?

It was four-thirty p.m. in the afternoon when he arrived home to their apartment.

"Hello, Babe!" Valery greeted while kissing him coupled with a warm smile, "How did your interview go?"
"Don't worry about the interview, Valery" Richard remarked unemotionally. "I need to talk to you."
He pulled her gently but firmly to their kitchen table. Valery in a state of puzzlement accompanied him willingly. After being seated, he nervously arose and prepared himself two jiggers of whisky and asked in mild anger,

"Why is it that we've never discussed marriage?! *Do you think for one minute I'll let you leave me now*? Is it because you still think I'm not worthy of you? Do you plan to marry someone else, Valery? Is this just a game to you?" he blurted.
"Richard!!" she stammered, "What are you talking about?"
"Us!" he emphatically replied with his head buried in his hands. "Us."

Suddenly he looked at her and intently asked while leaning across the table,

"Valery, do you love me?"

"Yes, Richard. I truly love you," she whispered, her eyes passionately melted upon his.

"*Then marry me, Valery. Please marry me!*" he pleaded. She cried.

Richard unseated himself and knelt by her chair.

"Richard, I was so afraid you would never say those words to me," she whispered while kissing his mouth as tears rolled down her cheeks and wet her lips.

"I was so afraid you'd lost some of your feelings for me, that you were content with this living arrangement. I was so afraid-"

"Wife," he interrupted with a whisper.

"Husband," she responded. "*My husband!*' she smiled, kneeling next to him on their kitchen floor cuddled within his arms.

The following Friday, Richard did not go to his classes nor to the garage the next day. He and Valery devoted this time towards the shopping and purchasing of their engagement and wedding rings.

****

The following Monday morning, Tadem Industries made arrangements for Richard's second interview as promised and thereupon coupled it with a generous job offer which Richard happily accepted.

****

Five weeks later, Sunday, June 15th, 1949, two weeks after his graduation, Richard and Valery were married in a simple holistic ceremony consisting of close friends and relatives at the home of his parents, William and Tina Washington.

CHAPTER XXX

July, 1950

"**W**ake up, Valery. . .Valery, wake up!" Richard whispered this nine-thirty Saturday morning. She was always the last to awaken in the morning. Nevertheless, after sleepily stretching her arms and receiving her expected short sweet kiss from Richard, Valery would arise from bed.

They had been ecstatically married for over twelve months and each month was invariably happier than the last. Valery's teaching position was secure and Richard conveyed great potential in the eyes of his superiors within Tadem Industries.

Today's activities had been pre-planned. Valery desired Richard's company at the shopping mall. She enjoyed dressing for him and discovered early in their marriage that his good taste for appealing color-coordinated garments was invaluable towards assisting her in making choice selections.

Prior to shopping, however, Richard desired a morning breakfast-he was starved. Upon dressing, they strolled out of their apartment, into the car and away to their favorite breakfast spot-in silence.

Valery was unusually quiet this bright Saturday morning, although Richard felt her eyes continually upon him. He was quite aware that something was lingering over his wife's mind.

"What is it, Babe?" he questioned while driving.

"What is what?" Valery asked coyly.

"What are you thinking about?"

"How much I love you," she answered softly while squeezing his hand tightly.

Richard could sense her mind was burdened but she obviously did not want to engage in conversation at the present time. He allowed her the privacy of her own thoughts.

They arrived at the restaurant at eleven o'clock. Upon being served, Richard became even more aware that neither Valery's mind nor appetite was on breakfast. Puzzled by her quiet and dismal behavior, he probed again, and again drew a non-responsive answer.

After breakfast they went shopping. Valery's spirit appeared to be lifted within the shopping mall. However, after four p.m. that afternoon, as he carried her purchases to their car, her solitude reappeared. As Richard laid the purchases in the car trunk and escorted his wife to the passenger side of the car, Valery impulsively kissed him.

"Do you want to talk about it now, Princess?" Richard questioned.

"No," she answered quietly while seating herself within the car's interior.

They then drove from the mall's parking lot toward the direction of home. While driving toward home, they passed the beach coastline and decided to walk the sands and watch the birds, seagulls, and boats now docking at the pier.

The sweet smell of the sea always rested Richard's mind and stimulated direction. After taking off their shoes and slowly strolling the cool sands of the beach, Valery questioned,

"Richard, is there any one particular possession you would like to have?"

"Sure," responded Richard, "One day I want to buy us a boat with-"

"Besides a boat, Richard!" she interrupted.

"Well, I would really like to own a fast, expensive sports car called a-"

"Richard I want a baby!" she interrupted.

"What?" he replied in a state of startled bewilderment at her response.

"I want your baby!" she flatly stated in desperation.

Richard could sense from his wife's behavior that she badly desired an affirmative response from him and thereupon whispered,

"If you want a baby, Valery, then we'll have a baby."

"When, Richard? When?" Valery hurriedly asked in a panicky state of fear.

Richard, trying to comfort Valery, took his wife into his arms and became puzzled by the manner her entire body was shaking. Maybe she was shaking from anger, he thought, although she never projected this type of anger before. What would she be angry about, anyway? Perhaps the air was too chilly for her, although the temperatures ranged near the mid-eighties.

Then he kissed her .. . softly . . . gently . . and she cried.

With his eyes planted upon hers he gently yet firmly demanded to know the reasons for her sporadic behavior.

"*I'm pregnant!*" she sobbed apologetically, "I'm pregnant!" she cried, beating her tiny fists softly upon his chest.

"*Great!*" he whispered, "*but why are you crying?*"

Valery appeared genuinely shocked. Her mouth opened. All tears subsided as she looked at her husband in dismay. For over a month, she had been worried sick daily because of her present condition. For over a month she had been dreaming of ways to inform him of a condition she felt he'd consider a premature burden; and he said, 'great!'

She looked at him and laughed. The more she thought about it the harder she laughed and the harder she laughed the more she felt love for him.

Richard, unaware of the reasons for his wife's strange behavior, began to feel sorry for her. The pressure of teaching those unruly students had finally gotten to her; they were driving his wife mad. Valery's eyes displayed a predatorily like intensity as she looked at him. She advanced toward him and Richard literally began to retreat. He had never seen these behaviors before as she launched on him and wrestled him to the ground. She kissed his hair, eyes, nose, lips, and neck continuously, even though all the visitors on the beach and on the pier were looking at them.

"Valery," he whispered smilingly, "Not here, Baby, people are watching."

"Shut up!" she laughed and continued as if he had said nothing.

He tried gently pushing her away in order to get up but she pursued him aggressively, still descending upon him her lips coupled with more robust bursts of laughter. An audience of amused by-standers began surrounding them as she continued. He again tried to get up but she stalked him relentlessly.

Valery tackled him; arms around his neck, wrestled him to the sands of the beach, and there kissed him long and sensuously while whispering unto him her most deeply rooted feelings of love for him.

Richard, seeing he was trapped, decided to surrender to the present predicament. He returned her ecstatic kisses and allowed her emotional course to run as the crowd of by standers continued to grow.

Valery suddenly realized the crowd of civilians being entertained by her impromptu show of affection. She was visibly embarrassed. Richard stood up and addressed the audience.

> "My wife's a little excited folks. We're going to have a baby!"

The crowd of strangers exploded with applause. Richard and Valery dusted each other's clothing, fell into each other's arms, and drove away.

That night, in front of their fireplace, they celebrated with red wine, cheese, soft music and laughter, the soon-to-be-delivered new member of their family.

CHAPTER XXXI

Thursday, April 25, 1951

Richard held and kissed the hand of his wife Valery within the delivery room as she gave birth to their six-pound baby boy. The following Sunday afternoon, under light falling snow, Richard brought his wife and son home to a welcomed apartment filled with parents, relatives, and friends who were impatiently waiting to see the new member of the Washington family. Richard and his father sat together within the confines of the kitchen drinking a whisky sour.

"Father," initiated Richard, "what do you think about your grandson?"

"Good job, Son," said his father in merriment, "good job. However, are you sure it's yours?" quizzed his father in seriousness.

"What do you mean, Father?"

"Well, Richard, that baby's extremely good looking and you…well…you know."

They laughed while looking at each other with pride, appreciation, and respect.

"Richard, Richard!" called Valery.

Richard answered her call with his presence. There, in the living room, Frank and his younger brother, Leonard, desired a special group picture of Richard, Valery, and their sleeping child. Leonard's request influenced more of the same type of requests by the other family members and friends of this close-knit group. Consequently, Richard and Valery found themselves blinded by dozens of snapped flash cubes directed at them and their sleeping child.

After Richard's presence was no longer required for the picture taking session, he decided to visit the corner winery because they were running low on white wine.

Richard's father accompanied him. After picking up the wine and driving back to his apartment, William initiated conversation,

"Well, how does it feel being a father, Richard?"

"I don't really know yet, Father. It's a big responsibility. I hope I have what it takes to be a good father."

"Are you ready for the child, Richard?"

"Yes, Father," answered Richard. "Valery always made it clear that children would be the core of our marriage. At first I desired the baby because Valery wanted a baby. However, the continued thought of having my son from her body and being involved in his deliverance stimulated a desire and love for our baby which is equal to or exceeds any man's love for his son."

William smiled at Richard and stated softly, while caressing his son's shoulder,

"Son, you'll be a great father, almost as good as I." Both gentlemen smiled at each other in warmth and respect while continuing t back towards the baby's homecoming party.

The homecoming party was growing larger and gregarious in their absence. It was six o'clock p.m. when the doorbell rang at the residence of Richard and Valery. Tina, observing Valery occupied and anticipating Richard and William at the door, opened the door. A good-looking, somewhat familiar male figure, appearing to be in his late forties or early fifties stood patiently outside of the door's entrance.

"Hello," Tina greeted, "How may I help you?"

"Hello," he replied with his head looking more at the ground than toward her, "Is Valery Washington home, please?"

"Yes, she is. Are you a member of Valery's family?"

"Yes…. yes, I am. I understand that she's a mother now, that she's delivered a child."

"Yes, she has, indeed?" smiled Tina. Please . .come in. It makes no sense for us to talk about that beautiful baby boy out here in the hall. C'mon in and take a gander at my beautiful grandson."

"Oh?" the stranger responded in surprise, "You must be Richard's mother."

"I am," she answered while extending her hand out for his acquaintance, "and you?"

He took her hand gently between the both of his, smiled, and asked, as if he had not heard her question,

"Is the baby healthy?"

Valery, holding her newborn, grew puzzled at seeing her mother-in-law conversing an extended period of time at the unbarred door. She wondered why no one had yet entered the apartment door. Her face and mood grew solemn, dark, as she laid the baby into the crib, excused herself from the women in her immediate presence and slowly walked toward Tina at the open door.

The guests, observing the sudden change in Valery's behavior, watched as she slowly walked toward the door.

A ' hush' fell over the apartment; a hush neither Tina nor the stranger were apparently aware of.

"He's healthy, fat, beautiful and a thousand other adjectives," answered Tina, still engrossed in conversation, "but this is not the place to discuss the baby. Please. . . come in."

Valery approached the doorway as the stranger walked within.

"Father!" she whispered, stunned and excited by his presence. They had not seen nor conversed with each other in almost three years.

"Valery . . . my dear daughter Valery?" he greeted in a low audible sincere tone, his voice breaking with warmth and grief.

"Father!" she again repeated, moving closer to him. "Daddy, Daddy, Daddy!! " she cried with glee, rushing into his welcoming arms.

He hugged and kissed his daughter over and over again.

"Forgive me, child," he whispered, while wrapping her tenderly in his arms. "I didn't mean to hurt you. I didn't know what I was doing ... we must talk. You're my baby. You know I wouldn't purposely do anything to harm you. Forgive me, daughter...please forgive me," he pleaded as his daughter cried tears of joy upon his shoulders.

"I love you, Father," she sobbed, "I love you."

Within moments she stepped away from his embrace and took his hand in hers.

"Come, Father, see your grandson-"

They seemed to have been totally oblivious of the intimate crowd of people observing their emotional reunion. Valery's aunt, Earlene, and Richard's mother, Tina, wept throughout the reunion.

Clifford walked behind his daughter's lead toward the nursery and looked upon the sleeping infant.

"He's beautiful!" Clifford exclaimed.

"Just like his father," Valery replied while looking at her son. "And just like his grandfather!" she added, while looking up into her father's eyes.

"You'll be a good mother, Valery," he stated.

"I hope so, Father. This is my chance to be the amazing mother that I lost."

The homecoming resumed in full swing. Against the noise and laughter, Clifford asked,

"Daughter, can you ever really forgive me? I've been such a fool. I have felt so ashamed to face you for the last three-"

"Father, please," Valery interrupted, placing a finger upon his lips, "I understand ... I really do. It's so easy to be critical when you're young but I'm a few years older now. I understand."

She then took Clifford to formally meet Tina, her friends, and father-in-law William upon his return from the winery. When Clifford's hands enjoined Richard's in a handshake, their eyes beamed with respect, admiration, and friendship.

Valery, dressed in a white chiffon ankle-length dress as her dark curls trampled below her small shoulders, sipped wine with her father Clifford and husband Richard within their dinette as the baby's homecoming continued to grow with more well-wishing guests and relatives.   Richard, sensing Clifford's desire to talk privately to his daughter, excused himself from their presence.

"Is it alright if I come by once in a while to see you and my grandson, Valery?"

> "Once in a while? Daddy, I expect to see you regularly or I'll scream. You seem to have lost weight, have you been eating properly?" she asked with concern.
>
> "Well . . . sort of. I do have a lady friend who has been seeing to it that I not starve myself too badly."

"Well, where is she?"
Clifford appeared embarrassed,

"Oh, no! Why…Out in the car! I didn't think I'd really go through with this or what type of reception I'd get so I had her wait for me in the car!"

"Go get her, Daddy!" she exclaimed, walking him in haste to the door to bring his lady friend from the car to the apartment. "How could you think it would be anything but a desired welcome?"

"I don't know, Valery . .   you know . .. it has been three years."

"But never again, Daddy," she whispered, "never again. . . okay?"

 "Never again, Valery," he smiled, "never again."

At around eleven p.m. that Sunday night, the relatives, grandparents, and friends were tired, fed, and frazzled. Tina and Earlene made coffee as the party concluded and the guests departed.   After everyone had left, Valery and Richard showered and prepared to go to bed.

Richard sat sleepily on the small sofa in their bedroom as Valery brushed her hair. They conversed about the future plans of their family. Tina had voluntarily agreed to stay with Valery and Richard during the child's first three months of life until Valery and baby were stronger.

Valery appeared to be restless and abruptly asked, "Richard, will you dance with me?"

"What did you say?" Richard responded sleepily in disbelief.

"Will you dance with me?" she repeated. "After all, Richard, I've basically been lying in bed for the last few weeks. Don't you want to dance with me, Richard?" she quizzed impatiently, putting him on the defensive.

"Valery, you just came out of the hospital," he gently reminded her.

"Ohhhh, I'm okay," she replied nonchalantly.

Valery stopped brushing her hair and walked toward Richard, took his hand and led him toward the front room of their home. She turned on the stereo and placed some of her favorite ballads on the turntable. She then walked toward her husband and asked,

> "Wouldn't you like to dance with me now? Just once? Instead of the little fat girl you've had to look at for the past few months, I mean, I am still beautiful to you . . . aren't I, Richard?" she asked in search of a positive reply.

"Valery, you'll always be beautiful to me," he whispered.

That night, prior to retiring to bed, they danced. They danced and romanced slowly under the influence of soft music while within the spheres of their sleeping first born. They were happy. They were in love.

CHAPTER XXXII

Richard, twenty-eight years of age, had been promoted to Marketing District Manager and proudly maintained an impressive six-figure income with the computer marketing firm of Tadem Industries. Valery resigned from her teaching position in order to address the role of full time mother and wife.

Valery, as most mothers of their firstborn, took the mother role a bit to extremes after little Ricky's birth. When Valery wasn't with their newborn physically, she was with the child emotionally and mentally. She became so focused on her child that there was little room for anything else; even Richard. Consequently, their time and dinners together generally lacked the emotional closeness, passion, playfulness and excitement that existed prior to their son's birth.

On or around the sixth month of Ricky's birth, Richard arranged for his parents to care for Ricky the entire week-end. Additionally, Richard scheduled an appointment with a respected therapist that he and Valery were socially acquainted with. Valery was angered to know that Richard had made the therapy appointment without her consent and had delivered their son to his grandparents for the weekend without her approval. She reluctantly attended the counseling session. The session was a dismal failure without signs of any compromise.

Richard had made reservations for dinner after their meeting with the therapist.
He had chosen Valery's favorite restaurant called, 'Room at the Top'. The name fit the venue in light of the fact that it towered on the 40th floor of the Financial District Building. Once within the restaurant, her temper softened and she appeared more receptive to discussion.

"Valery," initiated Richard softly over a late dinner," I apologize for unilaterally making the appointment with the therapist. It was a desperate move on my part."

"There is no need to apologize. I would just like to know why is it that you told her that you're being so neglected."

"Because I am neglected. You barely say more than three sentences to me during the course of a day," he snapped.

"That's not true, and even if it is, our son requires my attention!"

"All day and night??" he asked. "Valery, if you need more domestic support then we should-"

"I don't need more help and I don't spend all day and night with the baby, I'm just trying to see to it that our son is properly cared for."

"And who properly cares for me, Valery?"

"Richard, I have never denied you," Valery reasoned.

"*This is not about sex, Valery!*" he angrily responded. Gaining his composure, Richard continued,

"Valery, I realize that being a good mother is very important to you and I respect and appreciate you for it. Nevertheless, don't forget about being a good wife to me, Baby...I mean ...don't neglect me! Don't neglect this marriage! *Don't neglect us!!*"

She looked into his eyes and saw the hurt, the pain, the fear of losing the magic that they had. She grew quiet, deciphering the logic of his complaint. She got out of her chair and moved it closer to Richard and kissed him on his cheek. His pain moved her to tears.

"Okay, I won't neglect us. You've just got to help me, Richard. I'm just overwhelmed with this mother thing. Nevertheless, I promise, I won't neglect us anymore."

And from that day forward-she didn't.

****

Richard and Valery were increasingly becoming aware that their family was outgrowing the apartment dwelling of their residence. Consequently, a decision was made to initiate a search for a home. Valery, impressed with the home construction models she had viewed on the outskirts of town, was able to motivate Richard to review the area with her.

The third model home they viewed appealed to the eyes and emotions of both.   It was a beautiful brick contemporary property in excess of three thousand square feet positioned in a dead-end cul-de-sac on a hill overlooking the other seven model homes within its immediate vicinity.

The interior of the property had a large yet intimate open floor plan composed of a step-down living room area, a brick wall length fireplace, cathedral ceilings, a private bar area, dining area, and a spacious kitchen with the most modern conveniences and appliances. The second level held four bedrooms, including a master bedroom which also incorporated a second fireplace, California closet and a master bath. Lastly, it had a backyard far from the streets for their child to play within coupled with a peaceful suburban type environment.

This structure immensely pleased and excited them. They requested certain personal enhancements for their model home which were approved by the architectural engineer heading the site's construction.   Prior to Christmas, they moved into their new home.

****

Ricky, now one year of age, was the pride of his father's eyes. Each evening upon Richard's arrival home from the office, his son would struggle to free himself from his mother's arms to receive the embrace of his father. There were days that Valery exhibited jealousy of little Ricky's frantic efforts to leave her arms for his father's attention,

"Traitor," she would murmur while handing him over to Richard's awaiting arms.

Richard literally enjoyed crawling, playing, and wrestling with his infant son in the living room quarters while Valery completed dinner. This threesome was happy, they were lucky, they were in love.

It became increasingly evident to Richard of the need for an advanced degree in order to maintain his corporate officer status with Tadem Industries. Therefore, on the eve of little Ricky's second birthday, Richard formally began his academic pursuit for a graduate degree in Business Administration.

Graduate school coupled with the stresses and rigors of his employment proved   to be a mental and physical strain for Richard to handle. However, with Valery's emerging assistance, Richard found the program more tolerable to bear.

Valery would do the class research at the campus library with the company of her son.   With same data, Richard would prepare a draft of the graduate paper and Valery would formally edit and type his papers to perfection.

 It proved to be a winning combination.

Each Sunday afternoon, prior to dinner, Richard would study at the campus library of State University with the company of his son. Within a relatively short period of time, little Ricky became so comfortable within the library walls that he'd roam the library spaces in search of a picture book in order to mimic the intensive study habits of his father.

No man could love his son more than Richard loved Ricky. The child was the laughter and light of his father's eyes.

His son however, did everything backwards. He rode his tricycle backwards, he walked backwards, and preferred to sleep at the foot of his bed rather than at the head.

Ricky was now three years old. Although well-disciplined, Ricky was one of the funniest young rebels his parents had ever experienced-and they loved it. Ricky had guts, too. He thought nothing of hopping on the handlebars of the older boys' bikes for a ride or stealing their football in the middle of an important play, only to be chased by them around the neighborhood in hot pursuit. Nevertheless, the neighboring boys loved this independent, curly-haired nuisance and the nickname "Little Man" was bestowed upon him.

At around eight o'clock, Ricky's energy resources had usually burned themselves out and he would be bathed and tucked into bed by his parents. In these dark hours, Richard and Valery would cherish their intimate moments together in front of their fireplace. Intimate moments consisting of white wine, soft music, warm conversation, light laughter, and physically surrendering, feeding, eating, and calming the predatorily sexual appetites of each other.

****

On the eve of Ricky's fourth birthday, Richard received his graduate degree as expected, coupled with a desired surprise from his wife Valery-she was pregnant with their second child.

CHAPTER XXXIII

On January 3rd, the eve of Richard's thirty-second birthday and the heart of the snow failing winter, Jennifer was born. She was named in honor of Valery's mother.

Jennifer inherited the dark eyes, dewy dark hair and handsomely soft facial features of her mother. Jennifer was also the noisiest, most pampered driven and time-consuming child her father had ever experienced.

As one might imagine, Ricky grew a bit insecure as a result of having less and less of his mother's attention due to the new arrival, and clung even closer to his father after Jennifer's birth.

Initially, Ricky's insecurities were projected by extreme degrees of regressive behaviors. This four-year-old now desired to be carried through the falling snow by his father, although prior to Jennifer's birth he insisted on independently walking and playing through the freezing snows of the most harsh winter weather conditions.

Ricky also developed a strong need for a greater degree of verbal and emotional attention.

One winter Sunday afternoon, while Valery and daughter were napping and Richard was casually reading the Sunday paper, Ricky climbed upon his father's lap and initiated a direct conversation.

"Daddy, do you love Jennifer?"

"Yes," answered   Richard while flipping the sports pages, "of course I do."

"Do you love me?" quizzed Ricky.

"Yes, Ricky," answered his father, "I love you too."

"Well, who do you love the most, Daddy, me or Jennifer?" earnestly questioned Ricky.

This question captured Richard's attention. He had recently submerged himself within a juvenile dimension of thought and wondered where he stood on the hierarchy of love with Valery. There were days and nights, though infrequent and sporadic when she appeared to be just too tired for him. He was still number one to her. . . wasn't he?

Richard quickly dismissed what he considered to be ludicrous and immature thoughts and returned from his insecure daydream to the concerns of his handsome son and warmly responded,

> "You are my favorite son and Jennifer is my favorite daughter, therefore I love you both the same," he smiled.

Ricky appeared disheartened by the response. Richard could easily sense that his son was not satisfied with this reply.

> "*But you're my best little buddy, Ricky*," smiled Richard in sincere declaration.

> "*And you're my best buddy, Daddy!*" happily exclaimed little Ricky while jumping up into Richard's arms and extending his tiny arms around his father's neck for a warm embrace.

Without a doubt, Ricky loved his father beyond endurance. Each morning at the breakfast table, Valery and Richard's conversations were usually limited because of Ricky's monopoly over his father's attention prior to Richard leaving home for the office.

Each evening, Ricky would sit and sulk in front of the living room window, regardless of rain, sleet or shine, until the awaited arrival of his father from work within his late model blue Ford sedan.

Valery ordinarily allowed Ricky the liberty of his father's time. However, each night around eight, she was again growing adamant about having Richard to herself. After putting Jennifer asleep in her crib and Ricky in his bed, she would return to the peaceful, warm, loving arms of her husband to pamper and feed her emotional and physical needs – and he would.

****

As the cold winter season began to fade and the bright colored spring began to appear, Richard decided to materialize into existence his long-awaited desire to own a cruiser sea vessel. He longed for the free sea wind to blow through his hair while inhaling the salt exhilarating smell of the sea.

Hence, during the early weeks of the spring, Richard and Ricky would drive from pier to pier, boat shop to boat shop, and from dock to dock in search of a special dream cruiser to call their own. Richard even bought himself and Ricky identical sailing caps in order to give more realism to their quest to be navigators of the sea. Richard's boat interests quickly became Ricky's obsessions.   Ricky would mimic or try to mimic everything about his father; *everything.* They were inseparable.

On May 17th of that year, Richard's teenage and adult fantasies became a reality upon the purchase of a second-hand, black, thirty-foot tri-cabin cruiser. It was a fiberglass beauty with an upper exterior deck and a lower interior cabin. The upper deck contained the steering and control section coupled with a seating capacity for six.   The boat's interior quarters were large and spacious and incorporated a large dining   area for up to fifteen passengers, a moderate size refrigerator, princess oven, two large cozy sleeping quarters and a bath area with necessary conveniences.

However, Richard was unable to take the boat adrift the waters after purchase because he lacked the sea-mastery skills required to manage the vehicle. Consequently, many hours and days were expended on private week-end lessons.

Frank was quite impressed with the boat purchase and usually accompanied Richard and Ricky during their tutored training.

On a clear mid-June day, while taking a tutoring session on the sea, a conversation between Frank, Richard, and the early fiftyish sea tutor, John, was initiated.

"How is the family, Richard?" questioned John as they began the lesson and the boat moved slowly into the peaceful waters.

"Fine, just fine," answered Richard with a smile while zipping up his wind-breaker and buttoning little Ricky's jacket.

"Tell me, John, are you married?" asked Richard.

"No, Richard, I got divorced about six months ago," John answered in sorrow while slowly puffing a pipe which filled the deck with a rugged fragrant tobacco aroma.

"How long were you married, John?"

"Twenty seven years," he answered.

Richard was flabbergasted. "Why, John? Why did it take you twenty-seven years of marriage to realize that you weren't in love or compatible with your wife?" he quizzed in a joking and sarcastic manner.

John smiled while turning the wheel toward more open waters.

" Well… let's see..How do I explain this. During the tenure of our marriage, I did not focus on the marriage, my focus, *our focus*, was on our four children. We were comfortable enough in the marriage to believe that we could address and overcome any personal issues of dislike or discord later in the marriage or after the children were independent of us. Unfortunately, we discovered too late that we had grown to far apart."

Richard was suspect and perplexed by John's summary and conclusions.

"I don't get it. How did the two of you grow so far apart?"

John replied while keeping his focus on the waters.

> "Well…the people Sarah and I are today contrast significantly from the people we were when we got married. Our perspectives on life, politics, love, career, developed independent of each other's radar despite having lived together all those years of marriage. After our last child graduated from college, I discovered that I really didn't know Sarah and Sarah really didn't know me. She was a stranger to me and I felt very little physical or emotional appeal or comfort with this stranger."

Richard continued to probe.

"You seem to be an intelligent guy, John. I find it hard to believe that you were not aware of the erosion of your marriage until a couple of years ago."

John nodded in agreement to Richard's analysis.

> "I suspected that we had problems years ago, Richard. However, I didn't realize how far we had grown apart until my youngest left the house. At that time, we mutually realized that there was very little of the love remaining for the strangers we had become."

John's matrimonial experiences and philosophies both intrigued and fascinated Frank and Richard. Even though it was a beautiful day for lessons, Richard thirsted to hear more, much more.

"John, did you try to revive your marriage prior to the divorce?"

"Of course I did, Richard," John answered while turning the round wood steering wheel over and over again to direct it to the boat's dock.

"We tried for two years. However, you can't recreate in two years a love affair that was neglected and slowly devalued in twenty-five years. Sarah and I seldom looked at or substantively related to each other during those twenty-five years. Consequently, we found it extremely difficult to relate to one another as man and woman; lovers, when our children grew and left the home. You cannot be lovers unless you are in love. You cannot have a substantive love affair with someone you really don't know or like. If you go through a rediscovery process, you still must like the person you discover. It was just too hard trying to rediscover and fall in love with someone who had grown so far away from who you are… it was just too hard."

For a moment there was silence. Both Frank and Richard were digesting the heart of John's story and growing disturbed by its reality.

"That's sad, John," whispered Richard in sympathy. "However, Valery and I . . . we don't have that problem. We know the order of our priorities."

"Then you're a very lucky and fortunate man, Richard," replied John with a look of envy in his eyes.

"I know, John," sighed Richard with a warm smile, "I know."

CHAPTER XXXIV

Pressure. . .Pressure . . .Pressure cooker. . .   Pressure cooker. . . pressure cooker. . pressure cooker..pressure cooker pressure cooker pressure cooker pressure cooker pressure cooker pressure cooker pressure cooker.

Richard was promoted to Vice President of Marketing and Strategic Planning. He was responsible for the national planning, marketing, sales and support services of the varied lines of computer brands and software developed by the company.

The profession of computer marketing, particularly within the market research, sales, and strategic planning levels proved to be a pressure cooker of stress, unreasonable deadlines and sales quotas. Competing corporate suppliers strategized and fought to increase market share by finding new outlets to promote their products to a more diverse cross section of consumers and companies.

The barrage of demands placed upon him proved to be an unusually difficult task due to the growing complexity and maintenance of the machinery and the increasing cut throat challenges of competing companies.

Many high level administrators within Tandem Industries were regarded as heavy drinkers due to the pressures of the job. Richard was not a heavy drinker but his profession did drive him to drink more than occasionally.

Valery was now greeting her husband's arrival from the office with a kiss and a highball in her hand. Consequently, this increase in alcoholic consumption was yielding a small mid-section of weight in Richard's otherwise slim appearance and Valery insisted he exercise himself back into health.

Consequently, most mornings, Richard would rise one hour earlier to jog two miles before preparing himself for the office and jog two miles after dinner each evening.

Ricky, four years of age, insisted on jogging with his father every morning. Eventually, Richard and Ricky could be observed in the neighborhood jogging two miles in unison; one mile with his four year-old son and one mile carrying his exhausted four-year-old son.

Ricky was quite a character. Each Saturday morning, Richard and Ricky would rise to wash and polish the four-door Ford sedan.   One bright Saturday morning, Ricky voiced a desire to do more than assist or observe in his father's car-washing rituals.

"Daddy," he initiated, "I want a car."

"What did you say?" questioned Richard in disbelief.

"I want a car," declared Ricky while looking directly at his father.

"A bike is enough for you," responded Richard impatiently while continuing to wash the hooded area of his automobile.

"But that's not enough, Daddy. I need my own wheels!" he seriously emphasized with his hands clenched on his tiny waist.

Richard laughed without control. He then buried his face into his wet hands in order that his sensitive son would not feel that he was being laughed at.   Ricky, thinking his father was crying because his eyes were covered and his body was shaking, began to yell,

"What's wrong, Daddy? What's wrong? I'm sorry, Daddy! Forget the wheels!!"

Ricky began pulling on his father's arms; he didn't want his father to cry.

"Forget the wheels, Daddy! Daddy, forget the wheels!" he emphasized as Richard helplessly laughed harder. Pulling himself together, Richard asked of his son,

"Where did you get this `my own wheels' jazz from?"

"From Jimmy's big brother," smiled Ricky hurriedly in relief, "Jimmy's got his own wheels."

Jimmy was their neighbors' five-year-old son. Richard understood the type of car Ricky was talking about. It was a battery-operated moving vehicle for children.   Within a two-week period of time, Richard purchased the moving vehicle for his son and hence every Saturday morning both gentlemen would wash and wax their own cars, together.

The years continued to move on; glorious years. Jennifer was almost two years of age now with a quieting disposition and the facial expressions and mannerisms of an angel. She loved to sit on her father's lap and lay her head on his left shoulder. They shared many moments of verbal communication on an adult-like level on her own child-like topics of conversation.   Richard loved Jennifer and her existence was the joy of his life, because Jennifer was the living micro image of her mother; and her mother was indeed a very beautiful woman.

From Richard's perspective, however, no words of sweetness or beauty could describe Valery. She was a very unique married woman. Each year she appeared even more radiantly beautiful than the year before. Her body was well cared for and even more sexually vivacious and petite. Her coal hair flowed longer with body within the passage of time, and her soft feminine facial features conveyed the same gentleness of character, spirit, and compassion which captured Richard's heart nine years ago.

And he loved her-and she loved him.

Valery's eyes still sparkled at the sight of her husband's arrival home from the computer jungle and Richard's tired, pressure-beaten face lifted itself into a smile of love and affection whenever he viewed his precious flower. They provided onto each other the three necessary foods required to maintain the aura of love. They fed each other emotionally, intellectually, and physically with all of the sexual vigor their bodies could muster within their penetrations of each other.

It was a love that had endured, a love they felt nothing or no one could cause to put asunder.

Many beautiful women had tempted Richard with their charms but Richard never saw them-or their charms. Multiple scores of men had imagined the physical taste of Valery's body with theirs and earnestly beckoned for her attention. But her body was never to be touched, yet more tasted, for she was the sole treasure of Richard's-only Richard's.

Richard and Valery were able to attend more social functions as the children grew older. They enjoyed high caliber plays, musical concerts, dancing, good movies, intimate dinners within the city, and the social and professional functions of their close associates and friends.

Valery designated Sunday as 'Family Day'. It was a day of rest, reserved for church services, grandparents, family, and/or a tranquil day on the boat in the sea.

It was mid-year now and the children were visiting their grandparents, Tina and William, this Sunday afternoon. Valery desired to feel the freedom, peace, and freshness of the sea and thereupon requested Richard to fulfill her wish by taking her sailing adrift the waters. She baited her request with a promise of preparing a special steak dinner for him within the boat's cooking quarters. Richard was easily lured and captured by the bait.

As they began preparations to make their journey from home to the boat's dock, Frank and his wife Rita made a surprise visit and eagerly joined in the Sunday sea plans of Richard and Valery. It was an ideal peaceful day for sailing.

The women prepared the appetizing steak dishes for their husbands and the men provided a romantic atmosphere by springing forth several bottles of champagne coupled with abundant words of gratitude for their wives' domestic efforts.

After dinner, Rita received the impression that Richard and Valery might prefer the privacy of each other's company within the boat's interior quarters. She quietly departed from them to the company of her husband Frank, who was on the upper deck, handling the boat's controls.

"Richard did you really enjoy your dinner?" Valery asked proudly.

"Of course, Valery," he answered in warmth while embracing her tiny waist as she washed the dishes, "but I enjoy everything you prepare for me."

"Oh, you fibber," she teased, "You didn't look so happy about the roast I burnt last Friday night."

"Is that what it was?" he laughed while locking the boat's interior doors.

"Richard, why did you lock the door?" she seductively whispered with her eyes melted upon his, "You know we can't get together with company on board," she continued.

"Why not, Valery?" questioned Richard, while kissing her long and tenderly.

"Because that would be rude, Baby," she answered while retreating from him and the hunger within his eyes as Richard slowly pursued her within the tiny confines of the boat's quarters.

"So what," he murmured while reaching for and missing her in the chase. "They wouldn't know what we're doing down here anyway."

"Well, they might, dear," she declared unconvincingly, now caught by his embrace.

"Then let's be rude, Valery," he whispered, while unzipping the fashionable white pants glued to her figure and carrying her to bed within the boat's quarters.

Valery smiled at seeing the need, longing and intent within her husband's eyes for her and whispered,

"Well . . . Richard . . okay," in surrender as they embraced, initially tenderly, increasingly passionately, and thereupon wrapped their bodies into a massive ball of penetrating fire again and again until exhausted within the ambit of each other's arms. They then inadvertently fell into a mild retreating sleep.

Richard and Valery did not awaken until Frank and Rita began knocking on the locked cabin door for entry in order to get their jackets due to the cold and windy gusts of air developing on the boat's upper quarters.

Upon awakening and hurriedly dressing in laughter, Richard and Valery promised each other they'd return the following Sunday with the company of their children, to once again sail upon and enjoy a peaceful afternoon upon the sea.

CHAPTER XXXV

Six days had passed; six tranquil days.

Richard, hoping to spend a quiet weekend at home, overheard Valery informing their enthusiastic children that they would share the following Sunday afternoon boating on the sea. This was to be the family's second outing on the cruiser since it was purchased and Valery appeared intent to make it a special occasion. That Saturday night, Valery and Jennifer expended their time making an elaborate Sunday dinner and packed it in a large straw-type picnic basket.

Richard awakened before dawn the following Sunday morning. He tried to go back to sleep but could not. He rose from bed, shaved, dressed himself and prepared a pot of coffee. Feeling restless, he hopped in Valery's yellow convertible two-seat sports car and travelled in the darkness to the distant dock to initiate a check on the mechanical condition of the cruiser. Richard travelled with silence while taking in the sweet smell of the clean, invigorating air. After reaching the beach, he walked the peaceful sands at the edge of the boat's dock while enjoying the tranquility of the environment. The sea winds gently kissed his face as a glowing red sunrise made a quiet yet bold brilliant appearance before a lone appreciative audience. Richard stood still, motionless, awed by the sun's beauty and vigor and continued his walk toward the dock.

The sea-the sea the sweet, awakening mystical powers of the sea always performed wonders in soothing Richard's mind. The morning waves gently crashed upon the beach surface as he approached and climbed upon the cabin cruiser. Richard made a thorough check of the boat's controls, confirmed the levels of gas, evaluated the oil levels, and did a quick general cleaning of the wood-work within the cabin. He felt satisfied. The curly locks of his hair blew in the mild wind as he walked to the marina's towers to check the anticipated weather forecasts. The day's weather conditions reflected a good prognosis; warm, mild, and sunny with a slight overcast.

He hurriedly travelled back home, his mind at peace.

After church services, Richard, with Valery and the children, drove to the beach to enjoy a Sunday afternoon together-on the sea.

*The sea-the sea-*the warm quiet, peaceful waters of the sea-provided a peaceful Sunday afternoon for this peaceful family. Richard and Valery, engrossed in warm conversation coupled with the laughter of their children, had unknowingly sailed a great distance from the boat's dock. Once they became aware of this oversight and after noticing the overcast in the skies, began their journey back towards shore in laughter. The radio within the boat's lower deck played soft music to its listeners and a "*special alert*" news bulletin regarding a severe weather storm rapidly approaching the city limits. This bulletin, however, Richard and Valery *did not hear*.

While turning the boat's steering wheel toward the direction of the distant dock, Richard could feel the gusts of wind blowing a bit stronger, a bit harsher, a bit colder than before. However, he disregarded his observances as being messages of seriousness and proceeded to gently wrap his jacket around the bare shoulders of his wife Valery. The wind continued to flex its muscles by blowing more violently on the boat's loneliness, thereby urging Richard to petition Valery to take their children down to the warmth and safety of the boat's interior quarters. Valery, in childlike innocence, examined her husband's face and saw a small measure of worry in his eyes. She thereupon gathered and directed her two children down to the boat's interior quarters as requested.

A feeling of terror gripped Richard's soul. The helm appeared to be fighting with him for the boat's control as the waves of the waters rolled back and forth, side to side, as if in a confused state of direction.   Soft rains began to fall. They stopped. They began again.   Although the mists of rain were mild, almost meek, the feeling of isolation and the smell of danger in the air persuaded Richard to propel his engine into a full throttle.

The sun pushed the gray smoke-colored clouds away from its immediate vicinity and although the mild rains continued to fall, the sun illuminated a bright yellow cast over the seas. The yellow glow quickly disappeared to be replaced by even darker grey clouds, almost charcoal in color.

Richard glanced at his watch. It read 6 p.m., but the scenery was reading midnight. Richard visually searched for some sight of land but his visual search was fruitless.

He questioned and pondered upon how he could have sailed such a great distance from shore in such a short period of time.

The steering wheel jerked free of Richard's control with such force that he was thrown to the boat's deck. He quickly arose from his fallen position and wrestled with the cruiser's wheel for control. The rain stopped. The sea-waves softened. The sun reappeared and within a matter of moments the skies again cleared. Richard could feel the wickedness in the air. He looked at his compass and was appalled by what he saw; the dial of the compass was turning clockwise at an alarming rate of speed.

"What is going on?" he loudly questioned to himself.

Valery and the children were within the protection of the sea craft's quarters. She peered out of the oval-shaped windows and felt their boat begin to sway - - ever so slightly - - ever so lightly - - as a mild mist of rain began to descend upon the boat and sea waters. However, she expelled the possibilities of danger from her mind and returned to the laughter and happiness she gave and received when relating with her two active children.

Within a matter of minutes, the blue skies again turned dark as night. Valery became alarmed as the boat began swaying more severely as thunder boomed louder and the rains fell harsher upon the vessel's roof.   In a mild panic, she instructed her children to remain seated within the boat's quarters as she went up to the upper deck to assist her husband in whatever way possible.

"What's going on?" she murmured, climbing toward the upper chambers.

The blustering of the sea winds and the raging turbulence of the waters were now resounding as Valery yelled to her husband,

"Richard!! Richard!!" in a state of fear while approaching him at the boat's controls. However, the noisy, violent fiendishness of the sea was now uproarious and because Richard's back was against her, he could not hear her cries as the cruel winds unmercifully threw her to her knees upon the cruiser's deck.   She tried vainly to reach him. However, each time Valery rose in quest of her husband's attention, the ruthless sea winds and rains would keel the vessel side to side, thereby descending her again and again to her knees, forcing Valery to crawl toward Richard in a state of frenzied fear.

Valery, crawling, crying, screaming, pleading,

"Richard!! Richard!!!" was now within a few feet of her husband's back and her voice was finally audible to his ears.

In silence, he turned and peered into her eyes. The seemingly aged transformations of his rain-filled face informed her their position was cancerous as she screeched in horror,

"Oh, my God, my God!! Oh, my God!!!"

The devilish aggressive high waves of the waters were erupting in the storm's darkness and the boat was being spewed around the waters as if it was a giant match box. Their children, petrified with terror by the boisterous thunder and dark skies, rushed upon the boat's deck only to be thrown to their tiny knees by the tempestuous winds and rains as they screamed helplessly for their father's protection; a father who fought vainly against the storm for the boat's control.

Valery crawled to her fallen children and encircled them within her hysterical crying arms. Amid her tears and the screams of her children, Richard beckoned, pleaded, and screamed to Valery to take the children and return to the boat's dry quarters. But in her shocked state of insensibility, she could not move-*she could not move!*

The sea, the sea- the cruel, wicked, dark, demoniacally possessed hideousness of the sea-was now trying to swallow up the wholeness of its prey, but Richard would not give up his control of the helm. Although his body was drenched from the freezing flowing rains and he found it difficult to see against the storm's dark skies, he sensed that as long as the vessel could remain afloat, there was still a reason to hope.

"Take the children down to the shelter!!" Richard continued to yell in desperate anger to his wife, for he knew there was little chance the soft bodies of his family could sustain their balance upon the cruiser's exterior deck.

However, again, his plea   fell on deaf ears.

Valery was mentally lost. She could not react to reason or anticipate hope. She could only deal with the staunch reality of this nightmare.

She must listen to me! .. She must!

Richard took one of his strong hands off of the boat's manual reins and grabbed his wife by the arm trying to shake sense into her. But Valery, while kneeling and clutching their two children even tighter within the locks of her arms, could not relate to reason during this crucial dilemma as he shook her in vain.

They were being attacked by a tag-team of evil. The monstrous waves were twice the size of their boat and relentlessly trying to shake them into the water. The demonic winds appeared more vindictive and hostile by Richard's efforts. The intensity, continuity and volume of this spectacle was overwhelming.

The sea-the sea- the fierce, raging, devouring quickness of the sea- found its prey subject to capture in this moment of weakness. Hence a massive wave of disproportionate height and bloodcurdling terror drenched the boat and occupants in sea water, thereupon jerking the helm away from Richard's one- handed possession and smothering him, with family, in a pool of high pressured waters down to their knees.

The malevolent waters, the monstrous waves, the chilling winds and harsh rains held control of the boat's power and in the darkness were claiming their prey. The next slapping wave ripped the children out of Valery's screaming arms and flung this family of four out of the boat and into the awaiting mouth of the lusty sea.

They were then devoured below the waters of the sea. The powerful undercurrents, generated by the waves, forced them to be surfaced and swallowed, surfaced and swallowed, again and again, like yo-yos, against their wills, thus filling their lungs with death-drowning salty sea waters.

Richard, a strong swimmer, forcefully surfaced himself above the waters in search of his family. As the waves crashed against his strong body, he observed that the twenty-yard swimming distance between himself and his wife was almost equivalent to the distance between himself and his children, who were being toyed about like rag puppets around the mad, murderous sea arena.

Richard, dazed with fear, swam instinctively in the direction of Valery in pursuit of hopefully saving her life and then the lives of their children.

He commenced swimming against the darkness, thrashing the rolling waters painfully, crying fearfully at the thought of losing his precious wife, his jewel, his long love of youthful memories, as the thunderous lightning brightened the black skies.

Richard finally reached the radius of his drowning wife Valery. She was a decent swimmer but the power of this storm and tragedy to her family was too overwhelming. Valery, totally unaware of Richard's exerted efforts to rescue her, had given up all hope of living and surrendered to accept this nightmarish death by water-silently.

Valery was tired; her mind was beaten; her children were tragically dying, at least death would end her mental anguish;

Hurry, death . . . hurry!

With her eyes closed, Valery prepared to welcome her extinction by water when Richard yelled unto her,

"Valery! Valery! Take my hand! Take my hand!!!" and her eyes quickly opened, *only to witness the bodies of her two children, in distant proximity being thrashed, toyed, and buried by the maddening waves and waters of the sea.* With the last ounce of strength within her, Valery pushed Richard's arms and hands away from her drowning body and yelled imperatively in nerve-splintering hysteria,

"*No! No! Not me! Not me! Let me die, Richard! Let me die! Save the children, Richard!... **Richard, Save the Children!!!**"*

CHAPTER XXXVI

Richard, torn, crazed and mystified by her request, reluctantly turned his head to witness and hear his children screaming in death-drowning fear. They were again crying to their father for salvation as the sea tossed their bodies around like wooden puppets.

He then turned and swam away from his wife, nodding crazily in verbal agreement as she prepared herself for extinction under the waters,

"Yes, save the children! Right, Valery! Save the children!"

He thereupon commenced thrashing through the sea waters in defiance of death and swam towards his son, his daughter-his children. In a state of fatigue and physical exhaustion, Richard miraculously reached Ricky. . . then Jennifer, and clung them within the protective safety of his left arm while using his right arm to wade the waters.

Amid the ear-cracking thunder, wild waves and gusty winds, Richard lovingly smiled while wading through the water and looking upon his dependent shivering offspring.

He then began yelling in hysteria-type laughter,

"I've saved the children Valery! Valery, the children are saved!!"

But she did not answer.

He yelled again in laughter more maddening and frenzied than before,

"I've saved the children, Valery!!, Valery, the children are saved!!"

But again he heard nothing.

He then turned his head towards the vicinity where he last departed from his wife, *and as the thunder lighted the sky, he shockingly saw the wrist of her left ringed hand slowly descending into the devouring waters of the sea some ten yards away.*

And he thought out loud about the last words of his wife while looking into the eyes of his loving son Ricky, clinging to his father's neck,

"Save the children, Richard, Richard, save the children!"

As he saw the remaining fingers of his wife's hand vanish under the waters, he thought, *Save the children, Richard, Richard, save the children!!*

As the waters began burying the body of her sweetness within a liquid grave he whispered,

"Save the children, Richard, Richard, save the children, the children, Richard," he cried, "Richard, save the children-"

As the laughter, love, and memories he had shared with that jewel for so long were being violently washed away from him he thought, *Save the children, Richard, Richard, save the children.*

Coercing himself to accept the last words of his beloved wife's request, he began to yell out loud,

"Save the children, Richard! Richard, save the children! The children, Richard! Richard, save the children! Save the children, Richard! Richard, save the children! Save the children, Richard! ... *no!* - - Richard, save the children! The children, Richard! Richard, save.... no! the children! Save the. . *no!* . . . children, Richard! Richard! . . . no! Save the... no! children!! Richard! Richard! save no! the children no! Richard! save the no! children, the children, Richard!!! no! no! no! no! Richard, save the children!!"

267

The look on little Ricky's face conveyed fear as he looked into the eyes of his father. Was his father really pushing him back into the murderous sea waters? *No, not his father.*

With tears in his eyes, Richard began swimming without direction with the children in his arms as he thought, Save the children, Richard--- Richard, save the. . . no! children!

His two-year-old daughter, Jennifer, was now clawing the flesh out of her father's chest in order to maintain a grasp for safety. Her dark eyes questioned, was Daddy really pushing her into the awaiting mouth of the hungry sea? *No! not her daddy.*

The thunderous lightening and knife cutting waters were even more angry by the strength and rebellion of Richard's battle to survive.   Richard then tried to swim towards the vicinity of his drowning wife Valery; maybe, just maybe he could figure out where she slipped under the water and save her too. He could not; not with the weight of his two children against the weight of the treacherous storm.

 He screamed as he reminisced about the day he first saw Valery; the social/economic walls that kept them apart; the rebellious battles they fought for each other; the intense love they had for each other.

And Richard again proceeded to think out loud,

"Save the children, Richard! Richard, save the no! children. Richard!!! Richard!!!   Save   the   children, Richard! no! Richard!! no! no! no! no!

the children! Richard!!! Save! no! no? no! no! no? the no! children! Richard! Save the children! no! no! The children, Richard! no! no! no? no! no! Save the children! no!   Richard!   Save! no! Richard!!!!!!!   the children!!!!!!!!!!   no!   no!   no!   no! **NOOOOOOOOOOOOOOO!!!!!"**

With tears in his eyes, *Richard released his screaming, hysterical children from his arms into the oncoming rushing waves of the murderous sea and softly cried,*

"Valery!"   increasingly..."Valery!" ...louder...... *"Valery"*

louder   " *Valery!!!!!!!!!!!!!!"*

He swam alone against the thunderous lightning, dark skies, massive waves and heavy rains towards the general vicinity where he had last envisioned the vanishing of his wife's existence.

His body was near total physical exhaustion and his mind had collapsed. He turned for a second and witnessed Jennifer being thrashed and carried, swallowed and buried, under the sea.

But Ricky! - - - Ricky . . was Ricky?

"Oh, my God! Help me!! Jesus!Jesus! God!! Help me! Help me!!!" Richard pleaded.

Was Ricky really trying to swim? Was his son again trying to imitate his father?

And Richard paused momentarily, with tears in his eyes, and watched his son rotate his tiny arms in desperation as he had seen his father rotate his own arms, crying in disbelief at his father's actions and pleading for his number one buddy to save him.

For a split second their eyes met, and a piece of Richard's soul died.

But Richard continued against the storm towards the vicinity where he felt his wife lie, again crying,

"Valery!!! Valery!!!" until he reached the general locale where he believed her body was swallowed by the sea.

He submerged himself under the death-defying torrents of the sea waters in quest of her body. He was under the raging waters for seconds, seconds which seemed like hours until forced to ascend above the water without her. His body and mind was caving in; dying.

> "Heart, hold up, please," he pleaded to his exhausted body. "Please! Hold up, please!" he cried out loud to himself. *"Somebody, please! God! help me! help me!!"* as he submerged again deeper into the depths of the tempestuous mad sea waters in quest of Valery.

Again, the undercurrents of the waters forced him to rise to the surface.

As he surfaced, his eyes viewed little Ricky's body being mauled and prepared for death by the murderous sea. Again their eyes met . . . but this time little Ricky was not screaming -- - he had been betrayed. Little Ricky was crying softly as his four foot outstretched body rode the waves of the sea waters. With his mouth open in fear and his arms outstretched against that giant wave of the water like a boy being crucified, little Ricky accepted his death.

Ricky conveyed a cold betrayal of hatred toward his father as their eyes touched and his tiny body, *beckoning to his father*, was taken and wholly swallowed under the stormy sea waters.

At this point, Richard's mind collapsed. He began pulling and extracting large amounts of hair from the roots of his scalp with *his bare hands* and he felt no pain.

Again, Richard submerged himself into the sea in search of his wife Valery, somewhere within the turbulent, dirty, treacherous sea waters he knew her body lay.

Fifteen seconds elapsed… but Richard did not surface as the treacherous waters crashed and waved against each other. Forty-one seconds passed… and there was still no sign of Richard. Sixty seconds passed…rise, Richard! Rise! …and still there was no sign of Richard. Ninety seconds slowly passed by.. and still Richard was nowhere to be found. He must now be dead.

The water turned a sick, murky, bloodcurdling red as intestinal pieces of flesh ascended to the surface of the maddening waters.

And then,...like a ghost...there he was...spewing blood...gasping for air to fill his capsized lungs... with the body... yes...with the body of his wife Valery clutched tightly in his arms.

Richard screamed in the darkness as the massive storm sea waves battered his deranged body as he surfaced above the waters. He felt his eyes begin to roll up into his head as he seemingly began to fall into a coma of physical exhaustion, but he caught himself and loudly demanded to his body,

"Not now!! Dammit! *not now!!*"

And he swam and waded upon the maddening surface of the sea waters with his wife's body within his arms until a slight degree of calmness began to appear upon the storm-ridden waters.

The coast guard ultimately found and pulled Richard and Valery's limp, lifeless-like body upon the ship. It was at this time that Richard allowed his eyes to roll up into his head as he escaped into the peace of a deep, dangerous, critical coma.

****

The medical personnel on the ship initiated immediate CPR efforts to consciously revive them. Richard and Valery continued to have a weak pulse beat. They were immediately air lifted by helicopter to State's Hospital.

CHAPTER XXXVII

Fourteen days had passed. Richard and Valery were comatose and lay in the Intensive Care Ward of the hospital. The prognosis for Richard was bleak.

The upper cortex of Richard's brain was damaged as a result of the prolonged loss of oxygen experienced in that ordeal. Additionally, the neurological tests and scans indicated that he likely suffered a stroke as a result of same blood flow loss triggered by same oxygen deficiencies.

Valery's prognosis was critical. In fact, the doctors held little hope for Valery's revival. She suffered brain damage to both her upper and lower brain centers. Consequently, a respirator was required to help her breathe.

Richard's parents, William and Tina, were advised that the longer the coma, the less likely were the chances of survival and/or recovery of function.

Seventeen days had passed.

"Doctor! Doctor!! He's moving!! He's moving!!" excitedly beckoned the nurse within St. Joseph's Hospital.

First, his arm, then his hands, and suddenly his eyes opened to the sight or doctors and nurses gathered around his bedside, gazing down upon his awakening in disbelief.

His appearance was repulsive. The bald spots on his scalp, generated as a result of that living nightmare, contributed in aging the physical appearance of Richard considerably. The deep-seated lines of fear and worry upon his face were to be permanent scars of his facial appearance coupled with growing gray hairs protruding in abundance from his body.

He lay motionless, looking at them and trying to figure out where he was.

"Valery, where's Valery?" were the first words of question from his mouth toward the group of medical personnel looking upon him like he was a man arising from the dead.

"That must be his wife," a young doctor declared to his peers.

"Yes, my wife Valery, where is she? Is she alright?" Richard questioned in panic while trying to raise his head and get his body out of bed. The medical team grabbed and restrained him.

"Please, Mr. Washington," pleaded a plump, middle-aged nurse of gentle character. "You must rest! You mustn't upset yourself, your wife is fine-"

"Where is she?" Richard demanded.

"Here in the hospital," the nurse answered.

"In the hospital?" he retorted, "Then she's not fine! I must see my wife! I must see my wife!!" he screamed while attempting to pull himself up from the bed.

The group of doctors, observing the mental anguish his mind was undergoing, decided to inject him with a sedative to put his mind at ease. They did not want to risk the possibilities of him experiencing another stroke.

Against his protest, they wrestled him back into the bed and injected his resisting body with the medical drug thorazine.

That evening, around seven p.m., the sedative had worn off and Richard's eyes, heavy from drugs, drowsily opened themselves. Upon awakening, he forced his body out of the bed and began roaming the halls and wards of the hospital floor. Because of his drugged physical condition and mental deterioration, Richard walked somewhat drunkenly from ward to ward on the hospital floor.

The physical strangeness of his face provoked the in-hospital bed patients to become alarmed. Same patients signaled the medical staff to halt Richard from roaming within their private wards of the hospital floor.

However, the hospital staff could not find him. Whenever Richard saw a member or group of uniformed personnel, he would hide away into the empty orderly or hospital supply rooms. His mind was intent on seeing his wife.

Richard continued to hide and roam, roam and search from ward to ward, operating room to operating room, in quest of Valery until he finally found the private sector of the hospital where she was being treated- and he cried.

Her unconscious body lay within a huge plastic oxygen tent. Plastic tubes for intravenous feeding were attached to her veins. The machine under the tent made it obvious that she had been the recipient of more than one blood transfusion.

Valery was suffering from Pulmonary Edema. Her lungs had taken in too much of the sea water thereby creating an abnormality on her body heart functions.

Richard was still crying, face in his hands, when the medical staff found him.

He was then coaxed and assisted back to his private ward with a promise of being able to return to his wife's side daily.

Every day Richard returned to his wife's side for a period of six days and did something he wasn't really in the habit of doing; He prayed. His prayers were answered the following Saturday evening when, after twenty days of unconsciousness, Valery's eyes opened to behold her pajama-attired husband lightly sleeping at the foot of her hospital bed.

With all of the strength she could gather, she warmly whispered, "Richard... Richard," and Richard's tired eyes opened to the awakened drowsy pupils of his wife Valery, and he smiled.

"How do you feel, Baby?" he tenderly asked as water filled his eyes.

"Okay, Richard," Valery weakly replied with a mild smile. "Where are we? Did we die?"

"No, Baby," he smiled, "we're alive. We made it."

"Oh, Richard," she cried softly, "You're unbelievable. It's hard to believe any man could have saved the children and myself through that terrifying experience, but you did, I'm so lucky to have you!"

Richard shuddered. She thinks the children are still alive, she's too weak to be told the truth. How will she react when she learns he sacrificed the children for her?

"Are the children okay, Love?" she questioned.

"Yes, Baby, they're fine," he answered while ringing the hospital floor desk to inform them his wife had consciously recovered.

"Don't talk too much, Valery," he warmly whispered, "you need your strength."

"I love you, Richard," whispered Valery while reaching for his hand.

"I love you too, Valery," responded Richard as his wife drifted into the peace of a mild sleep.

During the last moments of their conversation, a doctor arrived and administered a brief examination upon her and noted the progress on her chart.

The doctor thereupon left Richard alone with his sleeping wife. Richard's body was shaking. How was he going to break the truth of their children's tragic deaths to Valery? How would he convey the essence of his choice? She had invested so much of her life in their upbringing.

He left her room to meditate on answers.

****

Richard visited his wife the following Sunday morning as the plastic tubes were being removed from her veins. She smiled in high spirits as he entered her room.

"Hello, husband," she cheerfully greeted while extending her hand to him.

"Good morning, wife," he answered solemnly while taking her hand and bestowing a kiss upon it.

"Dear, call the children," she requested. "I want to see the children. Who's taking care of them, anyway? Mother Washington, I bet, right?"

"Valery," interrupted Richard, "there is something we must talk about."

"Not now, Richard," she bubbled. "Don't get serious on me today, dear. You're always so serious. Smile for me, Love. We're alive! We made it! Call the children, Richard, call-"

"Valery, we must talk!" he interrupted.

Valery looked into Richard's face and for the first time became aware of its aged transformation.

"Okay, Love," she responded, "but before we talk, let me call Mother Washington. I want to talk to the children," she replied while picking up the telephone.

Richard gently took the telephone receiver from her hand and declared,

"You can't talk to the children, Valery."

"Why not, Richard?" she asked in exasperation, "I'm okay now, husband. Let me talk to my children," she replied while pulling the phone receiver from his hand.

"You can't talk to the children, Valery!" Richard repeated.

"And again I say why not, Richard!?" Valery inquired in exasperated anger while dialing the number of her mother in law, Tina Washington.

"Because the children are dead," he answered with solemn quietness while looking into her dark, deep eyes. The phone dropped from her hand onto the floor and her eyes turned into a watery coldness.

"What did you say?" she asked in shocked disbelief.

"Let me try to explain-"

"Explain what?" she coldly snapped."What are you saying to me, Richard? Richard, where are the children?"

"The children are dead, Valery," he quietly repeated with his eyes turned to the floor.

"But how, Richard? I distinctly remember seeing you swim to their safety so how are they dead?"

Her face turned a deathly pale,

"If they're dead, Richard," she shrieked, "then why am I still alive? Talk to me, Richard... *talk to me!*"

At this point the entire floor of medical personnel and hospital patients were aware of the piercingly loud argument between Valery and Richard. Her doctors, fearing a relapse of her cardiac functions, rushed to her room and vainly tried to relax and calm her heightening temper. They could not.

She was angry, very angry. Valery's right leg moved from the bed to the floor. Her left leg followed as she got up from the bed while crying,

"Where are our children, Richard? You didn't kill them, did you, Richard? Richard, did you kill my children?"

Valery was approaching Richard with venom. She continued to scream,

"Richard, did you murder our children?!?"

The doctors and nurse wrestled her to bed amid her screams, cries, and kicks. They quickly administered a sedative to her body and she fell asleep. Richard was asked by the medical team to leave the confines of his wife's ward, and he left.

****

It was three a.m., the following Monday morning. Valery felt the spirit of someone over her bed and her eyes opened, first slowly, then quickly upon recognizing Richard.

"I must talk to you," he whispered in the darkness.

With her eyes glowing with hatred she asked, "Did you kill our children, Richard?"

"I did not kill anyone," Richard answered defensively. "I saved my wife!"

"Richard, I distinctly remember telling you to save the children."

"At that time, Valery, it was not your choice to make."

"What do you mean it was not my choice to make?" she screamed. "It's my life!"

"But the choice was mine!" he retorted angrily in defense and frustration.

Richard calmed down and continued,

"Valery, there is no way I can describe to you the horror of that choice. I haven't slept a good sleep since regaining consciousness. I keep seeing Ricky's eyes upon mine while being devoured by the open sea. I keep hearing-"

"Richard! Stop it! Stop it! Stop it! Stop it! Stop it! Stop it" she yelled, "I neither care nor desire to hear the gory details of my children's death," she declared while again breaking down in tears.

"Richard, how could you?" Valery asked with her face buried in her hands.

"How could I what, Valery? How could I have saved your life over theirs? *Do you think the nightmares I'm experiencing would have been of a less degree had I sacrificed you for them? No way, Valery! No way!! Regardless of which choice I'd have made, I'd still suffer today."*

He moved closer to her and continued,

"Valery, listen to me, I need you now more than ever. Please don't turn on me now," he pleaded. "Please…not now!"

"Richard….please leave, she coldly responded.

"What!!!" he stammered in shocked disbelief. Was this his wife speaking? Was this the soft, sympathetic, mild flower he had known and loved for so long?

"Get out! Disappear! Vanish!" she yelled. "If you think for one minute that I'm going to comfort you after murdering my children, you are sadly mistaken!" she vindictively asserted while looking into his eyes.

Richard, shocked, pleaded,

"Valery!...Please!!!"

"Get out!" she screamed, her body shaking in anger as she buzzed for the medical staff to remove him from her ward.

"And don't bother coming back!!!" she yelled to his pale, sickly face as he was escorted from her room.

And Richard left her room-feeling very empty, very hurt, and very, very alone.

CHAPTER XXXVIII

The following Friday morning, four days after his verbal ordeal with Valery, Richard was discharged from the hospital in supposed fair health.

Prior to departing, Richard again requested to see his wife, but again she refused his request. He felt, however, that within a reasonable period of time she would understand the essence of that tragic choice and they would again be able to pull their lives back together.

On the evening of Richard's discharge, he slept in his father's home. William was a comfort to his son. Richard discussed the nightmarish ordeal he had experienced. Three times while telling the story, he lost his composure and sobbed.

"Father, tell me truthfully, was I wrong?"

William sympathetically looked at his prematurely aged son and decreed,

"Richard, in a situation such as that; there is no right or wrong decision."

Richard appeared comforted by his father's response, but not at peace.

William and Tina could hear their son walking and roaming the rooms and halls of their home until the early hours of the morning; another night he again could not sleep.

Several days later, Richard again visited the hospital with the hope of seeing his wife only to learn of her discharge from the hospital the night before.

His physical appearance was even more unpleasant. Sleeping nightmares of that tragic day at sea kept him from resting; nightmares which were always a reliving experience of the choice. He grew fearful of even considering sleep for he always awaken screaming in a cold sweat with excessive hairs pulled from his scalp lying in his hand.

Richard initiated a search for Valery. He felt that by now she could relate to the nightmare he went through; at least they would be able to talk. Richard searched for Valery for fourteen days. He visited relatives, close associates and friends where he felt she might seek recluse. His search was fruitless.

On the fifteenth day, Richard returned to his home; a home of emptiness and memories without the presence of his wife and children. As he unlocked and walked in the front door, Richard thought he heard noises emanating from what was once his children's bedroom. Richard had not entered their rooms since his discharge from the hospital. He had no desire of materially viewing the environment and treasures of their past existence, not yet.

As he climbed the stairs toward the second floor, the noises coming from within became more audible. Richard was now at his children's bedroom door. Who was in there? he pondered. A burglar? Had the children come back to haunt him? Richard swung the door open and saw Valery sitting on little Ricky's bed sobbing over the toy cars and dolls of her deceased children, deceased children who had once filled the room with so much warmth, so much love, so much laughter.

Her eyes were red and swollen from the excessive tears she had cried in mourning of her children's death. She was startled to see Richard at the open door and shocked by his appearance. His head was half bald with significant portions of grey hair sprouting on his scalp. Additionally, there were newborn fixed lines of age and worry engraved on this stranger's face. She saw a tired man with sagging facial muscles and fatigued sleepless red eyes. Was this Richard?

Was this the proud, tall, confident, handsome man she had known and loved so many, many years? And for a fleeting moment her face conveyed sympathy...pity... but it was only for a moment.

Richard walked toward his wife.

"You've come back!" he exclaimed with a broad smile across his face. "You've come back!!" he repeated in glee, caressing his wife within his arms.

However, when he looked at her, he did not see Valery-he saw scorn. He released her of his embrace.

"Richard, I'm leaving you," were the first cold words of greeting she voiced towards him.

"But why, Valery? Why?" he demanded.

"The reasons are obvious," she murmured. "I just came here to pick up my clothes."

Richard looked at the floor and saw her packed suitcases.

"Valery, we must talk!" he pleaded.

"There is nothing to talk about," she quickly responded while rising from Ricky's bed and taking her suitcases in her hands.

"Valery, we must talk!" he demanded.

"Good-bye, Richard," she replied while trying to exit from the children's door.

"Valery!" he screamed, blocking her exit with his body.

"Richard, forget it!!" she yelled. "Do you think for one moment that I can live in this house with all of its dead memories?"

"Then we'll move," he decisively answered.

"Richard, it would never be the same. I can never forgive you for the deaths of my children. I could never forget!"

"Valery!!" Richard bellowed. "They were my children, too, remember? Jennifer was my daughter! Ricky was my son! Do you think I can forget? Every minute I hurt with their memories. Every night I'm afraid to allow myself to sleep from fear of reliving the nightmares of their deaths. Every day I suffer! Help me, Valery! Valery, please! Help me!!"

Valery looked at Richard with mixed emotions and then sympathetically whispered,

"Good-bye, Richard."

"You can't leave me, Valery!" Richard snapped emphatically while circling the proximity of her presence.

At that precise moment, a physical battle was initiated by Valery. Richard, hoping to restrain Valery, not harm her, found that the lack of sleep had sapped him of his strength and she was able to release herself from his grasp. She then scrambled down the stairs of their two-level home with Richard in pursuit of her. Richard's emotional, mental, and physical strengths were depleted. Consequently, as Valery moved down the stairs and to their front door, Richard's legs buckled, and he stumbled and fell down the stairs to the hard granite first floor.

Too weak to immediately rise from his fallen position, Richard sat at the bottom of those stairs . . and he cried …. and he cried . . . and he cried.

****

Valery, fearing Richard would continue his search for her, left her home state with one thousand dollars in her purse and took a midnight plane the following Thursday night destined for New York.

She chose New York because it was a state of few relatives and friends and she could thereby start her life anew. In addition, New York was a state having a high population rate and was of such a complexity that Richard would have difficulty finding her.

The only individual who knew of her departure was her Aunt Earlene who unwillingly vowed secrecy.

****

Richard returned to his position with Tadem Industries. Prior to returning, Richard scrubbed and bathed his ill-kept body, laid out his finest suit, and practiced the flamboyant air of confidence and poise he possessed prior to the family tragedy.

He tried to be the man he once was but his efforts were in vain.

He was generally incoherent on the job. Within a short time, the mask of confidence wore off. Richard was lost; unmotivated; depressed.

He lacked the emotion-filled vigor which earlier magnetized his staff and peers toward him and this depletion of confidence exposed itself to all within his working environment. Consequently, Richard could no longer provide the stimuli, motivation, enthusiasm and energy to inspire the marketing division to reach their quota of marketing ideas and sales in his department.

Ninety non-productive days passed. After repeated warnings, missed meetings, unfulfilled sales quotas, unexcused absences, and consistent late arrivals to work, Richard was called into the office of Vincent Reynolds, Chief Executive Officer, and fired.

Richard was in free-fall.

His daily consumption of alcohol was now excessive-and he drank alone. He buried himself in his house, a house of haunting memories and nightmares, and he drank more; only to sober up to the same haunting house, and drink more.

No one saw him.

His father would drive to his son's home daily with the hope of emotionally lifting his son and getting him out of a home of dead memories, but Richard generally would not answer the door.

Once a week, however, he would allow his father to look at him. With the screen door locked, he would open the oak wood door and let his father observe him, just stare at him ….and he'd cry and shut the oak door on his father's face against William's protests.

William Washington seriously considered committing his son into a mental hospital for emotional help but declined to do so predicated upon a belief that within time, Richard would rise above this nightmare.

NEW YORK

Chapter XXXIX

Valery acquired a retail sales clothing position with one of New York's more prestigious women's department stores. She had been employed for two months. She worked twelve to fourteen hour days in order to exhaust herself of any idle time to reflect on her life.

Memories of Ricky and Jennifer consistently surfaced in her mind or in her dreams. The dreams of her children practically killed her. It literally required in excess of three days for Valery to cease crying and pull herself out of the depths of grief and depression whenever she experienced same dreams. Consequently, she learned how to self- medicate by totally blocking the memory of Ricky and Jennifer from her mind. Their memories were too painful to recall, so they never existed. She initiated efforts toward killing the memory of Richard, efforts which were growing more and more futile. Was her hatred and vengeance wrong? She had begged him to save the children.

The Christmas season had arrived and the department store was crowded. While assisting a group of disgruntled shoppers, her eyes met a handsome man of stature. He looked familiar. She shuddered and couldn't explain why, but continued to perform her selling duties, ignoring his persistent stares.

Five minutes later, Valery looked up and again observed the handsome stranger's eyes piercing into hers. She ignored his visual freshness and continued her work.

Moments later she lifted her busy eyes from her selling station to a new customer who had now approached the counter. Within two feet of her was the same handsome stranger, looking at her more intently than ever. The stranger then greeted,

"Hello, Valery."

Valery was shaken; the handsome stranger knew her name. However, she recaptured her cool headedness and commenced her programmed sales inquiry.

"Can I help you, sir?" she smiled.

"Don't you recognize me, Valery?" the stranger questioned.

"Sir?" she questioned.

"Valery, look at me," the stranger warmly requested.

And Valery looked … and thought… was it? No! Is it? And she verbally questioned,

"Damien?...you….yes…..Damien!!!" and they laughed while greeting each other with a warm, friendly embrace.

She had not seen Damien in over eight years. He was handsome at State University but the years had been even more kind to him. Damien quickly informed her that he had lived in New York for the last five years, was involved in stock market transactions, was unmarried, and desired the pleasure of her company over dinner that evening-a desire Valery was persuaded to accept.

By accepting Damien's dinner invitation, Valery was unknowingly rekindling the fires of an old romance.

****

Richard again renewed his search for Valery. He asked her closest associates for information regarding her whereabouts, friends who were reluctant to allow him into their homes because of his physical strangeness and growing eccentric means of behavior and instability. However, they knew nothing.

Richard went to her father, Clifford Hall, who wanted so badly to emotionally touch Richard, but in regards to Valery's whereabouts, he knew nothing.

Finally, Richard visited Earlene. She claimed a lack of knowledge regarding Valery's new place of residence, but after a desperate cry for help she informed him that Valery had moved to New York. However, Valery's exact whereabouts were unknown.

That night, Richard took a plane to New York City and arrived there at twelve o'clock midnight with five hundred dollars in his pocket. The clothes on his body were his only luggage.

****

Richard searched hard for Valery during the month of December. He assumed she would continue her career as a teacher. Consequently, he acquired a list of every New York elementary school and initiated a personal visit to each. Unknown to Richard was that Valery had purposely decided not to reenter the field of education in order to further hinder Richard's efforts of locating her. On Christmas Eve of that year, two hundred fifty dollars in his pocket, a lonely heart, and no stable place of residence, Richard began to fear that Valery would not be found and again this strong man cried.

As he roamed the cold windy streets of New York City, he'd quietly whisper to himself,

"Somebody, please tell me this is a bad dream ... please tell me this is a bad dream!!!"

****

The relationship of six weeks, shared between Damien and Valery, was silently growing stormy. Valery, always young at heart, accustomed to emotional warmth, displays of affection, attendance at good plays and musical concerts, found it hard to relate to Friday evenings of basketball games, emotional disconnects, and the nosy, bourgeoisie air of Damien's wealthy family. Emotionally she was starving.

Damien's good looks and charms, however, were such that Valery decided to stay with and remake Damien rather than end their revived relationship. She could no longer cope with being lonely. Loneliness triggered thoughts and memories of her lost life; her lost love; her lost children. Every night in her sleep, however, whether, she slept with Damien or slept alone, she'd whisper,

"Richard ….. Richard……."

Chapter XXXX

Richard's father, William Washington, a man of gentle character, having not seen nor heard from his son in more than four weeks, was informed by Earlene that Richard had departed for New York in search of Valery. William thereupon took a leave of absence from his garage and initiated a search for his son.

Leonard moved back home and looked after his mother, Tina, in his father's absence.

****

Upon arrival to New York City, William notified police of his missing son's appearance, gave them a picture of Richard for identification purposes, and hired two private detective agencies to assist him in his search. William then proceeded to conduct his own personal search for Richard.

He searched daily until near physical exhaustion, sometimes eighteen to twenty hours of a twenty-four hour day, hoping to find at least some clue of his son's whereabouts. It was a search that grew from days to weeks to now over a month. William visited major computer firms, hoping that his son had gotten himself back together and resumed his professional field of endeavor, but Richard had not. William frequented nightclubs and bars, hoping, begging, asking, pleading, for someone to recognize the photograph he bore of his son, but no one recognized the photograph.

He visited the city morgue weekly, now daily, praying that he would not find his son there, and he did not.

Eight weeks had passed. The search conducted by the two private detectives was fruitless. They tried to persuade him to give up his search. William paid them handsomely for their efforts and continued the search alone. The perpetual search extended on during the heart of the snow-covered winter through January but brought no sign of progress.

Richard, no job, little money, lost pride and a dying spirit, found it necessary to rest his body in the slum area flophouses of New York's downtown bowery.

The flophouse chosen was a large, empty, heated, rodent-infested, uncarpeted room where derelicts resided on a daily basis. The owner charged little more than a dollar a night for a soiled mattress, a spot on the floor, and a bowl of hot soup.

Richard possessed ten dollars within his pocket. After paying for shelter he began to budget how he'd manage the remaining dollars for his survival. Richard felt that if he ate little in the next few days, he might be able to rest in the stench yet heated house the remainder of the week and bulk of the next. He commenced to worry about survival once those remaining few dollars were gone.

Richard had come to New York City over two months ago wearing a black suit and white shirt. Outside of his recently purchased winter coat, the clothes he wore served as his street-walking and sleeping attire. The suit was now tattered and torn, one would never believe the shirt was once white, and his body projected a body odor equivalent to his appearance. He needed money. The freight train yards hired daily workers to load and unload the docks. However, the freight train yards would not hire such all ill-kept street tramp to work on the dock, nor in the yards. He didn't dare spend his remaining few dollars to clean his clothing because a clean suit on a street derelict was more of an oddball hindrance towards gaining employment at the train yards than an asset. He refused to spend the remaining few dollars he possessed on a chance. He felt trapped. He had to live day by day.

The following morning, Richard continued his fruitless search for Valery. At the end of that cold, late, January day, Richard walked with a limp. Severe frostbite to the lower extremities had done damage to his nerve endings. That frostbite had been left untreated and it was now severely infected.

Richard possessed nine dollars in his pocket. With one of those nine dollars he again paid for shelter at the bowery house. While asleep, a small group of three derelicts, having noticed the dollars in his possession, robbed Richard in his sleep and took his recently purchased winter coat. When Richard woke up the following Wednesday morning, he discovered himself penniless.

****

William continued to search in vain for his son. He awakened Wednesday morning and visited police headquarters with the hope that they had discovered some clues relating to the whereabouts of his son. They had discovered nothing.

William phoned Earlene and his wife, Tina Washington, praying that perhaps Richard had called; anything, something, just a clue- but nothing.

William's optimism of finding Richard was waning. A level of depression was surfacing. He went back to his downtown hotel room at approximately one-thirty p.m. that afternoon and rested his tired weary exhausted body. He awakened at six-thirty p.m. Darkness fell early over the state. William walked out of his hotel room and into the cold, windy, snow-laid streets in search of his son. He was losing his dogmatic confidence that Richard would be found. Although the snow fell lightly, the temperatures were reaching levels of sub-zero degrees. William slowly walked New York's downtown streets. His coat, wrapped tightly around his body, scarf secured around his neck, and boots zipped to the top in order to prevent the snow and slush from freezing his feet.

While passing an isolated downtown corner as the darkness heavily covered the sky, William heard a faint voice behind him ask,

> "Say, mister, I'm really not in the habit of doing this, but could you possibly loan me a quarter?"

William turned around in the darkness to view an obviously poor street tramp wearing a tattered black suit and dingy shirt for clothing. The tramp was not wearing an overcoat despite the freezing zero degree temperature and kept his head down as if he was too proud to visually accept charity. The tramp projected a bad body odor, maintained a fast running nose, and from what William could see in the darkness, he estimated the derelict to be a crippled old ill-kept graying man in his early sixties.

William felt sorry for the tramp, and though he was not in the habit of giving money to soliciting derelicts, he went into his pocket and gave the humble tramp a crisp one dollar bill. For some reason, he felt a spiritual warmth towards this street vagrant, he didn't know why, he just did.

As the headlights of an oncoming car drove by these two men, the tramp lifted his head with a broad smile of appreciation and said,

"Thank you, sir...thank-"

and as their eyes met, the tramp choked in astonishment before he could finish his words of appreciation.

The derelict was Richard, the donor was his father.

William, shocked to utter extremes at the condition of the man that he thought he knew, questioned,

"Richard? . . . Richard?"

Richard dropped the dollar bill and began to run. The limp in his frostbitten leg, more apparent now than ever, still carried his abused body as his elderly father ran in pursuit of his son through the isolated downtown New York streets yelling,

"Richard!! Richard! Stop! Stop! The least you can do for me now is stop!!"

Richard slowed down and abruptly stopped.

William, breathlessly exhausted, reached his son, whose back was turned against him. Richard would not turn around and face his father.

"Why did you come out here, Father?" he quietly asked, his nose flowing like running water.

"Why in the hell do you think?!"   His father angrily answered, still trying to recapture his breath.

"Do you know what you have put your family through, Son? Do you know how hard I have searched for you? Do you have any idea how many tears your mother has cried over you? Do you care!!? Will you ever stop wallowing in self-pity? Will you ever be the man I once knew? Look at me, Richard! Dammit, Richard!! Look at me!"

Richard slowly turned his cold, shaking, frost-bitten body around to the tired lines of hurt and sympathy within his father's eyes. Hurt because of how his son had fallen, sympathy because of how his son now physically appeared.

"I'm sorry that I've disappointed and hurt you so badly, Father," he softly sincerely responded.

William wept while wrapping his arms around Richard's cold, shaking body and kissed his beaten face tenderly.

"Son, let's get out of this cold weather," he petitioned, "We must talk."

Richard stepped away from his father and responded,

"No!!"

"Why not, Son? You don't have a coat or adequate clothing," he reasoned with a plea.

"Here, let me help you,'" he continued while taking his coat off and attempting to wrap it around Richard's shivering shoulders.

"No!!" Richard again adamantly responded refusing William's gesture of his coat.

"Dammit, Richard! You're still punishing yourself for some superficial crime you're not guilty of committing. Now you've punished yourself enough! Come home!"

"No!" Richard yelled. Then he quickly asked in a surprisingly soft manner,

"Have you heard from Valery, Father?'

William continued to talk as if he did not hear Richard's question.

"Son, Valery is now a part of the past, you must forget the-"

"Have you heard from Valery, Father?!" Richard repeated in anger, cutting his father off,

"Son, believe me! You'll forget in time. It just takes time!"

Richard, exasperated, frustrated looked at his father and inquired,

"*Time will help me forget what Father*?! Throwing my children into the sea?

Time will do what, Father?! Remove these old age lines of worry from my young face or the gray hairs growing over my entire body which remind me every day of that experience?

Time will do what, Father?!! Forget Valery's dying request that I save the children over her? A request I had no right to refuse!!

Time will do what, Father? Wipe away the look of hatred and betrayal in my son's eyes as the murdering waves played with his helplessness and buried his body under the sea?

No, Father, not time! I've tried to forget and I still remember. I remember as vividly today as if that living nightmare happened today. I still dream . . . I still cry… please, father, just leave me alone. I've embarrassed you and the family enough."

"Richard, it was your choice!" his father bellowed. "You followed your heart....she was the priority!"

"And now this lifestyle is my choice, Father!" Richard retorted.

William grew fearful. It appeared as if Richard was preparing to take flight and run again.

"I'm tired, Father. How is Mother?"

"She's fine, Richard," quietly cried William.

"Tell Mother I love her, Father," Richard sobbed, "Please tell Mother I love her,"

"Richard, listen to me!"

"I have to go now, Father," Richard replied as he began to run, limp in leg, against the icy snow-covered streets with his father in pursuit yelling, panting, puffing, crying, pleading, "Richard!! Richard!!!"

as Richard disappeared into the darkness of the night.

CHAPTER XXXXI

Because Richard dropped the dollar bill donated by his father during their chance encounter, he was again penniless and unable to seek warmth, food and shelter within the bowery.

The winds of that February winter night were cutting. The streets were covered with a heavy blanket of snow and the zero degree winter temperatures were attacking his infected frostbitten leg and body.

He found it necessary to seek shelter from within the train yards. Richard limped to the yards and found them closed and locked. Against the renewed snow-falling snow, he doggedly hopped the chicken-wired gates and discreetly limped around the train depot in search of an empty boxcar for shelter. Eventually he found a vacant baggage car and stole within the protective yet relatively cold interior of the roofed freight car. He buried himself within a mountain of straw for warmth.

Unbeknownst to Richard, this train of boxcars was to travel to Detroit, Michigan in the night.

The following morning, a railroad hand angrily discovered Richard asleep in the boxcar. He pushed Richard's cold, taut-nerved sick body out of the car and onto the cold, snow-laid railroad tracks of a strange surrounding environment.

****

"Richard! Richard! Richard!!"

"Wake up, Valery. Valery, wake up!" Damien loudly retorted at three a.m. this Thursday morning.

Trying to wipe the sleep from her eyes, Valery awakened to an angry man sitting on the edge of her bed.

"We must talk!" he thundered. "We absolutely must talk!"

The relationship shared between Damien and Valery had never been one of emotionalism or affection but one of trust and companionship. Lately it was becoming one of war. Valery continually tried to change Damien's cool nature into the warm character of someone he wasn't. His resentment toward these forced changes was only secondary to a complaint which should have been aired and discussed in the early days of their renewed acquaintance with each other.

Valery, unknowingly, had been calling out the name of Richard in her sleep. Initially it was only a whisper; a faint whisper which Damien felt would eventually vanish with time. Tonight, however, it was a scream, a continual scream, a plea, for Richard.

"What's wrong, Damien?" asked Valery innocently while wondering why he awakened her at three in the morning to talk.

Damien was sitting at the edge of the bed staring into space while shaking his head in disbelief. He was shaking in anger. His bare back was facing her. Valery touched his masculine shoulders in her attempt to persuade him to face her but he pushed her hand off of him in disgust.

"What's wrong, Damien?" she again asked in a demanding, frustrated tone.

"We're wrong, Valery," was his cold reply while putting on his pants and shoes as if preparing to leave her apartment.

"You still love him, don't you, Valery?"

"No!" she snapped without lifting her head to his.

"Then why do you continue to call his name over and over again in your sleep, even after I've made love to you?" he bitterly asked.

Her eyes widened. The sleep fell from her face as she lifted her head, momentarily speechless, and stared in shock at Damien.

"Whose name?" she asked in fear.

"Richard's name, Valery. Richard's name."

"How long have I been doing that? Why didn't you tell me before?"

"I don't know. I guess I felt that in time you'd forget him, Valery, but you haven't. You are now calling out his name even louder, even more clearly, than before. I'm convinced that at this point in your life no man can make you happy except Richard. You want him so badly that you've attempted to make me into some kind of carbon copy of the man. I've been playing the role that you've indirectly demanded of me to play and yet you're still not happy. *Face it, Valery, a carbon copy won't do!*"

It was obvious to both of them that this would be their last night together.

"What should I do, Damien?" she sobbed like a child looking for parental verbal direction. "What should I do?" she repeated while burying her sobbing shaking head into her tiny hands.

Damien took her hands away from her face and lifted her eyes to his. In softness and sincerity he voiced the most appropriate direction that he felt she should pursue.

"Go to him, Valery," he whispered. "Go to him before it's too late."

Valery looked up at Damien and smiled as he rose from bed, completed dressing, and left her apartment. She then called and awakened a surprised Aunt Earlene at four thirty a.m. that Thursday morning and learned of Richard's search for her and the downtown hotel where William was temporarily residing.

Valery dressed, hurriedly packed her clothes into her suitcases, called a cab, and left her New York City apartment-forever.

****

William had been visibly shaken by Richard's physical appearance and behaviors. Richard was mentally deteriorating. William gave up the exhaustive and fruitless pursuit of his son that cold late Wednesday night. After returning to his hotel room, William took out a bottle of commercial whiskey and drank the hot liquid recklessly from the bottle, spilling half of it over his face. He tried to sleep; he couldn't.

He called his wife Tina, in order to discuss the strange encounter he'd had with their missing son that night. However, upon hearing her weary voice of greeting, he hung up the telephone. Informing Tina of this night's shattering experience would only upset his wife more, not help the situation at all.

It was 12:00 a.m.; Thursday morning. William was still exhausted and unable to sleep. He rolled over on his bed, picked up the telephone and called Earlene in hope that she'd heard from Valery. Had she learned of Valery's whereabouts? Something? Anything? Nothing.

William gave Earlene information regarding his present place of residence at the Downtown New York hotel and pleaded of her to have Valery contact him if she should ever call. It was obvious that Valery's presence would be necessary in order for him to rationally relate to his son.

William had been in quiet pursuit of his son for two months now; a search that had ended only hours ago and was again to continue forward. He left the hotel and revisited the bowery sector of New York City wherein he had shared that chance brief encounter with his son. He was growing impatient, very impatient. He would stop or grab derelict after derelict, begging, shaking many of them to profess some knowledge of Richard. None of them could give him any information, not even those who were sober.

The time was two o'clock a.m. that Thursday morning. William returned to his hotel room totally physically exhausted and mentally drained. He lay across his bed, though heavily clothed in cold winter garments, and fell into an exhausting sleep.

The hours rolled by. The time was 4:00 a.m. Thursday morning. The skies were pillars of darkness as cold, violent gusts of windy winter weather beat at his bedroom windows. William was awakened by consistent, almost urgent, knocks on his hotel room door. He dragged his heavily clothed body out of the bed and staggered to the door.

"Who is it?" he sleepily asked.

The knocking continued.

"Who is it?!" he repealed in frustrated anger.

A tiny voice sobbed in question,

"Father? Father??"

William opened the door in welcome surprise and rejoiced,

"Valery! Valery!" As Valery fell into her father-in-law's strong arms and broad shoulders amid waves of love and desired relief.

There was still hope.

DETROIT

CHAPTER XXXXII

Richard's body lie upon the snow-covered railroad tracks for a period of five hours that past Thursday morning. Initially, he tried to stand but his legs would not support him.   A light mist of cold winter rain began to descend from the dark grey clouds over the city.   Richard's moist eyes were open, his lips slightly parted as he looked up at the constant motion of the cloudy skies.   The freezing pain had left his body. He felt nothing; numb. He was thinking about everything, yet he was thinking about nothing, He lost consciousness.

In passing, a small group of four Catholic nuns noticed his body across the tracks, they threw his arms around their shoulders and carried him inside the train depot offices while angrily wailing curses toward the male employees who had not lifted their hands to assist the helpless stranger.   Out of embarrassment, the men began initiating efforts to revive Richard into consciousness while the nuns of the church began ripping off his frozen clothing and preparing hot liquids to warm his body.

A small smile crossed Richard's tight lips.

Richard regained consciousness for a five minute span. They tried to feed him the hot soups but he could not orally retain anything. They searched his pockets for identification- there was nothing. He lost consciousness.   Again, he regained and lost consciousness.

A fire department team of paramedics were called in and Richard was taken by ambulance to the city's public hospital. Although the fire department authorized the medical staff to begin medical tests and operations for Richard, there were emergency cases pending that allegedly warranted consideration prior to addressing his needs.

It was now Friday afternoon, twenty-four hours later, and outside of two x-ray tests,
Richard had not received strong medical attention.

****

That same Friday morning, Valery and William searched the bowery houses of New York for Richard. The third house they inquired to proved rewarding.
The proprietor, John Sweeney, informed them of a man bearing Richard's description that had boarded within his wayward house but had not been heard from since registering a complaint of robbery while in his sleep. After more questioning by William, the owner informed them of the labor docks where many wayward men earned daily pay by loading and unloading freight. William and Valery left the bowery house, hailed a cab, and traveled to the labor yards.

Once there, they were informed by the yard employer of a man bearing Richard's description that had frequented the yards for work on many occasions but according to records had never been retained for daily employment. William then asked in vain around the yard for any relevant information leading to his son's whereabouts without success. Just prior to leaving the yards, William overheard an employed railroad laborer boasting about how he had kicked a stowaway out of the train's baggage car that past Thursday morning in Detroit. William questioned the employee and discovered that the description of the stowaway fit the description of his son Richard.
William and Valery hailed a cab to the airport and chartered a plane to Michigan.

****

The following Friday morning, upon arrival to Detroit, they searched the train yards and offices for information leading to where Richard might be. Their inquiries proved to be fruitful upon learning about a man fitting Richard's description who had been sent by ambulance to City Hospital. That afternoon they arrived at City Hospital and learned of a patient bearing Richard's description who had been checked into the hospital's emergency ward by the fire department.

The patient was alive. Their search was over.

****

William and Valery requested to see Richard but were told he was undergoing medical tests and examinations and not available to be seen by visitors. They thereupon took seats in the waiting room area. One hour went by... and another; still they had not seen Richard. William walked to the nurse's station and requested information regarding the type of hospital tests being performed on Richard in order to ascertain how much additional time might be required before he and Valery could visit his son.

The nurse could not give him this information-she did not know. William became puzzled. He returned to Valery and told her of the present state of events.

"I want to see Richard, Father," Valery whispered.

"He wants to see you too, Valery," William softly responded.

William then stole away from Valery and roamed the halls and walls of the city-financed hospital.

Valery had loved William Washington ever since their initial acquaintance nine years ago. William was everything her husband was. He was soft, yet tough. Gentle, but capable of being hard. Highly persistent, yet bending. So secure in his manliness that he found it easy to convey feelings of warmth . . . love . . . and tenderness.

306

Valery said little to her father-in-law this day. She was lost in thought. Thought about those earlier days when Richard pursued her as a coed. The laughter they shared when living together under the same roof and reaching for the sky. The happy years of marriage and childbearing they'd shared and enjoyed. They had so much going for them, so many happy memories . . . so much giving . . . so much love. She shuddered. Would it all end here?

"What have I done?" she cried out loud to herself. "What have I done?"

William hastily walked from hospital patient area to hospital patient area in search of Richard. He checked the emergency wards. Richard was not there. He knocked upon the doors of various x-ray departments and testing rooms searching for his son. Richard could not be found.

On the third floor of the hospital was a large open area of hospital beds where patients lay side by side, separated by white hospital curtains. William hurriedly went from hospital bed to hospital bed in search of his son.

He finally found Richard.

William shivered with fear. Richard's appearance seemed to have been aged by even more additional years. His unconscious body, clad in white hospital attire, lay wet and motionless in the bed. William touched his son's forehead and was shaken by the scorching high fever his son possessed and the apparent lack of oxygen being inhaled by his congested lungs. Richard was suffering with a critical case of pneumonia.

William ran to the nurse's station and adamantly demanded of her and a doctor present at her desk to give immediate attention to his son. They adhered to his demands. William, fearing Richard might die, ran back to Valery in the waiting room.

"Hurry, Valery! He's dying! He's dying! I'm begging you, Valery, please save my son! Please save my son!!"

They both ran up the flight of stairs to the third floor of the open hospital bed patient area to Richard's side. The doctor and nurse were exerting their best efforts but William could sense their despair. He sat in a chair, exhausted, and buried his sobbing head into his hands.

Valery gasped at the pitiful sight of her prematurely aged husband and pushed both the doctor and nurse away from Richard's unconscious body.

"Richard! Richard! Wake up, Richard! Please wake up, Richard!" she pleaded. There was no physical response.

"Richard! Richard!" she screamed. "For me! Please wake up!"

His fingers began to move and Richard's eyes slightly parted themselves as he whispered in a barely audible tone,

"Valery?....Valery??"

Valery sat on his bed and with a moist cloth began to wipe the heavy beads of moisture from his forehead.

"Valery ….Baby…where have you been?" he asked as tears began to trickle down his once handsome face.

"It's all right now, Richard, I'm here! I'm here!" she whispered. "Please don't die, Richard," she sobbed, "I'm here. I'm not going anywhere anymore. I promise, Richard," she whispered. "I promise!"

"We lost the kids, we lost the house, and I lost you," Richard wept, his body trembling with the chills of death.

"Richard, that's okay, Richard," Valery smiled. "We have each other. We'll have more children. We'll buy another house bigger and better than before. Everything's going to be fine, Richard."

Valery screamed as Richard drifted into unconsciousness.

"Please!" she screamed in hysteria while shaking his body to be coherent and conscious.

"Okay, Valery. Don't worry, Baby," he smiled, "I won't die. We'll have more kids, right, Valery?"

"Right, Richard," she responded cheerfully, "But first we have to get you well and cleaned up. You haven't been taking care of yourself," she smiled.

Richard's father, William, discreetly left the curtained room. His beaten mind could not deal with the game Valery and Richard were playing with themselves.

"Right, Valery," smiled Richard, "everything's going to be alright, everything's going to be fine. I've been looking all over for you, Valery. Baby!..Where have you been?!" he cried. "And I'll get another job even better than before, right, Valery?"

"Right, Richard," she answered while kissing his forehead.

"And we'll have children just as beautiful as Ricky and Jennifer, right, Valery?"

"Right, Richard," she again repeated cheerfully. "Everything is going to work out fine, Richard, I know it is. I just had to get away for a while, Richard. It's only been nine months, Richard. We'll pull our lives back together. We have time. We can do it, Richard. I just know we can."

"I love you, Valery," he whispered.

"I love you, Richard," she responded while gently kissing his lips.

And with his eyes half parted upon hers and the warm tears flowing down his cheeks- Richard died.

EPILOGUE

I don't really know what happened to Valery upon Richard's death.

I was told by one individual that she wasn't aware of his death (or didn't accept it) until thirty minutes after he had ceased living; that she talked those thirty minutes to his corpse. After visually learning of his death she suffered a nervous breakdown and was taken, while screaming, to a private mental hospital where she resides today.

I was told by another source that upon Richard's death, Valery suffered a cardiac arrest due to the heightened tension on her weak heart muscles and died of a heart attack at her husband's side.

Still another source informs me that upon his death, Valery quietly and discreetly stole away from the hospital and everyone associated with it, including William Washington, and hasn't been seen nor heard from since.

Like I said. . .I don't know.

I met Richard two weeks prior to his death. I remember being visibly shaken after hearing his 'choice' experience and numb upon learning of his death. It's tragic how one day in a man's life can drastically alter his physical and mental makeup.

Richard was faced with a dilemma. A synonym for dilemma is 'catch-22'; 'impasse'.
The synonyms for 'catch-22' are *no-win situation*; *vicious circle*.

Despite Richard's dilemma, I have heard a myriad of opinions praising and ridiculing Richard for his actions and the decisions he made. Was it the proper choice? I don't know. Is there a proper choice in a living nightmare such as that?

Irrespective of individual opinions, there is one thing I do know. Richard knew how to love and respect a woman.

I live for the day that I can love a woman as hard as Richard loved Valery. I live for the day that I obsessively desire a woman and that same woman obsessively desires me. I live for the day that I can feel the extreme depths of commitment and allegiance for any one woman that Richard felt for Valery.

As far as 'the choice', it must be your decision. You make the choice.

Me? . . . Like I said . . . I don't know.

I don't know. . .I don't know. . . I just. . . don't…know.